S0-BZQ-094

NEWS
IN A DIGITAL AGE

Comparing the Presentation of News Information over Time and Across Media Platforms

JENNIFER KAVANAGH | WILLIAM MARCELLINO

JONATHAN S. BLAKE | SHAWN SMITH

STEVEN DAVENPORT | MAHLET G. TEBEKA

RAND
CORPORATION

For more information on this publication, visit www.rand.org/t/RR2960

Library of Congress Cataloging-in-Publication Data is available for this publication.
ISBN: 978-1-9774-0231-8

Published by the RAND Corporation, Santa Monica, Calif.
© Copyright 2019 RAND Corporation
RAND® is a registered trademark.

Support RAND
Make a tax-deductible charitable contribution at
www.rand.org/giving/contribute

www.rand.org

Preface

The media ecosystem in the United States has experienced rapid technological changes over the past 30 years that have affected the way news is produced, consumed, and disseminated. This internally funded report seeks to assess empirically whether and how presentation of news in newspapers, television, and online has changed in light of these developments. We use RAND-Lex, a suite of RAND Corporation tools that combine text analysis and machine learning, to explore changes in news presentation over time and across platforms. It considers the implications of observed changes and of areas in which reporting has stayed the same. The report will be of interest to journalists, those who study news media and mass communication, and consumers who want to understand more about the media ecosystem and how it has evolved.

This report is one of a series focused on the topic of Truth Decay, defined as the diminishing role that facts, data, and analysis play in today's political and civil discourse. The original report, *Truth Decay: An Initial Exploration of the Diminishing Role of Facts and Analysis in American Public Life* by Jennifer Kavanagh and Michael D. Rich, was published in January 2018 and laid out a research agenda for studying and developing solutions to the Truth Decay challenge.

RAND Ventures

RAND is a research organization that develops solutions to public policy challenges to help make communities throughout the world safer and more secure, healthier and more prosperous. RAND is non-profit, nonpartisan, and committed to the public interest.

RAND Ventures is a vehicle for investing in policy solutions. Philanthropic contributions support our ability to take the long view, tackle tough and often-controversial topics, and share our findings in innovative and compelling ways. RAND's research findings and recommendations are based on data and evidence, and therefore do not necessarily reflect the policy preferences or interests of its clients, donors, or supporters.

Funding for this venture was provided by gifts from RAND supporters and income from operations. For more information about RAND Ventures, visit www.rand.org/giving/ventures.

Contents

Figures

Tables

Summary

Over the past 30 years, the way that Americans consume and share information has changed dramatically. People no longer wait for the morning paper or the evening news. Instead, equipped with smartphones or other digital devices, the average person spends hours each day online, looking at news or entertainment websites, using social media, and consuming many different types of information. Although some of the changes in the way news and information are disseminated can be quantified, far less is known about how the *presentation* of news—that is, the linguistic style, perspective, and word choice used when reporting on current events and issues—has changed over this period and how it differs across media platforms.[1]

We aimed to begin to fill this knowledge gap by identifying and empirically measuring how the presentation of news by U.S. news sources has changed over time and how news presentation differs across media platforms.

Our interest and motivation in investigating this topic—the presentation of news—emerged from observations in a 2018 RAND Corporation report, *Truth Decay: An Initial Exploration of the Dimin-*

---

[1] By *platform*, we refer to the means through which news is delivered and consumed. Newspapers, broadcast television, cable television, the internet, and social media are all platforms—as is radio, which was not a subject of this report. The term *news presentation* refers to the linguistic style of news and to relevant patterns in usage (e.g., contexts, relevant frames). The term is intended to encompass both the discourse of news and the style of presentation.

xii   News in a Digital Age

ishing Role of Facts and Analysis in American Public Life.[2] That report pointed to four trends—increasing disagreement about objective facts, data, and analysis; a blurring of the line between fact and opinion; an increasing relative volume of opinion over fact; and declining trust in government, media, and other institutions that used to be sources of factual information—that together have degraded factual discourse and called into question the meaning and purpose of news.

In this report, we further analyze the second and third trends of Truth Decay and explore whether existing trends in news presentation might match the expectations of the Truth Decay framework. We cannot directly measure the extent to which fact and opinion have blurred or quantify the relative balance of fact and opinion, but we are able to measure how characteristics of news presentation—such as personal perspective, subjectivity, and use of authoritative sources—have evolved. This report documents the results of our analysis.

Objective and Research Questions

Our objective was to explore how the linguistic style of news coverage (e.g., tone, subjectivity, ambiguity, emotion) in select print, broadcast, and digital media in the United States has changed over time and differs across platforms. To pursue this objective, we addressed four research questions:

- In what measurable ways did the style of news presentation in *print journalism* change between 1989 and 2017?
- In what measurable ways did the style of news presentation in *broadcast journalism* change between 1989 and 2017?

---

[2] Jennifer Kavanagh and Michael D. Rich, *Truth Decay: An Initial Exploration of the Diminishing Role of Facts and Analysis in American Public Life*, Santa Monica, Calif.: RAND Corporation, RR-2314-RC, 2018. The 2018 report is the first in a series of studies, including the one that this report focuses on, that RAND intends to produce on *Truth Decay*, the phrase that we use to describe the diminishing role of facts, data, and analysis in American public life. When used in this study, Truth Decay refers to RAND's larger research effort, not just to the 2018 report.

- How did the style of news presentation in *broadcast journalism* differ from the style used in *prime-time cable programming* over the period from 2000 to 2017?
- How did the style of news presentation in *online journalism* differ from that of *print journalism* over the period from 2012 to 2017?

Methodology

To address these questions, we began by examining how cable news networks, the internet, and social media are reshaping the U.S. media industry and ecosystem and radically changing not only how people consume information but also how that information is produced, shared, and disseminated. We also explored past research into how these changes are affecting news presentation across digital platforms. We found that most other examinations of news presentation, although valuable, are qualitative in nature and do not address the specific linguistic characteristics that we were most interested in exploring.

We then turned to quantifying the changes in news presentation and measuring these changes on different media platforms over time. To do this, we analyzed and compared the text or transcripts of news stories produced over different periods by three types of media: print journalism (the *New York Times, Washington Post,* and *St. Louis Post-Dispatch*), television (broadcast and cable), and online journalism (Breitbart News, BuzzFeed Politics, Daily Caller, HuffPost Politics [which until April 2017 was Huffington Post], Politico, and TheBlaze). We chose these sources because they are heavily consumed, generally representative of their media cohorts, and generate ample data that team members could analyze.[3]

---

[3] For newspapers, we chose the three sources with the longest available online, text-based archives. This sample also used two of the largest national newspapers and a leading regional one. For the newspaper analysis, we examined text from the three papers' front-page stories (along with the text of those stories that continued onto later pages), sampling each paper every eighth day from January 1, 1989, to December 31, 2017. For television, we used material from each major network news organization and the three largest cable outlets. For broadcast and cable television news, we collected transcripts of the flagship news programs

We made four specific comparisons: newspapers before 2000 with newspapers after 2000, broadcast television news before 2000 with broadcast television news after 2000, broadcast television news with prime-time cable programming in the years 2000–2017, and print with online journalism from 2012 to 2017.[4] Table S.1 shows the data sets that we reviewed to conduct these comparisons.

To compare text in the data sets, we used a suite of computer software tools designed by RAND called RAND-Lex, which combines machine learning with textual analysis to identify patterns in the use of words and phrases. The process works by calculating the frequency of certain words, phrases, or characters and then attaching a score to one of 121 linguistic measures or characteristics. This allows researchers to comb through large volumes of text (e.g., in the tens of millions of words) and to conduct both descriptive and exploratory statistical tests to analyze and interpret the meaning of those data. In this study, RAND-Lex enabled us to make reliable claims about how the presentation of news has (and has not) changed over time with specific reference to changes in tone, sentiment, and language used, on a very large scale.

---

on the American Broadcasting Company (ABC), Columbia Broadcasting System (CBS), and National Broadcasting Company (NBC) and of a selection of prime-time programs from the three major cable television news networks: Cable News Network (CNN), Fox News Channel, and Microsoft/National Broadcasting Company (MSNBC). For online journalism, we focused on six of the most highly trafficked online journalism outlets, three on the left side of the political spectrum and three on the right. We searched the archives of these six news websites, taking homepage stories stored by the Internet Archive (archive.org) for every eighth day from January 1, 2012, through December 31, 2017. If archived stories were not available for the selected date, the team took stories from the closest available date within four days of the original target.

[4] These dates were chosen in large measure because of two important changes in the U.S. media industry that took place around the year 2000. First, viewership of all three major cable networks (especially Fox News) increased dramatically starting around 2000. In the years after 2000, cable programming solidified its position as a major source of news for U.S. audiences. Second, 2000 marks a turning point in the growth of the internet. It was around this time that internet usage among Americans first passed the 50-percent mark. Internet use escalated rapidly after that, and roughly 90 percent of Americans are online today.

Table S.1
Data Sets

Analysis Name	Sample 1	Articles/Segments (Sample 1)	Words (Sample 1)	Sample 2	Articles/Segments (Sample 2)	Words (Sample 2)
Newspapers						
Full newspaper sample	*NYT, WP, SLPD* pre-2000[a]	12,272	11,360,227	*NYT, WP, SLPD* 2000–2017[a]	15,342	17,072,668
National newspaper	*NYT, WP* pre-2000	8,091	8,791,100	*NYT, WP* 2000–2017	11,082	13,617,145
New York Times	*NYT* pre-2000	4,736	4,698,501	*NYT* 2000–2017	5,821	7,085,705
Washington Post	*WP* pre-2000	3,355	4,092,599	*WP* 2000–2017	5,261	6,531,440
St. Louis Post-Dispatch	*SLPD* pre-2000	4,181	2,569,127	*SLPD* 2000–2017	4,260	3,455,523
Television						
Broadcast news	ABC, NBC, CBS pre-2000	4,223	1,513,175	ABC, NBC, CBS 2000–2017	6,502	2,299,085
2000–2017 television comparison	ABC, NBC, CBS 2000–2017	6,502	2,299,085	CNN, MSNBC, Fox News Channel 2000–2017	4,232	12,278,437
Cross-platform						
Full internet/full newspaper sample	Online 2012–2017 (Politico, HuffPo, Breitbart, Daily Caller, Blaze, BuzzFeed Politics)[a]	38,252	21,238,215	Newspapers (*NYT, WP, SLPD*) 2012–2017	4,609	5,611,270

Table S.1—Continued

Analysis Name	Sample 1	Articles/ Segments (Sample 1)	Words (Sample 1)	Sample 2	Articles/ Segments (Sample 2)	Words (Sample 2)
Reduced internet/ national newspapers	Online 2012–2017 (Politico, HuffPo, Breitbart, Daily Caller)[b]	26,020	15,798,570	Newspapers (NYT, WP) 2012–2017	3,398	4,358,964

NOTE: We conducted several different versions of most analyses, using variations in the samples to assess the robustness of the results and assessing the influence of specific sources within the analysis. HuffPo = HuffPost Politics; NYT = New York Times; SLPD = St. Louis Post-Dispatch; WP = Washington Post.
[a] Data sets were halved (taking alternating stories from source data sets) before compilation into the analytical corpora because of computing capacity constraints.
[b] Data set was quartered (taking every fourth article) before analysis because of computing capacity constraints. Sample counts are before halving or quartering. Unless otherwise noted, data collection periods started in 1989 and ended in 2017.

Key Findings

In What Measurable Ways Did the Style of News Presentation in Print Journalism Change Between 1989 and 2017?

We found that although much of the language and tone of reporting in the *New York Times*, *Washington Post*, and *St. Louis Post-Dispatch* remained constant over the past 30 years, there were quantifiable changes in certain linguistic areas between the pre- and post-2000 periods. For example, the three newspapers' reporting before 2000 used language that was more heavily event- and context-based; contained more references to time, official titles, positions, and institutions; and used more-descriptive, elaborative language to provide story details. In contrast, we found that post-2000 reporting engaged in more storytelling and more heavily emphasized interactions, personal perspective, and emotion.

In What Measurable Ways Did the Style of News Presentation in Broadcast Journalism Change Between 1989 and 2017?

Broadcast journalism went through changes similar to those of newspaper journalism in the same period. Our analysis found a gradual shift in broadcast television coverage from more conventional reporting in the pre-2000 period, during which news stories tended to use precise and concrete language and often turned to public sources of authority, to more subjective coverage in the post-2000 period, which relied less on concrete language and more on unplanned speech, expression of opinions, interviews, and arguments.

How Does the Style of News Presentation in Broadcast Journalism Differ from the Style Used in Prime-Time Cable Programming over the Period 2000–2017?

We found a starker contrast between broadcast news presentation and prime-time cable programming in the post-2000 period. Compared with news presentation on broadcast television, programming on cable outlets exhibited a dramatic and quantifiable shift toward subjective, abstract, directive, and argumentative language and content based more on the expression of opinion than on reporting of events. This was accompanied by an increase in airtime on cable channels devoted to advocacy for those opinions rather than on balanced description of context. It should be noted, however, that some of this contrast is to be expected based on the very different objectives and business models of the two platforms. Cable programming, particularly during prime time, is geared toward a narrower audience and uses opinions and provocative material to attract attention; broadcast television aims at a wider audience and sticks closer to traditional forms of reporting.

How Does the Style of News Presentation in Online Journalism Differ from That of Print Journalism over the Period 2012–2017?

Comparing newspaper and online journalism in the 2012–2017 period, we found that the news presentation style in newspapers sampled remained far more anchored in what could be considered traditional reporting than the online media outlets sampled. News presentation in newspapers tended to be more strongly characterized by use of characters, time, and descriptive language (to describe events or issues) and by a more narrative context. It also appeared to be more strongly characterized by the use of concrete objects, numbers, references to duration, and connections to individual roles, spatial relationships, and retrospective reasoning. In contrast, language in the online journalism sample tended to be more conversational, with more emphasis on interpersonal interactions and personal perspectives and opinions. Appeals were less narrative and more argumentative, with an eye toward persuasion.

Implications of Findings

The general trends observed in our analysis provide initial evidence of a gradual and subtle shift over time and between old and new media toward a more subjective form of journalism that is grounded in personal perspective. In each of the analyses that considered changes over time, we found evidence of a shift from a journalistic style based on the use of public language (e.g., sharing of talk, descriptions of groups), academic register (e.g., formal style, citing precedent), references to authority figures and sources, and event- and context-based reporting to a style of journalism based more heavily on personal perspective, narration, and subjectivity. We saw this trend in broadcast news and, to a lesser extent, in newspapers.

In comparing the characteristics of new and old media, we found that prime-time cable programming is more highly interactive and subjective than broadcast television news and relies on arguments and opinions intended to persuade and debate, a stark contrast from the more academic style and precise language employed in broadcast television in the pre-2000 period. Similarly, our online journalism sample was characterized by a personal and subjective style that, in many cases, emphasized argument and advocacy and was very different from the pre-2000 print journalism sample, which relied more heavily on event-based reporting that often referred to authoritative institutions or sources.

Although we found measurable evidence of more widespread use of opinion and subjectivity in the presentation of news than in the past, the change has been subtle, not wholesale. News reporting has not shifted from Walter Cronkite–style serious reporting to fiction or propaganda—even in the biggest contrasts we saw, there was still much similarity over time and across platforms. Future research could extend this analysis to other types of media, such as local newspapers and television news, news radio programs, video content, and photographs that appear alongside news stories.

Acknowledgments

We are grateful for the support of many colleagues in the writing of this report. We are especially indebted to Michael Rich for his support of this work and for his insights and feedback on early drafts. James Dobbins, Geoffrey McGovern, and Samantha Cherney provided valuable input during the project's early stages. Craig Bond and Sarah Meadows guided the report through the quality assurance process and their comments improved the report. Gordon Lee provided expert assistance on the report's summary. The authors are also appreciative of comments from their three reviewers, Sandra Evans and Todd Helmus of RAND and Tom Johnson of the University of Texas. Their observations greatly improved this report.

Abbreviations

ABC	American Broadcasting Company
ANOVA	analysis of variance
CBS	Columbia Broadcasting System
CMU	Carnegie Mellon University
CNN	Cable News Network
LIWC	Linguistic Inquiry Word Count
MSNBC	Microsoft/National Broadcasting Company
NBC	National Broadcasting Company
NYT	*New York Times*
POV	point of view
SLPD	*St. Louis Post-Dispatch*
WP	*Washington Post*

CHAPTER ONE

Introduction

Over the past 30 years, the way that Americans consume and share information has changed dramatically. The days of waiting for the morning paper or the evening broadcast are gone; smartphones are ubiquitous, and the average person spends hours each day online, looking at news or entertainment websites, using social media, and consuming many different types of information.[1] News consumers have an array of choices—newspapers, broadcast television, cable programming, online journalism, and social media—all of which provide different types of information in different ways. Some of the changes observed in the way that news is produced and disseminated can be quantified. For example, newspaper and television audiences have measurably declined while social media sites and online sources have gained users and followers.[2] The growth of online-only journalism outlets also can be tracked. A recent assessment of trends in this area highlighted not only a marked increase in traffic to online journalism sites but also expansion and diversification by the sites themselves, with more than 60 percent of these sites having at least one mobile app and more than 70 percent also having podcasts.[3] Data provide insight

---

[1] Jeffrey Cole, Michael Suman, Phoebe Schramm, and Liuning Zhou, *Surveying the Digital Future 2017*, Los Angeles, Calif.: Center for the Digital Future at USC Annenberg, 2017.

[2] Pew Research Center, "Newspapers Fact Sheet," State of the News Media project, webpage, June 13, 2018c; Pew Research Center, "Network News Fact Sheet," State of the News Media project, webpage, July 25, 2018d.

[3] Pew Research Center, "Digital News Fact Sheet," State of the News Media project, webpage, June 6, 2018b.

into the growth of such platforms as Twitter and Facebook, and public opinion surveys measure how often these sources are used for news.[4] Analyses identify sources of disinformation and track their spread, and surveys assess what people want out of media outlets and whether they are satisfied with the choices they have.[5]

What has gone less explored is how the *presentation* of news (in terms of its linguistic elements and characteristics) has changed over this period and how it differs across platforms or types of media.[6] Our interest and motivation in investigating this topic—the presentation of news—emerges from the observations of a 2018 RAND Corporation report, *Truth Decay: An Initial Exploration of the Diminishing Role of Facts and Analysis in American Public Life.* That report defines Truth Decay as comprising four specific trends: increasing disagreement about objective facts, data, and analysis; a blurring of the line between fact and opinion; an increasing relative volume of opinion over fact; and declining trust in institutions that used to be looked to as sources of factual information, such as the government and the media. In that report, we argue that the phenomenon is driven by the interaction of four primary drivers: characteristics of human cognitive processing, such as cognitive bias; changes in the media ecosystem; competing demands on the education system that challenge its ability to prepare students for this new media ecosystem; and political, social, and demographic polarization. We posit that Truth Decay creates at least four challenges to the foundations of American democracy: the erosion of civil discourse, political paralysis that results when policymakers do not share a set of facts, political alienation and disengagement, and uncertainty for individuals and policymakers who lack the objective benchmarks they need to make individual and policy decisions. Within each of these areas, that report describes

---

[4] Kurt Wagner and Rani Molla, "Facebook Is Not Getting Any Bigger in the United States," *Recode*, March 1, 2018; Elisa Shearer and Jeffrey Gottfried, *News Use Across Social Media Platforms 2017*, Washington, D.C.: Pew Research Center, September 7, 2017.

[5] Gallup and Knight Foundation, *American Views: Trust, Media, and Democracy*, Washington, D.C.: Gallup, January 2018; Katie Langin, "Fake News Spreads Faster Than True News on Twitter—Thanks to People, Not Bots," *Science Magazine*, March 8, 2018.

[6] We use the terms *platforms* and *types of media* to refer to different means of information transmission and sharing—for example, newspaper, television, and radio.

what can be learned from existing research and identifies key empirical and theoretical gaps (i.e., areas in need of more or different data and new theories) that create obstacles to a full understanding of Truth Decay and its implications.[7]

Among the gaps mentioned in that report is the lack of good empirical data on each of the four trends that define Truth Decay, with the partial exception of declining trust in institutions, for which there is extensive polling data. The other three defining trends suffer a lack of empirical data that would allow researchers to track the phenomenon over time, to understand where it is most severe, and to devise policy solutions. This report aims to begin to fill this gap, focusing specifically on the second and third trends—the blurring of the line between fact and opinion and an increasing relative volume of opinion over fact.

There have been efforts to characterize differences in news presentation using qualitative and descriptive analyses.[8] These efforts provide significant insight, but they do not quantify the size or significance of observed changes, and they provide limited precision about what identified differences look like in context.[9] In this report, we seek to fill this gap by identifying and presenting empirical measurements both of changes in the presentation of news in U.S. sources over time and of the differences that exist across platforms.[10]

We are particularly interested in anything that provides insight into how the use of or reliance on authoritative and fact-based information has changed or how it differs across platforms because this factor is most directly relevant to Truth Decay and its characteristic trends. For exam-

---

[7] Jennifer Kavanagh and Michael D. Rich, *Truth Decay: An Initial Exploration of the Role of Facts and Analysis in American Public Life*, Santa Monica, Calif.: RAND Corporation, RR-2314-RC, 2018.

[8] We use the term *news presentation* throughout this report to refer to the linguistic style of news and to relevant patterns in usage (e.g., contexts, relevant frames). The term is intended to encompass both the discourse of news and the style of presentation.

[9] Robert W. McChesney, *Rich Media, Poor Democracy: Communication Politics in Dubious Times*, New York: New Press, 2015; Cass Sunstein, *#Republic: Divided Democracy in the Age of Social Media*, Princeton, N.J.: Princeton University Press, 2018.

[10] In this report, we focus only on media produced within the United States for U.S. audiences. Future work could consider these questions from an international perspective.

ple, in Chapters Three through Five, we provide evidence of changes over time in the frequency of, on the one hand, references to authority figures, institutions, and event-focused coverage (proxies for "authoritative sources") and, on the other hand, uses of personal perspective and subjectivity (proxies for "opinion-based sources"). However, our analysis does not directly or definitively answer the question of how that information is used or how its use has changed. First, the suite of computer software tools that we used, RAND-Lex, combines machine learning with textual analysis to identify patterns in the use of words and phrases and can measure many different linguistic characteristics (described in Chapter Two), but it does not directly assess reliance on facts or measure the accuracy of information. Second, our samples of text do not support broad generalizations, which we will explain further in our discussion of results and implications in the final chapter.

The Changing Media Ecosystem

Before considering changes in news presentation specifically, it is useful to explore some of the ways that the media ecosystem has changed more generally in the past 30 years. In that time, the media industry and ecosystem have been reshaped by significant technological changes: The players, ways of doing business, and types and amount of content available are all fundamentally different now than they were three decades ago. The emergence and spread of cable news networks, broad access to the internet, and the rise of social media radically changed the ways that news information is produced, shared, disseminated, and consumed.[11] In 1989, it was presented in three major forms: newspa-

---

[11] In this report, we use *information* as a general term to refer to all types of material conveyed to an audience through any media channel. We use *news* to refer to information focused on current events, social and policy issues, and the interactions of these events and issues with people and places. News is a type of information, but not all information would be considered news. Recipes, for instance, are information but would not be considered news by our definition. Opinion pieces and editorials are another form of information that would not be counted as news. For more information on this, see Kavanagh and Rich, 2018, Table 1.1, pp. 8–10.

pers, broadcast television, and radio. Newspapers were a central part of the market, with a circulation of more than 62 million, just below its peak in the 1970s.[12] This began to change during the 1990s. By 2000, weekday circulation had fallen to less than 56 million. By 2010, this number stood at only about 45 million, and by 2017 it had fallen to a little more than 30 million.[13]

Broadcast television news also was affected by changes in the way people consume information, with viewership declining even as the medium remains the most popular way for people to get news.[14] Specifically, broadcast networks lost 4 percent of their evening news viewers between the 2015–2016 and 2016–2017 seasons, falling to 23.1 million total.[15] Prime-time cable viewership, which is smaller than the broadcast television audience overall, also has declined, although at a slower rate. In 2017, Fox News led the pack with 2.4 million prime-time viewers, followed by MSNBC at 1.6 million and CNN with 1.1 million.[16] About 50 percent of Americans report turning to some kind of television programming for news—in 2017, 26 percent of Americans reported that they often get news from network television; 28 percent reported often getting news from cable television.[17]

There are several reasons for these declines. The most significant, perhaps, is the rise of the internet and the spread of social media as a way to produce, consume, and share news. The use of online sources of news has become ubiquitous; in some cases, online use has grown faster than consumption of other media has declined. In 2018, 90 percent of adults reported using online media as sources of

---

[12] Pew Research Center, State of the News Media project, homepage, undated.

[13] Pew Research Center, undated.

[14] Pew Research Center, undated.

[15] Stephen Battaglio, "'ABC World News Tonight' Takes Ratings Crown but Broadcast News Audiences Continue to Shrink," *Los Angeles Times*, September 26, 2017.

[16] Lisa de Moraes, "FNC Tops Cable in 2017, MSNBC Grows Most, CNN Bags Best Total Day on Record," *Deadline*, December 19, 2017.

[17] Although we mention radio as a major form of news, we do not analyze it in this report. We had hoped to feature radio transcripts but were unable to locate a systematic database of such transcripts that would allow us to conduct a rigorous evaluation.

news. Web traffic on online news outlets (in the aggregate) also has increased slightly over the past five years. The 35 most-trafficked online sites received an average of more than 20 million unique visitors per month in 2017.[18] Online news consumption is rapidly catching up with broadcast television in terms of the number of users who report "often" getting news from those platforms, with 43 percent of users reporting they often get news from online sources and 50 percent reporting the same for television.[19] Use of social media sites as sources of news also has increased significantly. In 2018, approximately 67 percent of individuals used social media as a source of news, with Facebook being the leading source.[20]

A final key change, directly related to this shift toward online platforms, has been an increase in the use of mobile devices for news consumption. A 2017 Pew survey found that 60 percent of respondents report that they often get news on their mobile devices and that 85 percent report that they have accessed news on their devices at least once. The survey found that mobile news consumption and sharing are highest among younger demographic groups but are also growing among older Americans.[21] It is also worth noting that most traditional news outlets have an online presence, and this bridge could somewhat moderate any effects that news publishers and producers might experience as a result of more consumers shifting to online news consumption. Increased web traffic to the online platforms of newspapers has partially offset losses in print subscriptions, but even outlets that charge subscription fees for access to online content have been unable to fully replace print subscription revenues.[22] Data from the Pew Research Center show that the decline in print subscriptions to

---

[18]   Pew Research Center, undated.

[19]   Kristen Bialik and Katerina Eva Matsa, "Key Trends in Social and Digital News Media," Pew Research Center, October 4, 2017.

[20]   Shearer and Gottfried, 2017.

[21]   Sophia Fedeli and Katerina Eva Matsa, "Use of Mobile Devices for News Continues to Grow, Outpacing Desktops and Laptops," Pew Research Center, July 17, 2018.

[22]   Dan Kennedy, "Print Is Dying, Digital Is No Savior: The Long, Ugly Decline of the Newspaper Business Continues Apace," commentary, WGBH News, January 26, 2016.

major newspapers has far outpaced the increase in web traffic, even over the period since 2010.[23] This could partly be the result of a greater variety of choices available online and the prevalence of free content.

Technological changes also have shaped the economics of the new media ecosystem, the incentives for news producers, and the fundamental ways in which news is produced.[24] First, the emergence of cable television and the rise of the internet and social media have lowered barriers to entry, allowing citizen journalism and online news outlets to flourish and contributing to a rise in consumer choices.[25] This has increased competition for audiences and advertising revenue that have remained constant in size, resulting in squeezed profit margins for many outlets. This is particularly significant because as income from subscriptions has fallen, advertising revenues have become increasingly important and essential. At the same time, consumers have significantly more choices, putting additional pressure on media companies to produce more content and to attract more attention to that con-

---

[23] Pew Research Center, 2018c.

[24] Seth C. Lewis and Nikki Usher, "Open Source and Journalism: Toward New Frameworks for Imagining News Innovation," *Media, Culture & Society*, Vol. 35, No. 5, 2013.

[25] Dianne Lynch, "The State of American Journalism," in *Looking at the Future of Journalism Education*, Miami, Fla.: Knight Foundation, 2015. It is worth noting that there are really two trends in media market structure. Winseck (2008) makes the useful distinction between numerical diversity (number of channels or outlets) and source diversity (number of media owners). While numerical diversity in terms of number of outlets has increased markedly, source or owner diversity has appeared to decrease over time. Despite the increasing diversity and number of sources in the market at the level of specific outlets, there has been a simultaneous shift toward consolidation at the upper, ownership level—acquistions by the large tech companies Google and Facebook are two examples. We do not focus on the consolidation aspect because existing research has not found a strong relationship between market structure and news presentation in the aggregate. Dwayne Winseck, "The State of Media Ownership and Media Markets: Competition or Concentration and Why Should We Care?" *Sociology Compass*, Vol. 2, No. 1, 2008. Also see Matthew A. Baum and Yuri M. Zhukov, "Media Ownership and News Coverage of International Conflict," *Political Communication*, Vol. 36, No. 1, 2019; Daniel E. Ho and Kevin M. Quinn, "Viewpoint Diversity and Media Consolidation: An Empirical Study," *Stanford Law Review*, Vol. 61, No. 4, 2009.

tent.[26] Finally, technology has led to the development of new news-gathering styles, such as journalistic outfits that operate collaboratively and through networks of individuals rather than large corporations or that operate through the use of crowdsourced and open information.[27] These crowdsourced outlets create yet another source of competition for more-traditional outlets that have a very different publishing model. Furthermore, past research has shown that technology has an influence on news presentation through its effect on the intensity of economic competition and norms of news production.[28]

As models of news production and the players involved have changed, so have business strategy decisions made by news producers. In most cases, business strategies also vary across platforms. For example, broadcast television has sought to appeal to broad audiences (as have newspapers, to some extent); by contrast, cable channels, such as Fox News and MSNBC, have tried to appeal to specific audiences that might feel underserved by more-traditional outlets, offering these groups more-specialized and tailored products.[29] The rise of online news has increased this push toward niche audiences. Specifically, with such low barriers to entry, online journalism comprises an increasing

---

[26] Lynch, 2015. Even more than competing for audience, media companies must compete for advertising revenue—typically the primary source of funding for media outlets. Advertising revenue tends to follow audience share—outlets with larger audiences can command higher ad prices. As consumers increasingly shift online, however, so does advertising spending. Specifically, trends in advertising revenues show a shift from traditional media (broadcast television and newspapers) toward digital media. Newspapers have experienced the largest drop in advertising revenue—from just under $50 billion in 2006 to about $16.5 billion in 2017 (Pew Research Center, undated).

[27] William H. Dutton, "The Fifth Estate Emerging Through the Network of Networks," *Prometheus*, Vol. 27, No. 1, 2009; Lewis and Usher, 2013; Nikki Usher, "Breaking News Production Processes in U.S. Metropolitan Newspapers: Immediacy and Journalistic Authority," *Journalism*, Vol. 19, No. 1, 2018.

[28] Phil MacGregor, "Tracking the Online Audience," *Journalism Studies*, Vol. 8, No. 2, 2007; Carly T. McKenzie, Wilson Lowrey, Hal Hays, Jee Young Chung, and Chang Wan Woo, "Listening to News Audiences: The Impact of Community Structure and Economic Factors," *Mass Communication and Society*, Vol. 14, No. 3, 2011; Hong Tien Vu, "The Online Audience as Gatekeeper: The Influence of Reader Metrics on News Editorial Selection," *Journalism*, Vol. 15, No. 8, 2014.

[29] "The Foxification of News," *The Economist*, July 7, 2011.

number of outlets and voices, each of which seeks to differentiate itself from other channels. These efforts often take the form of expressing more-partisan positions, emphasizing opinion and anecdote, or using a personal and informal tone.[30] Online journalism also has come to be characterized by citizen journalists, collaborative and open-source journalism, and even crowd-funding, all of which create an entirely different set of news production norms and practices that also likely influence news content and presentation.[31]

In this report, we are most concerned with measuring differences in news presentation over time and across platforms (rather than explaining why these differences occur). However, this discussion of current trends in consumption and the economic dynamics of the media industry provide a backdrop and a useful frame for this analysis.

News Presentation in a Digital Age: Past Research

We are not the first to ask how the presentation of news has changed over time and how it differs across types of media. Past research on these questions has most often considered differences through the lens of a specific issue area, such as exploring differences over time and across platforms in coverage of climate change, politics and elections, health issues, or race and crime. Insights from this work are valuable but often not generalizable across an entire given medium. Other analyses look more generally at differences in specific linguistic characteristics, such as tone or use of emotion. These analyses are more widely generalizable and more similar to our approach, described in Chapter Two.

Both single-issue and more-general assessments of changes in news presentation specifically explore differences over time and across platforms in content and in *framing*, which is the way that news is packaged, interpreted, and presented. Framing includes such

---

[30] "The Foxification of News," 2011; Nic Newman and David Levy, eds., *Digital News Report*, Oxford, England: Reuters Institute for the Study of Journalism, 2014.

[31] Usher, 2018; Lewis and Usher, 2013.

elements as word choice, what information is emphasized, how it is organized, and even what other stories or information is presented nearby—or omitted.[32] Even when different sources cover the same topics, those sources might present information in different ways, with different cues, words, and context—that is, with different frames. Frames are important in the context of this report because many of the linguistic differences on which we are focused and that we are trying to detect are also differences in frames—different ways of presenting the same basic information, with different points of emphasis. Another framing issue relevant to our sample selection is partisanship. As we describe in the next chapter, some sources that we analyzed provide news that is oriented toward one side of the political spectrum,[33] and this partisanship could affect linguistic characteristics and style in ways that were picked up by our analysis.

We are interested in the different comparisons, results, and issues covered in existing literature and what this information indicates about how news presentation differs across time and type of media. Specifically, we used this previous research to inform our analysis and to develop expectations for the types of differences we might observe over time and across platforms.[34]

Changes over Time

Past research approaches the question of how media changes over time from several angles. First, there is research that considers how the changing economics of the media industry, as described, have influenced the presentation of news over time. One version of this approach

---

[32] Daniel Kahneman and Amos Tversky, "Choices, Values, and Frames," *American Psychologist*, Vol. 39, No. 4, 1984; Porismita Borah, "Conceptual Issues in Framing Theory: A Systematic Examination of a Decade's Literature," *Journal of Communication*, Vol. 61, No. 2. 2011.

[33] Kevin Coe, David Tewksbury, Bradley J. Bond, Kristin L. Drogos, Robert W. Porter, Ashley Yahn, and Yuanyuan Zhang, "Hostile News: Partisan Use and Perceptions of Cable News Programming," *Journal of Communication*, Vol. 58, No. 2, 2008.

[34] This literature is vast and we could not capture every relevant study that uses content analysis to look at news presentation. Instead, we focused on those with research questions and methodologies most similar to ours and aimed to provide representative examples for each of the main types of literature that we identified.

considers the impact of bottom-line pressures on news presentation, particularly on newspaper coverage. Research completed in 2010, for instance, suggests that reductions in staffing affect the quality and style of newspaper journalism. Specifically, the study indicated that newspaper staff layoffs force journalists to cut corners in ways that affect the content and characteristics of news presentation, such as citing fewer sources and generating fewer specialized features.[35] A 2017 analysis of newspaper journalism focused more explicitly on changes in content and found an increase in the diversity of subjects covered in newspaper journalism over time, which the authors say is a reaction to competitive pressures and a desire to "mimic" the diversity found in online content.[36] However, we should not assume that increased competition in the media industry will always lead to changes in news presentation. In fact, some research suggests stability in certain types of reporting. For example, a review of science coverage in three major newspapers—the *New York Times*, *Washington Post*, and *Chicago Tribune*—over three decades (the 1970s through the 1990s, during which time media economics changed dramatically) found that although the number of articles produced did increase over the period, the nature of the coverage did not change substantially in terms of depth and the details omitted and included.[37] It is worth noting, however, that this study predates the digital age and does not capture all the dynamics of the current media period.

Another body of research looking at changes in news presentation over time focuses on technology, specifically the rise of the internet and what it has enabled in terms of new mechanisms of communication and news presentation. This set of studies is not entirely independent of the effect of economic changes. As noted previously, technological and

[35] Scott Reinhardy, "Downsizing Effects on Personnel: The Case of Layoff Survivors in U.S. Newspapers," *Journal of Media Business Studies*, Vol. 7, No. 4, 2010.

[36] Bozena I.Mierzejewska, Dobin Yim, Philip M. Napoli, Henry C. Lucas Jr., and Abrar Al-Hasan, "Evaluating Strategic Approaches to Competitive Displacement: The Case of the US Newspaper Industry," *Journal of Media Economics*, Vol. 30, No. 1, 2017.

[37] Marianne G. Pellechia, "Trends in Science Coverage: A Content Analysis of Three US Newspapers," *Public Understanding of Science*, Vol. 6. No. 1, 1997.

economic changes are closely intertwined when discussing the media ecosystem; technological changes drive economic ones, and economic changes can encourage additional technological evolution. However, one set of studies focuses less on the economic implications of technological change and more on how new technologies have sparked the development of fundamentally new forms of news production and creation and have led to changes in news presentation. Dutton, for example, argues that social media and the internet allow for collaborative forms of news production that rely on networks of individuals and informal channels rather than formal ones.[38] Lewis and Usher similarly describe a new collaborative journalism that operates across news organizations and at the local, individual level, creating what they call "open source" journalism.[39] Related work argues that the use of hyperlinks and more-frequent updating and revisions, some of which are crowdsourced and driven by users, have made online journalism more current and more interconnected than print or television journalism ever can be.[40]

Another aspect of the technology-focused approach is how the speed of the news cycle and overarching political dynamics might have affected the presentation of news. For instance, a 2018 study explored changes in broadcast television reporting specifically about the U.S. Supreme Court, finding this coverage has changed in terms of the language and frames used to present information. Specifically, the authors found reporting about the Supreme Court increasingly focused on political winners and losers ("the game frame" as they refer to it), using words that emphasize strategy and partisan competition.[41] Related work has shown a similar increase in the use of the "game frame" in

---

[38]   Dutton, 2009.

[39]   Lewis and Usher, 2013.

[40]   Michael Karlsson, "Charting the Liquidity of Online News: Moving Towards a Method for Content Analysis of Online News," *International Communication Gazette*, Vol. 74, No. 4, 2012; Andreas Widholm, "Tracing Online News in Motion: Time and Duration in the Study of Liquid Journalism," *Digital Journalism*, Vol. 4, No. 1, 2016; Usher, 2018.

[41]   Matthew P. Hitt and Kathleen Searles, "Media Coverage and Public Approval of the US Supreme Court," *Political Communication*, Vol. 35, No. 4, 2018.

other types of reporting over time, including congressional and election coverage more generally.[42]

A final set of studies that look at changes in news presentation over time focuses more narrowly on individual issues and examines how the presentation of a single issue varies as the issue goes from one that is unfamiliar to one that is more widely understood. For example, one study considered the evolution of media coverage of marijuana legalization over the 2010–2014 period and how narrative frames used to discuss the issues changed over time and across platforms.[43] This research, although interesting and important, is less relevant to our analysis; we are concerned with changes over time across issues and types of media rather than how each individual issue narrative might evolve.

Cross-Platform Differences

In addition to changes over time, past research has explored whether there are clear linguistic differences across types of media. Research focused on cross-platform differences starts by asking whether different platforms cover the same or different issues. For instance, a 2010 analysis compared the topics covered by newspapers, television, and radio with topics covered by online journalism. The study found that about 60 percent of stories on news websites correspond to those stories published in more-traditional outlets, but that the other 40 percent of news coverage is distinct.[44] This information is a little dated, given the changes that have occurred since 2010, but it still provides a

---

[42] Johanna Dunaway and Regina G. Lawrence, "What Predicts the Game Frame? Media Ownership, Electoral Context, and Campaign News," *Political Communication*, Vol. 32, No. 1, 2015.

[43] Emma E. McGinty, Hillary Samples, Sachini N. Bandara, Brendan Saloner, Marcus A. Bachhuber, and Colleen L. Barry, "The Emerging Public Discourse on State Legalization of Marijuana for Recreational Use in the US: Analysis of News Media Coverage, 2010–2014," *Preventive Medicine*, Vol. 90, 2016.

[44] Scott Maier, "All the News Fit to Post? Comparing News Content on the Web to Newspapers, Television, and Radio," *Journalism & Mass Communication Quarterly*, Vol. 87. No. 3–4, 2010.

useful point of reference and underscores the existence of both overlap and divergence in the topics covered by different types of media.

Studies that directly compare the coverage of a single issue across several platforms provide useful insights into when and how digital and print media diverge in their coverage. However, as alluded to previously, the focus on specific issues means that the results of any one analysis might not be generalizable. Still, this research provides useful insights and context for our analysis in Chapter Three. For example, a 2009 report focused on sports journalism in print and online media found that online sports journalism did not have the same types of gender bias in its coverage of the NCAA March Madness tournament that print journalism was found to have.[45] Other research has compared radio and television news presentation differences. A 2011 study of the level and types of outrage displayed on different forms of media, for instance, found that instances of outrage were most common on cable news programs (being present at least once during every hour) and talk radio; online blogs and columns were somewhat less likely to have instances of outrage.[46] The study also found that mockery was most common in blogs and columns and less common on television and radio.[47] As a final example, a 2018 analysis of coverage of the Tea Party by cable news, online sources, and newspapers found that each type of media framed the party in a different way. Specifically, the authors found that cable news described the Tea Party in a more simplified way as an integrated part of the Republican Party with coverage tied to key events; newspaper coverage was more variable and nuanced in theme and framing of the group and in the timing of coverage.[48]

---

[45] Edward M. Kian, Michael Mondello, and John Vincent, "ESPN—The Women's Sports Network? A Content Analysis of Internet Coverage of March Madness," *Journal of Broadcasting & Electronic Media*, Vol. 53, No. 3, 2009.

[46] *Outrage journalism* can be defined as journalism that displays and is intended to provoke anger. Sarah Sobieraj and Jeffrey M. Berry, "From Incivility to Outrage: Political Discourse in Blogs, Talk Radio, and Cable News," *Political Communication*, Vol. 28. No. 1, 2011.

[47] Sobieraj and Berry, 2011.

[48] Patrick Rafail and John D. McCarthy, "Making the Tea Party Republican: Media Bias and Framing in Newspapers and Cable News," *Social Currents*, Vol. 5, No. 5, 2018.

Not all comparative studies find significant cross-platform differences, however. For example, a 2015 analysis of the treatment of race and crime on cable and network news found no significant differences across the two.[49] As another example, a comparison of disaster coverage on Twitter by professional journalists with disaster coverage on broadcast television found significant similarity in terms of topics and themes covered and frames used. The authors suggest that this similarity is to be expected as a result of feedback between these different forms of media as they operate in the same space. The authors also note that each medium influences the other, with Twitter influencing broadcast journalism more than the other way around (in the cases considered for this analysis).[50] These two studies are reminders that although we do have examples of cross-platform differences in past research, we also have research that finds no meaningful difference across types of media. In our analysis, we try to provide more-complete and holistic comparisons across types of media by considering news coverage writ large rather than coverage of a specific issue and by identifying areas where differences do exist and where they do not.

Limitations of Existing Work and Contributions of This Report

Existing literature focused on news presentation is already extensive. Past research has considered how various sources of news have evolved over time and compared different platforms with each other. It has also provided insight into the possible causes of some of these differences. However, there are several remaining gaps in this literature that we seek to address in this report. First, previous work has focused on qualitatively describing how news presentation differs (or is the same) across

---

[49] Travis L. Dixon and Charlotte L. Williams, "The Changing Misrepresentation of Race and Crime on Network and Cable News," *Journal of Communication*, Vol. 65, No. 1, 2014.

[50] Sebastián Valenzuela, Soledad Puente, and Pablo M. Flores, "Comparing Disaster News on Twitter and Television: An Intermedia Agenda Setting Perspective," *Journal of Broadcasting & Electronic Media*, Vol. 61, No. 4, 2017.

media platforms. In our assessment of news presentation, we aim not only to identify linguistic differences between different forms of media or over time, but also to measure and quantify those differences so that we can say how large the differences are and how relatively significant one linguistic change is compared with another. Without this quantitative measurement, it can be hard to assess how meaningful and substantive observed changes are. Second, previous work has identified some elements of how news presentation differs across platforms and over time, but the assessment has been qualitative for the most part. As an example, online journalism is said to be more interactive and dynamic than print journalism—or to be characterized by a greater degree of outrage.[51] But past research does not always then show what those differences mean in practice. In our report, we aim to provide contextualized information and a more fine-grained analysis that provides insight into what changes in news presentation actually look like.

The final contribution of our report is methodological. Past research has relied on a variety of methods, such as content analysis, interviews, and surveys; the use of some form of content analysis is a fairly common approach. Content analysis uses many different means—humans, coding software, automated programs—to analyze textual data for common themes, tone, style, or other characteristics.[52] Until recently, the majority of coding analysis was done by human coders, limiting both the feasible sample size and the consistency of the coding.[53] Of course, machine coding is not perfect either; machines could miss important nuance that a human coder might appreciate. However, the advantages of machine coding, especially the ability to handle a larger sample size, are significant. In this report, we use RAND-Lex, which combines machine learning with content analy-

---

[51] Sobieraj and Berry, 2011; Karlsson, 2012.

[52] Kimberly A. Neuendorf, *The Content Analysis Guidebook*, Thousand Oaks, Calif.: Sage, 2016.

[53] For another study using automated coding, see Ilias Flaounas, Omar Ali, Thomas Lansdall-Welfare, Tijl De Bie, Nick Mosdell, Justin Lewis, and Nello Cristianini, "Research Methods in the Age of Digital Journalism: Massive-Scale Automated Analysis of News-Content—Topics, Style and Gender," *Digital Journalism*, Vol. 1, No. 1, 2013.

sis that has both quantitative and qualitative elements. The use of a machine-learning tool allows us to include tens of thousands of articles in our sample and then look for patterns and trends across these larger data sets. This tool makes patterns and trends, where they exist, more visible. It also lends robustness to our analysis that work based on a smaller sample might lack.[54] By also featuring a human element, we are able to capture nuance and content, capturing the best of both methods. We describe our method in more detail in the next chapter.

Objective of This Report

The objective of this report is to provide an empirical assessment—quantitative and qualitative—of how the presentation of news has changed over time and varies across platforms. The report is guided by the following research questions:[55]

- In what measurable ways did the style of news presentation in *print journalism* change between 1989 and 2017?
- In what measurable ways did the style of news presentation in *broadcast journalism* change between 1989 and 2017?
- How does the style of news presentation in *broadcast journalism* differ from the style used in *prime-time cable programming* over the period from 2000 to 2017?
- How does the style of news presentation in *online journalism* differ from that of *print journalism* over the period from 2012 to 2017?

---

[54] Appendix A provides details on the RAND-Lex taxonomy, along with examples and definitions.

[55] The set of comparisons made in this report is certainly not exhaustive and there are others that we could have run. We made our selections as follows. First, we had resources to do only four analyses (each features at least one and sometimes several separate comparisons). Second, we wanted some analyses conducted over time and some comparisons across platforms. Broadcast television and newspapers covered the longest time frames and so were best suited for the comparisons across time. We chose to anchor the comparisons across platforms on how news was consumed, meaning comparisons of news that an audience watches and the news that an audience reads. This led to the online-newspaper and broadcast-cable dyads.

In addressing these questions, this report describes empirical evidence that can be used to measure the style composition of newspaper reporting, television, and online journalism (e.g., online-only news outlets such as Politico, Breitbart, Huffington Post) and quantitatively assess the degree and scope of these changes. By *style*, we mean the word choices that reflect speakers' stances or perspectives.[56] For example, in one sense, the words *regime* and *government* are denotatively similar, but the former often has a more negative connotation of illegitimacy and authoritarianism. We can think of these style choices as linguistic variables—emotion, values, social relationships, levels of certainty, etc.—and thus measure style as linguistic behavior.

As noted, we also aim to address some of the remaining gaps in existing literature on news presentation. First, we combine software-based text analysis with human-based content analysis to produce a more complete picture of media changes over time at scale, using large data sets of thousands of news articles and millions of words spanning decades. This process allows us to present a more holistic approach to understanding the evolution of the linguistic presentation and character of media content. It also allows us to present a replicable methodology and to begin to develop a quantitative empirical foundation that can be used in the future to track changes over time and to describe the current and future state of news presentation. Second, we consider a longer time frame, starting in the 1980s and continuing through the present, which allows us to track changes more reliably and to detect a wider set of changes. Third, we explore changes across issues rather than across platforms, providing a more complete perspective of the diversity of this presentation across multiple platforms.

In this report, we focus explicitly on changes in the presentation of information, with a particular focus on the language choice, using empirical data. We do not try to attach a normative value to any changes or to link these changes to any possible effects on individual

---

[56] Scott F. Kiesling, "Style as Stance," in Alexandra Jaffe, ed., *Stance: Sociolinguistic Perspectives*, New York: Oxford University Press, 2009; Stefania Degaetano and Elke Teich, "The Lexico-Grammar of Stance: An Exploratory Analysis of Scientific Texts," *Bochumer Linguistische Arbeitsberichte*, Vol. 3, 2011.

political attitudes. Future research should evaluate these questions; the data collected and described in this report might be useful in such investigations.

This report is intended for a wide audience, including researchers studying mass media communication and those already analyzing changes and dynamics in the current media ecosystem; journalists and media professionals seeking to better understand how their industry has evolved over time and the overall implications of choices about tone, subjectivity, and word choice in news coverage; and members of the general public interested in understanding more about how changes in the presentation of news might affect what they consume. We present our findings in several different ways, using different visualizations, tables, and specific examples to make the results more accessible to a wider audience.

Outline of This Report

The remainder of this report is as follows. The next chapter describes the data and methodology used in our analyses. Chapters Three through Five present results of our analysis of changes in newspaper and television journalism over the past 30 years and the changes that emerge as we shift from print to online journalism over that time. Chapter Six summarizes and discusses key insights from our analysis and their implications for Truth Decay. We also provide several appendixes. Appendix A provides details on the RAND-Lex taxonomy, along with examples and definitions. Appendix B provides graphs from subsample analyses used as robustness checks of the analyses presented in the body of the report. Appendix C provides the analysis of variance (ANOVA) tables from all analyses.

CHAPTER TWO

Data and Methodology

To assess how news presentation has changed over time, we focused on three primary types of news: television, print journalism, and online journalism. These three sources are the primary ways that Americans currently get news and (with the exception of online journalism, which is still relatively new) the primary ways that they have consumed news in the past.[1] We did, however, exclude two important forms of news: radio and social media. As mentioned in Chapter One, we had hoped to feature radio transcripts but were unable to locate a systematic database of such transcripts that would allow us to conduct a rigorous evaluation. Examining the tone, content, and sentiment of news coverage on social media, on the other hand, is feasible.[2] In fact, it is an essential question that deserves further investigation. However, it is also such an expansive undertaking that it warrants its own project rather than being folded into this one. For each of the three types of news media used in this analysis, we built a corpus of textual material—articles and transcripts—and then analyzed the textual data using RAND-Lex, a tool for textual analysis that combines machine learning used to iden-

---

[1] Amy Mitchell, Elisa Shearer, Jeffrey Gottfried, and Michael Barthel, "Pathways to News," Pew Research Center, July 2016.

[2] Elizabeth Bodine-Baron, Todd C. Helmus, Madeline Magnuson, and Zev Winkelman, *Examining ISIS Support and Opposition Networks on Twitter*, Santa Monica, Calif.: RAND Corporation, RR-1328-OSD, 2016; Todd C. Helmus, Elizabeth Bodine-Baron, Andrew Radin, Madeline Magnuson, Joshua Mendelsohn, William Marcellino, Andriy Bega, and Zev Winkelman, *Russian Social Media Influence: Understanding Russian Propaganda in Eastern Europe*, Santa Monica, Calif.: RAND Corporation, RR-237-OSD, 2018.

tify patterns in word use, tone, and sentiment with qualitative content analysis. In this chapter, we describe our data and discuss the methodological approach used in our analyses.

Data Collection

Newspapers

Newspaper articles and television transcripts came from the LexisNexis database.[3] We were able to use three newspapers—the *New York Times*, *Washington Post*, and *St. Louis Post-Dispatch*—each of which has an archive that extends from 1989 to the present in LexisNexis. The three newspapers provide a mix of national newspapers from major media centers (the *New York Times* and *Washington Post*) and a regional newspaper from outside the Northeast (the *St. Louis Post-Dispatch*). Admittedly, this sample is less diverse and representative than would have been optimal and will not be generalizable across all U.S. newspapers. We encountered various data limitations that affected the sample selection and that we seek to address by taking multiple cuts at the data that we have. First, we wanted to use about 30 years of data to ensure that our time frame prior to the rise of the internet was sufficiently long to permit a before-and-after comparison, and this limited our choices to newspapers with sufficiently long, digitized, and searchable archives in LexisNexis. Each of the papers we used had archives going back to 1989, which gave us 29 years, falling one year short of our goal. We would have liked to include more newspapers with greater geographic diversity, but there are reasons why our sample might be reasonably representative of the news that at least a substantial portion of national or regional newspaper consumers receive. First, the *New York Times* and *Washington*

---

[3]   We chose to use LexisNexis despite some limitations, such as missing dates and limited sources. ProQuest provides an alternative, but articles are available only as PDFs. RAND-Lex requires text files and the process of converting all PDFs into text files would have been prohibitively time-consuming. We also looked into using the archives of individual newspapers. However, getting full text access would have been prohibitively costly to do at the scale we hoped to achieve. Although LexisNexis coverage might be imperfect, we expect that these imperfections are random and thus unlikely to bias the results of our analysis.

Post are two of the leading papers in terms of print circulation and rank in the top five in online traffic as well.[4] Both are large, national newspapers that are broadly representative of news coverage of this type and their wide reach indicates that they are representative of the specific types of information that newspaper consumers are receiving. The *Post-Dispatch* is much smaller, but it does still rank among the top 50 largest U.S. newspapers.[5] It is also a regional paper, introducing some diversity and a different perspective from the other two sources, and it represents a more mid-size market. In addition to the full-sample analysis, we also conduct two additional analyses: The first is a national sample using only the *New York Times* and *Washington Post*, which will measure the change in news presentation style specifically for national newspapers. Second, we consider each individual paper separately, as a robustness check, to understand whether changes within any one paper are driving the results.[6]

Because our focus was on news, we collected only the front-page stories (including the segments of those stories that continued on inside pages). We sampled each newspaper's front page every eighth day from January 1, 1989, to December 31, 2017. This sample composed the basis for our newspaper analysis.[7]

Television News

The television news we studied consisted of both broadcast and cable samples. We collected transcripts of the flagship news programs on the American Broadcasting Company (ABC), Columbia Broadcasting

---

[4] Amy Mitchell, ed., *State of the News Media, 2015*, Washington, D.C.: Pew Research Center, April 29, 2015; Lewis Dvorkin, "Inside Forbes: The State of the Digital News, or 25 Web Sites Captured in 3 Revealing Charts," *Forbes*, January 2016; Douglas McIntyre, "America's 100 Largest Newspapers," 24/7 Wall Street, January 24, 2017.

[5] Mitchell, 2015; Dvorkin, 2016; McIntyre, 2017.

[6] Because our sample is not fully representative of all newspapers, the results will be interpreted cautiously as applying only to the specific samples considered.

[7] RAND-Lex can analyze corpora only up to 5 million words because of computational constraints. Corpora larger than 5 million words were halved or quartered as needed to ensure computational feasibility. For newspapers, this meant that we randomly selected every other story and used this reduced sample in the analysis.

System (CBS), and National Broadcasting Company (NBC) and of a selection of prime-time programs from the three major cable television news networks: Cable News Network (CNN), Fox News Channel, and Microsoft/National Broadcasting Company (MSNBC). The different networks are in LexisNexis with different start dates (dates reflect available transcripts as of November 2017): 1979 for ABC; 1989 for CBS; 1996 for Fox News, MSNBC, and NBC; and 1990 for CNN. All six networks are archived through December 31, 2017. We collected data from each network beginning with the dates their transcripts appear in the database. We used different procedures for collecting data from broadcast television and cable television.

For each news channel, we collected the written transcripts provided by LexisNexis for a 30-minute segment of news coverage from one day each month. The same day was used for all six networks, and it rotated through weekdays (weekends were excluded). For broadcast television, we collected the transcripts from each network's flagship evening news program: *ABC World News Tonight*,[8] *CBS Evening News*, and *NBC Nightly News*. For the cable television networks, however, we collected a sample of their evening prime-time programming. To do so, we collected all programming between 8 p.m. and 10 p.m. (Eastern time) on CNN, Fox News Channel, and MSNBC.

By focusing on prime-time coverage for cable networks, we intentionally captured the most popular programming and created a sample precisely tailored to our research question. However, these programs tend to be opinion-based shows led by pundits, not news reporting–based programs. Our analysis was designed to detect any systematic differences in the presentation of news in these two types of shows. (Because of their different intents, we expected such a difference to exist.) Previous work has suggested that prime-time cable programming tends to be more heavily opinion-based than network news.[9] As

---

[8]   ABC's flagship news program has changed its name several times during the period we examined: *World News Tonight* (1979–2006), *World News* (2006–2009), *ABC World News* (2009–2014), and *ABC World News Tonight* (2014–2017).

[9]   Mark Jurkowitz, Paul Hitlin, Amy Mitchell, Laura Houston Santhanam, Steve Adams, Monica Anderson, and Nancy Vogt, *The Changing TV News Landscape*, Washington, D.C., Pew Research Center, March 17, 2013.

a result, even when covering the same topics as broadcast television or newspapers, prime-time cable shows present a different form of information that relies on the opinions and arguments of individual pundits to define and shape issues under discussion. We chose the prime-time period for cable programming because doing so allowed us to explore the cable news-channel shows with the greatest exposure. Our comparison of prime-time cable programming with broadcast television news aims to assess empirically how prime-time cable programming and broadcast news are different in terms of the language each uses. The empirical data we collected allowed us to describe the linguistic implications of these differences and to track the relationship between the two over time.[10]

Online Journalism

The online journalism in our sample focused on web-only online journalism sites from across the ideological spectrum. Web-based platforms are an increasingly common source of news. In 2017, 43 percent of the general public reported getting news online.[11] Our selection of sources was intended to study a sample of the *most-consumed* online outlets on each side of the political spectrum.[12] We did not collect data from the websites of print outlets (e.g., www.nytimes.com) or major television networks (e.g., www.foxnews.com) because we were already capturing these through our search of newspapers and television transcripts. We chose three outlets on each side of the spectrum, taking into account both political orientation and online traffic.[13] On the conservative side of the spec-

---

[10] Chapter One contains relevant usage statistics for both broadcast and cable television.

[11] Jeffrey Gottfried and Elisa Shearer, "Americans' Online News Use Is Closing In on TV News Use," Pew Research Center, September 7, 2017.

[12] We did not try to create a representative sample that was fully balanced in type or partisanship of coverage. Such an effort would have been complicated by the tremendous diversity of online journalism and the difficulty that comes with trying to precisely rate the partisan bias or "quality" of any source. This means that the results of our analysis are not broadly generalizable but do provide insights into how some of the most-consumed online news sources present news. Future analysis could consider whether a more representative sample could be collected and whether the insights would be substantially different.

[13] The choice of six total outlets was governed by project resources.

trum, we relied on a January 2018 list of the most-trafficked conservative websites, which ranked Fox News first (as noted, this was excluded), followed by Breitbart and the Daily Caller. TheBlaze, our third source, ranks eighth.[14] Outlets ranked third through seventh were excluded either because they did not adequately cover our 2012–2017 time frame or because they were affiliated with print news sources. Another advantage of TheBlaze is that, according to two sources that rate media bias, it tends to be a little bit more toward the center than Breitbart and the Daily Caller, giving us additional diversity in the sample.[15] There are, of course, many different rankings of news websites, each slightly different. We cross-checked these three sources across these lists and found that all three appeared on each list, usually within the top ten sources. Our sample of conservative sources, then, represents a sample drawn from some of the most broadly consumed conservative-leaning information online. Certainly, there could be consumers who rely on smaller outlets with different perspectives, but this content reaches and affects a smaller audience of consumers.

For left-leaning sources, the choice was complicated by an even greater number of rankings of online journalism sites, each ranking with slightly different criteria. We ultimately settled on three that appear near the top across multiple lists and that also met our criteria for the time frame. We selected BuzzFeed, Politico, and Huffington Post as sources that represent some of the most highly consumed left-leaning online journalism sources.[16]

Table 2.1 provides readership numbers for our six sources.

Finally, we considered the relative bias of our selected sources.[17] Comparing across several different sources that rate media bias, we

---

[14] Howard Polskin, "Who Gets the Most Traffic Among Conservative Websites," MediaShift, January 18, 2018.

[15] Shawn Langlois, "How Biased Is Your News Source? You Probably Won't Agree with This Chart," *MarketWatch*, April 21, 2018. Also see Media Bias/Fact Check, homepage, undated.

[16] Dvorkin, 2016; Aelieve, "List of the 20 Most Popular Liberal News Sites," webpage, 2018a; Aelieve, "List of the 20 Most Popular News Sites," webpage, 2018b.

[17] As noted elsewhere, online news is often more openly partisan than newspapers, partly because of structural and economic features of the media industry. Television news also is

Table 2.1
Readership for Online News Outlets

	Monthly Visits (millions) (average, August–October 2018)	Total Visits (millions) (August–October 2018)	Unique Visitors (millions) (August–October 2018)
Breitbart	78.03	234.1	17.66
Buzzfeed Politics	26.68	80.1	10.41
Daily Caller	29.26	87.8	7.1
Huffington Post	133.4	400.4	48.21
Politico	60.28	180.9	19.5
TheBlaze	13.35	40.1	3.19

SOURCE: SimilarWeb, homepage, search thread for each outlet, conducted August–October 2018.

found that our six sources tend to be reasonably far to the right and left of the political center. According to two separate sources that rate the bias or slant of news programming, the sample of right-leaning sources is somewhat further to the right than the left-leaning sources are to the left, which means that the full sample of data is not fully balanced in terms of partisanship.[18] That our sample of some of the most-used online journalism outlets does not include a larger number of centrist sources is not surprising. Many of the most-balanced news sources according to bias ratings are associated with either print media (or at least have a print version, such as The Hill) or major television networks. Our analysis might reveal linguistic markers of this bias, but that is consistent with our intention to assess a sample drawn from the most highly consumed sources of online journalism. Because this

often affected by partisanship but there are fewer outlets, allowing us to use all of them. There is substantially more diversity for online sources, so partisanship is a secondary selection criteria, after readership. We do not conduct any comparisons of left-leaning and right-leaning sources. We chose to use three sources on each side of the spectrum but did not try to achieve full balance in partisanship because circulation or readership was our priority selection characteristic.

[18] Langlois, 2018; Media Bias/Fact Check, undated.

content is likely more affected by partisan bias than that of the newspaper sample (as rated by these same bias rating tools), our comparison of online journalism with print journalism might provide some insight into the extent to which partisanship affects the way news is presented in terms of linguistic elements and characteristics. It will also provide insight and collect empirical data on how the presentation of information differs across print and online platforms. However, the diversity of online sources means that our results should be viewed as a first cut only and not a fully generalizable result.

To collect our digital journalism data set, we searched the archives of the six news websites, taking homepage stories stored by the Internet Archive (archive.org) for every eighth day from January 1, 2012, through December 31, 2017. If archived stories were not available for the selected date, we took stories from the closest available date within four days of the original target. When no archive was available to match that request, the week was skipped. During the analytical period of 2012–2017, this method yielded URLs to front-page (i.e., homepage) archives for almost every request, with the exception of a four-month outage from Politico (January 2014 through April 2014) and a one-month outage from the Daily Caller (December 2012).

For each of these homepages, we designed customized sampling frames to identify all potential links to story pages, excluding non-news content (e.g., links to advertisements, comment threads, or website subsections).[19] Importantly, we did not screen out sports or other information if it was featured along with news; however, website sampling frames were designed to minimize these types of stories.[20]

A small number of URLs contained valid news text but could not be scraped effectively by the algorithm because of inconsistent webpage formats. To ensure data quality, pages that were successfully scraped were then checked for several potential exclusion conditions. To prevent the double-counting of stories that appeared on multiple "front pages"

---

[19] By *sampling frame*, we refer to the code specified to scrape text from the selected outlets and pages on identified dates. Because the structure of each outlet is slightly different, a separate code must be used for each outlet.

[20] As for print journalism, this would have been prohibitively time consuming and costly.

archived for different dates from the same outlet (especially important for websites with long-lived front pages and slow publication rates), URLs were checked for duplicated content. We also removed stories with fewer than 500 characters—primarily video-based content—and stories hosted on a different domain. Stories that passed all of those verification steps were admitted into the preparatory analytical data set for further text cleaning. Table 2.2 summarizes the amount of data collected by this process, including the number of stories scraped from each source.

Table 2.3 lists the full set of analytical comparisons completed with the online journalism sample and the amount of data in each. First, we compared the full online sample with the full print journalism sample. Then, we considered a reduced sample of internet outlets (excluding the left-leaning and right-leaning outlets with the lowest readership (TheBlaze and Buzzfeed Politics) and the national newspaper sample to assess robustness of the results to specific analyses.[21]

Preparing the Data for Analysis

Once all the data were collected, we "cleaned" them. This consisted of removing all of the metadata so that only the news story remained and verifying that the sampling procedure did indeed collect the desired types of news articles. As part of the cleaning process, we removed such text as the author byline, publication date, reporting location, and stage directions (in the case of television). We also removed information provided by LexisNexis, such as the word count and publication language. The process was imperfect—especially so for the online journalism sources because website designs vary over time and across outlets. We retained the headline and text of each article for newspapers and internet news or the transcript of the television segment.

---

[21] To ensure analytical feasibility, we used only one-quarter of the data, drawn randomly, from the larger corpus.

Table 2.2
Details of Online Journalism Data Collection and Validation Process

Outlet	Homepages Analyzed	Story Links Detected	Stories Successfully Scraped	Unique Stories	Stories With More Than 500 Characters of Text-Based News	Total Words from Each Source (millions)	Average Words per Story
Buzzfeed Politics	256	8,794	7,295	6,174	5,220	3.1	415
Breitbart	227	19,397	18,257	17,094	16,234	7.5	464
Daily Caller	221	17,740	15,476	15,253	14,290	5.5	388
Huffington Post (Politics)	270	13,341	12,845	11,181	10,834	10.0	926
Politico	249	13,605	12,095	11,290	10,684	9.7	918
TheBlaze	260	21,511	21,090	19,940	19,243	8.0	605

Table 2.3
Data Sets

Analysis Name	Sample 1	Articles/ Segments (Sample 1)	Words (Sample 1)	Sample 2	Articles/ Segments (Sample 2)	Words (Sample 2)
Newspapers						
Full newspaper sample	*NYT, WP, SLPD* pre-2000[a]	12,272	11,360,227	*NYT, WP, SLPD* 2000–2017[a]	15,342	17,072,668
National newspaper	*NYT, WP* pre-2000	8,091	8,791,100	*NYT, WP* 2000–2017	11,082	13,617,145
New York Times	*NYT* pre-2000	4,736	4,698,501	*NYT* 2000–2017	5,821	7,085,705
Washington Post	*WP* pre-2000	3,355	4,092,599	*WP* 2000–2017	5,261	6,531,440
St. Louis Post-Dispatch	*SLPD* pre-2000	4,181	2,569,127	*SLPD* 2000–2017	4,260	3,455,523
Television						
Broadcast news	ABC, NBC, CBS pre-2000	4,223	1,513,175	ABC, NBC, CBS 2000–2017	6,502	2,299,085
2000–2017 television comparison	ABC, NBC, CBS 2000–2017	6,502	2,299,085	CNN, MSNBC, Fox News Channel 2000–2017	4,232	12,278,437

Table 2.3—Continued

Analysis Name	Sample 1	Articles/Segments (Sample 1)	Words (Sample 1)	Sample 2	Articles/Segments (Sample 2)	Words (Sample 2)
Cross-Platform						
Full internet/full newspaper sample	Online 2012–2017 (Politico, HuffPo, Breitbart, Daily Caller, Blaze, BuzzFeed Politics)[a]	38,252	21,238,215	Newspapers (NYT, WP, SLPD) 2012–2017	4,609	5,611,270
Reduced internet/national newspapers	Online 2012–2017 (Politico, HuffPo, Breitbart, Daily Caller)[b]	26,020	15,798,570	Newspapers (NYT, WP) 2012–2017	3,398	4,358,964

NOTES: We conducted several different versions of most analyses, using variations in the samples to assess the robustness of the results and assessing the influence of specific sources within the analysis. HuffPo = HuffPost Politics; NYT = New York Times; SLPD = St. Louis Post-Dispatch; WP = Washington Post

[a] Data sets were halved (taking alternating stories from the source data set) before compilation into the analytical corpora because of computing capacity constraints.

[b] Data set was quartered (taking every fourth article) before analysis because of computing capacity constraints. Sample counts are before halving or quartering. Unless otherwise noted, data collection periods started in 1989 and ended in 2017.

Periodization and Comparisons

Stance comparison, a way of detecting the stylistic choices that writers and speakers make as they represent the world through language, is contrastive in RAND-Lex between two corpora of text. Thus, to study change over time, we needed to divide the data into contrastive collections: in this case, an earlier period and a later period, or two samples from different media. We used January 1, 2000, as our cut point, creating pre-2000 and post-2000 data sets for newspapers and network television news, the two media sources for which we had data that extended prior to 2000. Table 2.3 summarizes all the analyses conducted—those that look at differences over time and those that look across platforms.

Two important changes in the U.S. media industry were taking place around the year 2000 that make it a good place to divide the data. First, viewership of all three major cable networks (especially Fox News) increased dramatically starting around that year. This increase is less sizable for CNN and MSNBC, but when taken together, cable news viewership does appear to increase markedly around this date.[22] In the years after 2000, cable news programming solidified its position as a major source of news for U.S. audiences. Second, 2000 marks a turning point in the growth of the internet. It was around this time that internet usage among Americans passed the 50-percent mark.[23] Internet use escalated rapidly after that, and roughly 90 percent of Americans are online today. Relevant to this study, important political news websites, such as the Drudge Report and Daily Kos, were founded around this time, in 1995 and 2002, respectively.[24] Both cable programming and online options increased competitive pressures on existing media outlets and introduced new forms and styles of news reporting. These new media also provided news 24 hours a day, which changed the relationship between news media organizations and

---

[22] Pew Research Center, "Cable News Prime Time Viewership," webpage, March 13, 2006.

[23] According to Pew surveys, 52 percent of Americans used the internet in 2000. Pew Research Center, "Internet/Broadband Fact Sheet," webpage, February 5, 2018a.

[24] Kavanagh and Rich, 2018.

the public and created new demands on media producers to fill the extended time with additional content.

A key news event occurred around this time that also might have played a role in changes in media content. The contentious presidential election that pitted George W. Bush against Al Gore and the subsequent Supreme Court case settling Florida's recount dispute quickly became a partisan dividing line that exacerbated political polarization. This rise in polarization led directly to increased partisan content in media coverage, reflecting another important change that affected how stories were depicted and consumed. The September 11, 2001, terrorist attacks in the United States were another crystallizing event that changed much about the country's political, military, economic, and media domains. We cannot fully disentangle the effects of these different events and changes within the media ecosystem. In reality, all of the above probably had some effect and their confluence might be most important to understand how the presentation of news has changed over time.

The 2000 cut point makes intuitive sense for this comparative analysis because of trends in internet and online news use. Importantly, our analysis will provide a comparison of the pre- and post-2000 samples rather than a time series assessment of how things evolve more continuously over time. Furthermore, the cut point does not imply that things drastically changed precisely in 2000; rather, it allows comparison of the overall characteristics of the pre-2000 period with the overall characteristics of the post-2000 period. The cut point does not work for all the changes that we would like to capture in our analysis, however. First, the rise of social media and online journalism occurred after 2000 but had significant impacts on the way news is disseminated and consumed. We do not include social media data, but we do include online journalism. For the comparison of online and print journalism, we instead use the 2012–2017 period because most digital journalism was fairly well established by 2012. Second, cable news outlets really came into being in their current form only in 1996, so we have only a full post-2000 sample. Therefore, we do not do a pre- and post-2000 analysis for cable programming; instead, we compare it with only the post-2000 broadcast sample.

Table 2.3 lists the full set of comparisons we conducted along with some details about the number of articles and words in each. It is worth noting that there are size variations for each source corpus (that is, the set of all articles from a given source). For example, we have considerably less text from Buzzfeed than from other online outlets and less from the *St. Louis Post-Dispatch* than other newspapers. Differences in size were less of an issue for the television sample, although we clearly have a smaller corpus of cable programming than broadcast television news. To assess the effect of these differences, we conduct additional analyses, looking at each newspaper individually and comparing the results using the full set of online sources with the results of analysis using only two of those sources and excluding the third (Buzzfeed, as shown in Table 2.3). We discuss the results of these analyses in later chapters but note that we find no meaningful changes from these sample alterations. However, given the imbalance in source material, we choose to present our results in terms of frequencies, statistics, and comparisons rather than in terms of the numbers of specific linguistic characteristics across two corpora.

Analysis

Software

To conduct our analysis, we used RAND-Lex,[25] a suite of text analysis and machine learning tools designed for scalable, human-in-the-loop analysis of unstructured text data.[26] RAND-Lex allows researchers to look at very large collections of text data (e.g., in the tens of millions of words) and conduct both descriptive and exploratory statistical tests to analyze and make meaning of those data sets. This kind of computer-assisted analysis extends and leverages human expertise and

---

[25] See Appendix A for an explantion of RAND-Lex.

[26] Human-in-the-loop approaches can leverage the reliability and scalability of fully automated text analysis with the high-context meaning-making of human interpretation. Specifically, the role of the human analyst is to review blocks of text, look for patterns of linguistic variables, and interpret those patterns in context. This is akin to what a human coder would do in a typical coding exercise.

attention—for example, identifying how Arabic-speaking populations across the world talk about the terrorist group ISIS online or how Russian speakers in the near abroad use social media to argue about the Russian annexation of Crimea.[27]

RAND-Lex was purposefully designed to avoid preprogrammed analysis and instead leverage the kind of context-rich analysis that humans are capable of. In this hybrid human-computer reading model, the role of computers is to detect "deep patterning . . . beyond human observation and memory . . . observable only indirectly in the probabilities associated with lexical and grammatical choices across long texts and corpora."[28] This bird's-eye view description can allow human researchers to bring their deep domain knowledge to bear and interpret the meaning of those patterns.

Text Analysis Method

To detect changes in *how* the news is reported as opposed to changes in *what* was reported (we assumed that the topics would change over time), we used stance comparisons. For example, an increase in first-person pronouns (i.e., "I," "we," "us"), or a decrease in hedging language (e.g., "maybe," "it's possible," "some degree of") can be statistically tested for even though it might not be obvious to a human reader—especially if a meaningful shift was spread over a very large, multi-million word corpus. Essentially, RAND-Lex looks for patterns across thousands of articles and is able to identify trends from this large-*n* analysis that a human coder of several hundred articles might not. These types of changes, taken together, can be indicative of more-systemic changes in the media ecosystem.

The stance analysis module in RAND-Lex uses a model and taxonomy of linguistic characteristics that was developed at Carnegie Mellon University (CMU) and has been usefully applied across a range

---

[27] Bodine-Baron et al., 2016; Helmus et al., 2018.

[28] Michael Stubbs, *Text and Corpus Analysis: Computer-Assisted Studies of Language and Culture*, Oxford, England: Blackwell, 1996, p. 15.

of language analytics domains.[29] This taxonomy is useful, but it is also complex and not always intuitive for new users. The stance dictionary contains 121 fine-grained *linguistic characteristics* divided into 15 higher-order *linguistic parent categories*. Some of these parent categories will likely make more sense at first glance (e.g., *emotion* or *personal perspective*) than others (e.g., *public values* or *elaboration*). Table 2.4 provides these 15 categories and their definitions along with selected examples to help give readers a sense of what the software is coding. Because RAND-Lex tags multiword phrases in addition to words, we provide examples of both for each parent category. (See Appendix A for a detailed discussion of the taxonomy and the literature surrounding the taxonomy's use and for definitions for all fine-grained linguistic characteristics.)

The taxonomy of language variables shown in Table 2.4 comes from functional linguistics and rhetorical theory. This theory-based approach treats language as social, pragmatic, and contextualized (culturally, interpersonally, and physically and spatially). Different categories of our taxonomy capture different aspects of the language in a given corpus of text. Different genres and discourses make more or less use of these categories and the more-specific linguistic characteristics that make them up. It is these differences in the prevalence of different linguistic categories and characteristics that we look for and assess in our analysis. RAND-Lex picks up on differences in individual categories and characteristics, but for the purpose of interpretation, we take a more holistic approach, considering categories that capture similar or complementary linguistic elements together to characterize the underlying linguistic style and to contextualize changes over time and differences across platforms.

The parent categories can be grouped in several ways to provide this more holistic understanding of what we are looking for in our analysis. First, there are categories associated with physical and spatial context. These include characters, descriptive language, elaboration, reporting directions, and time. This group of categories is focused on

---

[29] For more information on the CMU taxonomy, see Carnegie Mellon University Department of English, "DocuScope: Computer-Aided Rhetorical Analysis," website, undated. We provide a detailed set of application references in Appendix A.

Table 2.4
RAND-Lex Linguistic Parent Categories and Definitions

Linguistic Category	Definition	Selected Examples for Each Category[a]
Personal perspective	Language from a subjective perspective, including personal certainty, intensity, and temporal experience (e.g., first-person language, autobiography, immediacy, personal disclosures)	• I feel that; I believe that; I'm sorry • It seems; it appears; I think it is • Right now; maybe; definitely
Time	Temporality, including temporal perspective (e.g., duration, date, looking back, looking to or predicting the future)	• Next week; last month; for two years • We will; there will be • In her youth; seems like yesterday
Emotion	Affective language (e.g., anger, fear, sadness, positivity, negativity)	• Regret that; sorry that • Joy; fear; petrified; livid • I've failed
Descriptive language	Descriptions of the world (e.g., motion, dialogue, orality, concrete properties)	• She said; uh-huh • Soft; prickly; sour; nearby; far away • Run; jump; dance
Interpersonal relationships	Text about or constructing the social world (e.g., promises, agreement, social closeness)	• I accept; I agree; I promise • Given credit for; attributed; condemn; denounce • Don't worry; it's ok; good going
Public values	Language about the public good (e.g., public virtue and vice, social responsibility)	• Justice; happiness; fairness • Human rights; civil rights • Take care of; accountability
Public language	Public sharing of talk, sources, and opinions (e.g., rumors, authority sources, popular sources and opinion, magazines)	• The courts; the police • Some hold that; some believe • I recognize that; I agree with
Academic language	Formal, academic style (e.g., abstract concepts, citing precedent, undermining sources, metadiscourse)	• Speaker; listener; audience • According to; sources say • Has a long history • Fulfillment; satisfaction; understanding; disillusionment

Table 2.4—Continued

Linguistic Category	Definition	Selected Examples for Each Category[a]
Reasoning	Language used to frame and discuss arguments; to persuade (e.g., resistance, contingency, denial, concessions)	• Suppose that; imagine that • If X, then Y and so, Z • She counterargued; the rebuttal • Even if; owing to; because of
Interactions	Language indicating a linguistic exchange between two or more people (e.g., feedback, follow-up, question, "you" reference, prior knowledge, attention grab)	• Do you know? What should we make of it? • As you know; in response to • I advise you; I urge you; he asks me
Elaboration	Adding details or explication to talk (e.g., numbers, examples, exceptions)	• All; every; for example • An exception; the only one • More; fewer; in particular; specifically • Resembles; looks like
Reporting	Reporting states, events, and changes; reporting causal sequences (e.g., reporting events, sequence, causality, consequence)	• Again, recurred • The candidate spoke, laughed, and then argued • The meeting began and so she left • By means of; as a result of • It was established; she instituted
Directions	Instructions and guidance (e.g., imperatives, procedures, body movement)	• Must respond by; take your; use only; go back to step one • Ought not; should never; need to • Now you will • Clasp; grab; lift up
Narrative	Language of storytelling (e.g., narrative verbs, asides)	• Came; walked; biked • By the way; anyway
Characters	Characters in the social and physical world (e.g., personal roles and pronouns, neutral attribution, dialogue cues)	• He; she; the • You guys • Farmer; scientist; actor; father

[a] More examples provided by linguistic characteristic in Appendix A.

describing physical locations and spaces, the people and things within those spaces, and how those people and things move through that space. Some of the more specific linguistic characteristics within these categories provide additional insight. For example, the linguistic category of "time" includes characteristics focused on the passage of time, looking forward or backward in time, duration, the individual experience of time (i.e., biographical time), and shifts in time (e.g., "next week").[30] These different conceptions of time can be used together or apart. In assessing the prevalence of the "time" linguistic category in any corpus of text, RAND-Lex would measure instances where these concepts were used or referenced and then compare this with other corpora. The human part of the analysis involved interpreting usage patterns in one characteristic alongside others and providing a holistic understanding of observed differences and changes across characteristics.

Second, there are categories associated with personal and interpersonal relationships and constructions, such as emotion, personal perspective, narrative, interpersonal relationships, and interactions. The categories in this group capture internal dialogues and thoughts, storytelling and narration, and the interactions and interplay between and within individuals. While the first set of categories is largely focused on describing the physical, external, objectively observed world, this second set is more inwardly focused, emphasizing the personal and subjective constructions and interpretations. As an example, the category "personal perspective" includes such characteristics as use of first person, personal disclosure, personal thinking, uncertainty, immediacy, and subjective talk. Each of these characteristics captures some element of personal perspective. In interpreting the RAND-Lex output on this characteristic and similar ones, we were interested not only in the fact that personal perspective was used, but in what contexts and with what frequency. We could then interpret that usage alongside other related characteristics and categories.

Third, there are linguistic categories used to describe societal-level interactions, institutions, and phenomena. Such categories as public lan-

---

[30] While we do not discuss all individual characteristics here, Table 2.4 features many examples. In Appendix A, we define each characteristic in detail.

guage and public values capture discourse at this more communal level, often focused on the common good, shared experiences, social responsibility, and the institutions that define and order societies, such as sources of authority. Finally, there are linguistic categories centered around elements of metacognition and the abstract, such as reasoning and academic language, that are used heavily in argumentation, interpretation, and advocacy. In the academic language category, we looked not only for abstract concepts but also citing of precedent, citing or countering sources, and use of quotations. Combined with such categories as reasoning, we were able to use the academic language category to understand the style of exposition and learn about the intended audience.

To summarize, the RAND-Lex tool detects differences at the characteristic and category level by looking at words and strings of words. The synthesis and interpretation of these differences, however, is more holistic and the "human" part of the process. In the following sections, we describe these analytical processes in more detail.

Software Environment

Stance comparison in RAND-Lex gives the users both a corpus-level view of differences between two collections of text data and an in-text view that uses color-coding to tag strings by stance variable. Figure 2.1 shows the corpus-level view for a stance comparison of newspaper journalism (2012–2017) with a comparable period of online journalism, using RAND-Lex's built-in ANOVA testing.[31] In our analyses, each text collection was cut into 2,000-word chunks, allowing for distributional testing of language variables across the collection.

ANOVA comparisons allow us to identify statistically significant differences between two samples of text. In Figure 2.1, the blue and red boxplots indicate the distribution range between the compared data sets.[32] In each of the graphs, the black dots (most visible in the abstract

---

[31] RAND-Lex produces the results of all ANOVA analyses in a set of .csv files that make comparisons straightforward. We use these tables to determine which corpora differences are statistically significant and which are not. We provide all relevant ANOVA tables in Appendix B.

[32] We found that confidence measures seemed less informative than effect size measures because any difference is likely to be statistically significant in such large data sets.

Figure 2.1
Corpus-Level ANOVA View

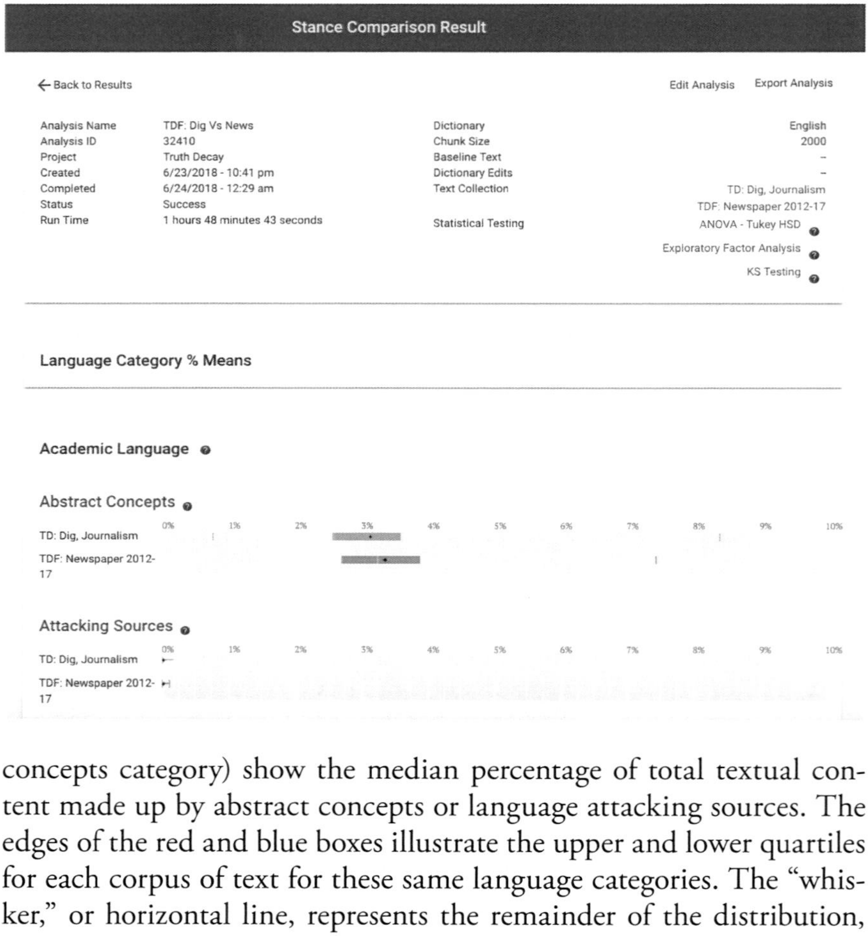

concepts category) show the median percentage of total textual content made up by abstract concepts or language attacking sources. The edges of the red and blue boxes illustrate the upper and lower quartiles for each corpus of text for these same language categories. The "whisker," or horizontal line, represents the remainder of the distribution, the top 25 percent and lower 25 percent. For example, for newspapers in the 2012–2017 period, a median of about 3.3 percent of text refers to abstract concepts; 50 percent of the data fall between about 2.6 and 2.8 percent, but the full range has a maximum of 7.5 percent and a minimum of 1.1 percent. The ranges for the other categories are much smaller. We can apply this procedure to any two bodies of data to observe differences across the sample.

But what does this difference in use of abstract concepts look like in practice, specifically in terms of this text collection? Within the RAND-Lex software, a user can click on any of the language categories (e.g., "Abstract Concepts" in Figure 2.1) and see a ranked histogram list of the most feature-rich chunks of text for that variable. Figure 2.2 gives a sample screenshot of text that is tagged (by highlighted color) by the software when that chunk is clicked.

Such words as *system*, *nonprofit*, and *revenue* are tagged as abstractions; so are such phrases as *income taxes* and *sources of.* The RAND-Lex analysis, therefore, not only shows that these phrases and concepts are systematically less common in online journalism but also gives examples of this in context. Figures 2.1 and 2.2 represent just an illustrative example of how the analysis and software work; they also illustrate the human and machine hybridity of RAND-Lex: the analyst can rapidly switch between the top level of computer-detected statistical descriptions and the human level of interpretation.

We also found meaningful differences in stance both *within* media over time (e.g., newspapers changing over time) and *between* media (e.g., broadcast news and prime-time cable programming differing over the same period). In Chapters Three through Five, we will lay out our empirical findings on stance differences and offer illustrative examples from news media to help make these differences clear. This should aid in understanding media content shifts and stance comparison as a method.

Mixing Methods: Qualifying Quantitative Descriptions

Our analysis is grounded in a quantitative description of the language used in various reporting media over time: We used machines to count language category usage across the various analytical categories into which we divided the data. These counts were then subjected to ANOVA testing to determine whether differences in these language categories were statistically significant.[33] But because significant differences are not the same thing as meaningful differences, we then cal-

---

[33] RAND-Lex uses a Tukey's Test, a post hoc ANOVA to find meaningful differences in pairwise comparison of linguistic categories between text collections. See Appendix A for more information.

Figure 2.2
Tagged-Text View

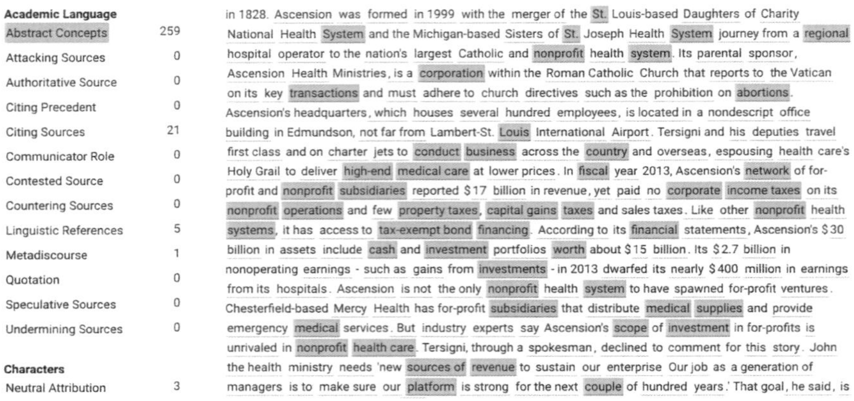

Academic Language		
Abstract Concepts	259	
Attacking Sources	0	
Authoritative Source	0	
Citing Precedent	0	
Citing Sources	21	
Communicator Role	0	
Contested Source	0	
Countering Sources	0	
Linguistic References	5	
Metadiscourse	1	
Quotation	0	
Speculative Sources	0	
Undermining Sources	0	
Characters		
Neutral Attribution	3	

in 1828. Ascension was formed in 1999 with the merger of the St. Louis-based Daughters of Charity National Health System and the Michigan-based Sisters of St. Joseph Health System journey from a regional hospital operator to the nation's largest Catholic and nonprofit health system. Its parental sponsor, Ascension Health Ministries, is a corporation within the Roman Catholic Church that reports to the Vatican on its key transactions and must adhere to church directives such as the prohibition on abortions. Ascension's headquarters, which houses several hundred employees, is located in a nondescript office building in Edmundson, not far from Lambert-St. Louis International Airport. Tersigni and his deputies travel first class and on charter jets to conduct business across the country and overseas, espousing health care's Holy Grail to deliver high-end medical care at lower prices. In fiscal year 2013, Ascension's network of for-profit and nonprofit subsidiaries reported $17 billion in revenue, yet paid no corporate income taxes on its nonprofit operations and few property taxes, capital gains taxes and sales taxes. Like other nonprofit health systems, it has access to tax-exempt bond financing. According to its financial statements, Ascension's $30 billion in assets include cash and investment portfolios worth about $15 billion. Its $2.7 billion in nonoperating earnings - such as gains from investments - in 2013 dwarfed its nearly $400 million in earnings from its hospitals. Ascension is not the only nonprofit health system to have spawned for-profit ventures. Chesterfield-based Mercy Health has for-profit subsidiaries that distribute medical supplies and provide emergency medical services. But industry experts say Ascension's scope of investment in for-profits is unrivaled in nonprofit health care. Tersigni, through a spokesman, declined to comment for this story. John the health ministry needs 'new sources of revenue to sustain our enterprise Our job as a generation of managers is to make sure our platform is strong for the next couple of hundred years.' That goal, he said, is

culated effect sizes from the ANOVA test results.[34] This allowed us to make reliable claims about how media has (and has not) changed over time with specific reference to changes in linguistic stance variables used, at a very large scale. Thus, we can be confident of the existence of the changes and differences we detected and report here, and we have a way to measure the size of those changes.

On their own, these changes and differences represent a limited set of claims. We can be confident, for example, that newspaper reporting has had a modest but meaningful shift away from directive language, public authority sources, and numbers and toward language about characters and narrative time. But what does that mean, and what does it look like in practice? Where the quantitative *counting* required machines because of scale, the qualitative *description* to make meaning requires a human ability to bring contextual knowledge to bear on the numbers. To do this, we look at feature-rich samples (chunks of text that have the highest frequency of the linguistic characteristics in question) for recognizable subgenres: Exposés, in-depth

---

[34] We use a *Cohen's distance* (measure of effect size) with thresholds for differences that are small (Cohens D, 0.2–0.5), medium (Cohen's D, 0.5–0.8), and large (Cohen's D, more than 0.8). Jacob Cohen, *Statistical Power Analysis for the Behavioral Sciences*, Abingdon, England: Routledge Academic, 1988.

profiles, crime reporting, human interest stories, and others are familiar patterns of language variables found in newspapers.

In the preceding example of newspapers, feature-rich examples from pre-2000 newspapers can be described as centered around important policy issues, such as a federal (authority source) requirement to provide (directive) $1 billion a year over five years (numbers) to fund state programs studying juvenile crime, whereas the post-2000 collection can be described as featuring more of the language of personal profiles, such as a crime victim (a character) sleuthing to understand why a juvenile offender was not in school "on the day of" the robbery (time).[35] In other words, in addition to identifying differences at the level of linguistic characteristics, we can also say something about how these linguistic characteristics are used (such as which other characteristics are used alongside them and in what contexts). Describing and interpreting how these language variables are being used in context is the human qualitative complement to the machine quantitative counts. In other words, the quantitative, machine-driven portion of the analysis measures differences between two corpora, but it is the human analysis of linguistic markers in context that allows us to understand what these changes mean for how language feels and might be interpreted.

In this sense, combining human and machine reading is highly complementary, with machine-based *distant reading* and human *close reading* allowing for the best of both worlds. Combining quantitative text mining with qualitative analysis of discourse is a well-established mixed method that has been applied to a variety of problems, such as military socialization, the role of gender in labor markets, and Arab stereotypes in news reporting.[36]

---

[35] Quotations indicate that it is the phrase that captures the time characteristics rather than any one word.

[36] Amal Al-Malki, David Kaufer, Suguru Ishizaki, and Kira Dreher, *Arab Women in Arab News: Old Stereotypes and New Media*, New York: Bloomsbury Academic, 2012; William M. Marcellino, "Talk Like a Marine: USMC Linguistic Acculturation and Civil–Military Argument," *Discourse Studies*, Vol. 16, No. 3, 2014; Maida A. Finch, Peter Goff, and Courtney Preston, "Language, Gender, and School-Leadership Labor Markets," *Leadership and Policy in Schools*, Vol. 17, 2018.

The quantitative analysis is completed by the software, but the ANOVA output itself does not provide the contextualized understanding of how specific differences play out between two corpora. This understanding requires qualitative analysis of the text and interpretation of linguistic choices. Being able to reliably measure the stylistic and representational choices of the news media at this scale advances an understanding of how changes in the way news is disseminated (with the rise of cable news, social media, and the internet) might shape the way news is reported. Understanding these stylistic and representational choices might provide useful insights as we explore why confidence in public institutions has eroded.[37]

We used this human-and-machine mixed approach precisely because of labor limits. Ideally, we would have thousands of scholars able to individually pore over the approximately 60 million words of text we collected and build a fine-grained and robust typology of story types through qualitative coding methods. Instead, we relied on machines to do the heavy lifting for the entire data set to describe language variables, and human analysis of feature-rich samples of the variables in question to understand and illustrate those variables.

A Deductive Approach to Qualitative Analysis

When thinking about qualitative analysis, readers might be most familiar with such qualitative descriptive methods as content analysis and thematic analysis: micro-inductive processes of recognizing repeated patterns in unstructured data.[38] These processes essentially refer to coders doing very close reading of data, trying to find the pattern variations within the data (e.g., the different ways that military service members being interviewed might express feelings of survivor guilt), labeling those patterns with codes, and then building up a kind of hierarchical knowledge representation of those patterns in a code-

---

[37] The other advantage of the human review is that it allows for a check of face validity to ensure that the RAND-Lex output's coding makes sense and appears to be appropriately tagging key words with relevant stance variables.

[38] Mojtaba Vaismoradi, Hannele Turunen, and Terese Bondas, "Content Analysis and Thematic Analysis: Implications for Conducting a Qualitative Descriptive Study," *Nursing & Health Sciences*, Vol. 15, No. 3, 2013.

book. The qualitative analysis embedded in RAND-Lex is slightly different. We used a holistic deductive process of finding the highest-ranked examples of already-established variables. This means we used RAND-Lex to do a distant reading, followed by a human doing a close reading of feature-rich examples to derive insights about context, usage, and other patterns.

After conducting the statistical analysis, we took each statistically significant variable and looked at between 20 and 25 1,000-word blocks of text ranked by the software as richest in that particular feature, until we had a qualitative sense of how that variable was being used. This involved looking for patterns in usage, such as content, context, and other linguistic characteristics consistently used nearby. Making decisions about when we had viewed enough text to make a final assessment required experience and expertise but corresponded roughly with a point of saturation—the point at which additional analyses confirm previous assessments but do not identify new insights. In addition to reviewing these feature-rich examples, we also explored a similar number of randomly selected examples for the purpose of comparison. In cases where randomly selected examples had wildly different usage from the feature-rich samples, we reviewed additional samples to confirm or refine our results. This was a two-person process in our project, with two analysts reading the same samples of text in order to understand, label, and choose illustrative examples that are presented in each of the chapters.[39]

The qualitative analysis, then, focuses largely on "feature-rich" blocks of text, chosen for their analytic value. The examples in the text are chosen to be illustrative. To provide the clearest example of how various linguistic features are used and how they vary across corpora, we have intentionally provided feature-rich examples that we carefully selected. These blocks of text will not be representative of all blocks of text in the sample, but our characterization of linguistic characteristics,

---

[39] To add rigor, our analysts conducted reconciliation, checking their qualitative interpretation of text examples for the different linguistic variables found to be significantly and meaningfully different in comparisons. Future efforts could increase rigor through formal inter-rating reliability testing.

how they are used, and how they differ across comparative corpora will be broadly representative and generalizable.

Because stance is cumulative over what we read,[40] we think it makes sense to qualify and illustrate examples of reporting that demonstrate linguistic features and characteristics of note. As pointed out later in our analysis, the changes we discuss are detectable and meaningful, but they are not wholesale. News reporting has not shifted from Walter Cronkite–style serious reporting to fiction or propaganda—even in the biggest contrasts we saw, there was still much similarity. But there were changes, and we have taken a deeper dive to understand and bring to light those changes using rich examples.

---

[40] Susan Hunston, "Using a Corpus to Investigate Stance Quantitatively and Qualitatively," in Robert Englebretson, ed., *Stancetaking in Discourse*, Philadelphia, Pa.: John Benjamins Publishing, 2007.

CHAPTER THREE

Changes in Newspaper Reporting over Time

The analysis described in this chapter compares newspaper content published prior to January 1, 2000, with content published after January 1, 2000. We consider several different analyses using the pre- and post-2000 frame: one with all three newspapers, referred to as the "full sample" (the *New York Times, Washington Post,* and *St. Louis Post-Dispatch);* a national newspaper analysis with only the *New York Times* and *Washington Post;* and, finally, a subsample analysis that considers each paper on its own. To preview the results, we focus this discussion on things that have changed but wish to emphasize that a clear observation that emerges from our analysis of newspapers is just how much print journalism has remained the same over time in terms of language and tone of reporting. Of the media comparisons we conducted, newspaper reporting over time showed the smallest differences and much consistency. We did, however, find some meaningful shifts in how news is reported in newspapers, specifically a shift away from a focus on events, time, and references to public authority and values and toward a more narrative approach featuring more personal perspective and emotion. However, the differences in newspaper reporting that we do observe should be viewed less as radical departures and more as subtle shifts in emphasis and framing. Nevertheless, even these subtle changes could have significance when taken together and in the context of other changes in the media industry.

Results

Understanding and Interpreting the Results

We present our results in two primary formats and then provide a third presentation (the raw, ANOVA results) in Appendix C. RAND-Lex works by looking at the frequency of certain words, phrases, or characters and then attaching a score to one of 121 linguistic measures or characteristics of the language in question. These 121 characteristics can be grouped into a smaller number of parent language categories. The results present the differences first by aggregated parent category and then by specific linguistic characteristic. (Appendix A provides the full list of linguistic elements and their definition.) We focus on statistically significant comparisons; thus, there is a statistically significant difference between the two samples for each of the linguistic comparison items we present. We are also interested in the substantive significance of the effect size. To measure this, we use *Cohen's D*, a measure of standardized effect size. We focus our discussion on factors for which differences are statistically significant and substantively meaningful. We also provide some discussion of those factors that are the same across the two blocks of text at the level of the parent category.

As an example, Figure 3.1 displays values at the parent language category level (parent categories consist of linguistic characteristics), and Figure 3.2 displays them at the linguistic characteristic level (the linguistic characteristics are on the left side of each figure, the parent categories on the right). The bars in Figure 3.1 show the weighted average of these statistically significant measures (Cohen's D scores), grouped by each parent language category (this value is also shown in Figure 3.2 as a vertical dashed line). The bars in Figure 3.2 mark the Cohen's D score for each linguistic characteristic that is statistically significant.[1] For Figure 3.2, the color fill of the bars also indicates the magnitude of the Cohen's D. Specifically, darker bars indicate a larger

---

[1]   As an example of how to read the results in Table 3.1 or 3.2, consider "neutral attribution" in Figure 3.2. This has a Cohen's D of just over 0.2 on the positive side of the axis, indicating that it is more common in the post-2000 period and that the effect is of moderate size; i.e., there is more neutral attribution (descriptions of individual actions and behaviors without value attributions) in the post-2000 sample.

effect size. In this example, the Cohen's D tells us how substantively large the difference is between the pre- and post-2000 data sets on each linguistic element. A Cohen's D between −0.2 and 0.2 is commonly interpreted to indicate a small difference, even if statistically significant. Cohen's D scores between −0.2 and −0.5 and between 0.2 and 0.5 indicate a moderate effect. Scores between ±0.5 and ±0.8 are moderately large, and scores above 0.8 or below −0.8 are very large.

We focus our discussion on the most sizable differences, generally discussing only those linguistic factors with a Cohen's D of at least 0.2, although we do also list factors that are close to the cutoff (~0.15) to avoid arbitrarily excluding meaningful results. Effects of this size are moderate in terms of substantive importance but still meaningful from the perspective of understanding how the presentation of news has changed over time. We also describe some of the more notable things that have not changed to underscore the degree of similarity. However, we do not discuss every factor in every table.

Full Newspaper Sample (New York Times, Washington Post, St. Louis Post-Dispatch)

We start with an assessment of the full newspaper sample, which encompasses all three newspapers, the *New York Times*, *Washington Post*, and *St. Louis Post-Dispatch*.

Figure 3.1 provides the summary view of effect sizes with larger Cohen's D values indicating more sizable differences between the two samples. Bars on the right-hand side of the figure identify parent categories that are more common in the post-2000 period; bars on the left-hand side identify parent categories that are more common in the pre-2000 period.

A first observation concerns the relatively smaller sizes of changes in reporting style between the pre- and post-2000 periods (the length of the bars). This emphasizes the consistency over time in the newspaper sample. However, there are a few factors that manifest slightly larger differences. First, text in our sample from the pre-2000 period exhibited more public language (references to authority sources), directive language, and academic or abstract concepts. It also exhibited more language of immediacy (e.g., "right now"). Meanwhile, the post-

Figure 3.1
Significant Linguistic Factors by Group: Newspapers Pre- Versus Post-2000
(Full Sample)

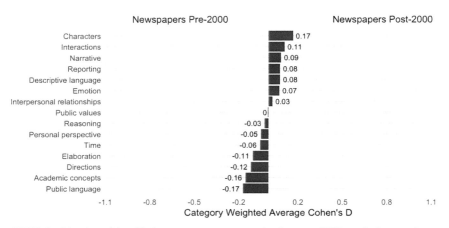

NOTE: Positive bars identify factors more common in the post-2000 period; negative bars identify factors more common in the pre-2000 period.

2000 language in our sample seemed to have a comparative emphasis on interactions, characters (narrative), and emotion.

Figure 3.2 illustrates these same trends but in more detail, highlighting specific linguistic characteristics on the left-hand side. Bars oriented toward the right of the figure identify factors that are more common in the period after 2000; those on the left side of the figure are more common in the pre-2000 period. Before 2000, newspaper reporting in the three sources we considered was marked by three distinctive kinds of language compared with post-2000 reporting. One was directive language (e.g., imperatives that order, foster, or require behavior). The second distinctive feature was elaborating through numbers (e.g., measuring or denominating). Finally, pre-2000 newspapers were marked by identifying authority sources—legislatures, courts—for public life. In reporting around public-sector issues involving money and policy, for instance, coverage from the pre-2000 period was typically marked by imperatives, a heavy focus on measurement and numbers, and identification of relevant authority figures.

Figure 3.2
Detailed Metrics for Newspaper Analysis (Full Sample)

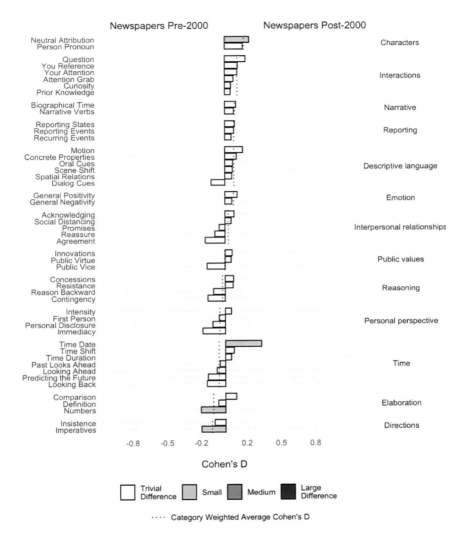

Figure 3.2—Continued

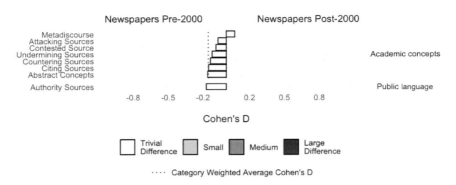

NOTE: Bars on the right identify factors more common in the post-2000 period; bars on the left identify factors more common in the pre-2000 period. Right-hand labels identify parent categories.

Coverage after 2000 in these three sources had fewer of these elements. Instead, post-2000 newspaper coverage was marked by two elements of narrative storytelling. The first is simple, value-neutral attribution of behavior to characters: telling the audience what a character did, said, or thought. The second feature was a tendency to place stories in dated time (e.g., Thursday, the next week, or September 11, 2001). A good example of those types of language combined in one story is the in-depth profile, laying out the day-to-day life of someone whose circumstances illustrate a pressing public issue. Even as many aspects of newspaper coverage remained the same, then, there does seem to have been a shift from coverage focused on numbers, authority, and imperatives to coverage that uses storytelling and such contextual details as dates to portray an issue. This change is subtle but meaningful and represents a shift in narrative style that is less definitive or directive.

Table 3.1 lists the key cross-period differences and provides specific examples of each, highlighting specific words and phrases that are associated with each of the listed linguistic characteristics in each of the two periods.

We can use specific examples from the text to highlight some of these changes in context and to provide a more nuanced illustration of

Table 3.1
Characteristics of Newspaper Reporting, Pre- and Post-2000 (Full Sample)

Language Category	Subcategories	Example Strings
Newspaper reporting pre-2000		
Direction	Imperatives	"require;" "establish;" "encourage"
Elaboration	Numbers	"one;" "$;" "20;" "million"
Public Language	Authority sources	"legal action," "department of," "committee"
Newspaper reporting 2000–2017		
Characters	Neutral attribution	"she has;" "he sees;" "she noticed"
Time	Time date	"in May;" "Dec.;" "on the day of"

what the findings just described mean in practice.[2] Based on our analysis of the data, directive language in the pre-2000 corpus of newspapers was often used to describe policy issues or to provide lists of activities, events, or demands.[3] Numbers were also more prevalent, primarily in denominating cost or in describing the world demographically (e.g., "1 in 5 country residents," or "5% whites"). Similarly, public language was more present, with cultural, legal, and moral sources of authority invoked (e.g., "chief justice," "the government," or "congressional

---

[2]   We have tried to use longer blocks of text to capture more examples of the linguistic characteristics and differences that emerged from our analysis. In addition, we have selected examples that clearly demonstrate the pre- and post-2000 changes in our sample. It would be incorrect to assume that all reporting in either period exactly mirrors our chosen examples. Our analysis identifies broader patterns across thousands of articles; many of the trends that this analysis can pick up might not be apparent after reading only a handful of articles. This is one of the benefits of our approach: the ability to detect trends that would not be apparent if we had to rely on manual coding. Our examples are chosen to illustrate the general trends that emerge from this large-n analysis. Text samples in the report were chosen to be illustrative, which means that they were intentionally selected out of the full text data set to provide clear examples of multiple linguistic characteristics and factors. Although the specific examples chosen are representative of the quantitative findings in the aggregate, they might not be representative of all text in the corpora.

[3]   When discussing examples of language categories, we have put quotation marks around the word or phrase tagged and counted by RAND-Lex.

approval"). We provide a good example of each of these three types of changes together in a public policy discussion that lays out costs, the public-sector authorities involved, and policy directives. We break out the specific examples of relevant linguistic characteristics in Table 3.2.[4]

> City park officials estimate the sewer work at about $20 million. Overall, they estimate that the park probably needs about $50 million worth of work just to fix up what's there now. City parks director Gary Bess is co-chairman of the park planning committee. Bess sees today's report as a kind of halfway mark. In the coming months, he said, the committee will hold even more public meetings. The next step: Using the goals and policies in the report as a framework for writing a park master plan, with specific projects and designs for how the park should look in the future. . . . Make Forest Park a separate unit with its own managers and budget, within the city's Department of Parks, Recreation and Forestry. Establish a Forest Park board, appointed by the mayor, with city officials and citizens. Explore establishing a metropolitan tax district including Forest Park. Take legal action if necessary to force the Metropolitan Sewer District to repair and maintain all sewers and take over storm-water management. Pursue use of the city-owned Arena prop-

Table 3.2
Textual Examples of Pre-2000 News Presentation

Linguistic Characteristic	Example
Public language/appeals to authority figures	"City park officials estimate the sewer work at about $20 million."
Directive language	"Make Forest Park a separate unit with its own managers and budget; Explore establishing a metropolitan tax district including Forest Park."
Enumeration	$20 million, $50 million

---

[4] The text blocks, tables, and text describing them provide the summary of our qualitative analysis. There is no standard qualitative output from the qualitative analysis conducted through RAND-Lex. The full set of qualitative results would be a larger set of feature-rich text samples with an assessment and summary describing how these text features are used. Presenting the full set of text samples is not possible in the context of this report, so we present a more limited but broadly representative sample of feature-rich text samples and discuss the key insights that emerged from the human analysis.

erty for expansion of park institutions, new activities and parking. Balance need for adequate parking with reservation of park setting district, bond issue, obtaining more private contributions and state money.[5]

A textual example from the post-2000 period provides a contrast, but also allows us to identify some similarities. The pre-2000 reporting relies on references to authority structures, events, and rules to describe policy issues (city park space in this case); post-2000 reporting uses narration to portray the issue of homelessness. This article and the previous one focus on different topics, but they are also very different in their expository styles and provide different types of information to the reader about the events or issues at hand, which is what we focus on here. The balance of styles is different in the two articles, with the result of a stronger emotional appeal in the post-2000 period and a more straightforward report in the pre-2000 period. In Table 3.3, we break out some examples of key post-2000 characteristics.

On the day of the tryout, he treats her children to lunch at a local bodega, joined by Malcolm X's grandson Malik, a friend of the team. Malik congratulates Dasani, handing her a bottle of peach-flavored Snapple. She carries the bottle with both hands, later stashing it in her dresser at Auburn. The next day, when

Table 3.3
Textual Examples of Post-2000 News Presentation

Linguistic Characteristic	Example
Placing characters in calendar time	"She wakes at 5 a.m. for the long-awaited school trip to Washington. Still feeling glum, she boards the bus on an empty stomach, sitting alone with a thin blue blanket laid carefully across her legs."
Attributing action to character (narration)	"On the day of the tryout, he treats her children to lunch at a local bodega, joined by Malcolm X's grandson Malik, a friend of the team. Malik congratulates Dasani, handing her a bottle of peach-flavored Snapple."
Attributing understanding	"He checks his phone, looking for a response. He shakes his head. Dasani goes to sleep feeling crushed."

[5] Charlene Prost, "Bosley Gets Data on Park; Panel Drafted Report After Heavy Debate," *St. Louis Post-Dispatch*, November 7, 1994.

Dasani's siblings tag along to practice again, Giant senses that Chanel expects him to repeat the invitation. He skips the meal, but reassures Chanel that her daughter, like his other team members, will be compensated for events. The first one is a training clinic this Thursday. All Chanel needs to do is bring Dasani. The rest is Dasani's job. "That's why we got the word 'responsibility,'" Giant tells Dasani in front of Chanel. "Response"—he holds up his right hand—"Ability"—then his left. "So respond to what? Your ability. Not your mom's ability." On Thursday afternoon, Dasani asks if her mother has heard from Giant. Chanel is tired after a long day and cannot imagine taking Dasani all the way to Harlem. "He never called." Up in Harlem, Giant had been calling repeatedly. He checks his phone, looking for a response. He shakes his head. Dasani goes to sleep feeling crushed. She wakes at 5 a.m. for the long-awaited school trip to Washington. Still feeling glum, she boards the bus on an empty stomach, sitting alone with a thin blue blanket laid carefully across her legs. Five hours later, as they approach the Capitol, Dasani presses her face to the window. Trees, monuments, water. She can see off into the distance, her view unobstructed by skyscrapers.[6]

Despite these changes, the overarching pattern for our newspaper analysis is one of stability. Slightly more than 60 percent of the linguistic characteristics that we assessed showed no statistically significant difference between the two corpora. Table 3.4 provides the number of linguistic characteristics found to have no statistically significant differences across the two corpora. The areas with the most significant number of changes are the treatment of time, use of characters, and such things as descriptive language. Areas where newspaper coverage remained more constant are the overall use of personal perspective, the use of emotion, and the use of public language. The relatively high nonsignificant percentages underscore the observation of overarching stability as a backdrop to the changes in style that were identified. We provide the full list in Appendix B; here, we emphasize the parent

---

[6]   Andrea Elliott, "Amid Repressed Hopes, Reasons to Dream," *New York Times*, December 13, 2013.

Table 3.4
Nonstatistically Significant Language Characteristics (Full Newspaper Sample)

Language Category	Characteristics Not Significant (%)
Personal perspective	73
Time	22
Emotion	86
Descriptive language	43
Interpersonal relationships	73
Public values	50
Public language	75
Academic language	58
Reasoning	58
Interactions	63
Elaboration	69
Reporting	75
Directions	72
Narrative	100
Characters	40

categories most consistently represented among nonstatistically significant variables.

National News Sample (New York Times, Washington Post)

To understand the robustness of these results and to understand how the full sample (including a regional paper) compares with a sample that focuses only on national sources, we next assess a sample that consists of only the two major national newspapers. Our analysis suggests only a few differences between the full sample and the national news sample. Figures 3.3 and 3.4 show the summary and detailed graphs illustrating a comparison of pre-2000 and post-2000 coverage for these two samples. Rather than repeating similarities, we focus on identifying and contextualizing meaningful differences between the national news and full sample results and do not discuss significant areas of overlap.

Figure 3.3 presents the results at the level of the parent category. There are relatively few differences between this and Figure 3.1. Figure 3.4 shows the results at the level of the linguistic characteris-

Figure 3.3
Significant Linguistic Factors by Group: National Newspapers

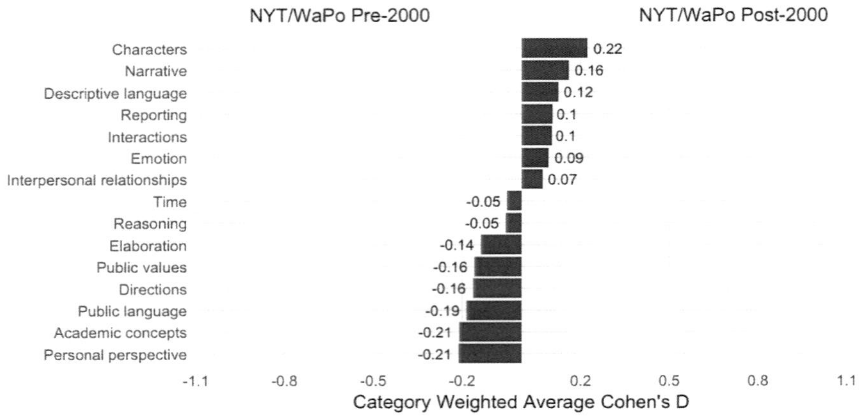

NYT/WaPo Pre-2000   NYT/WaPo Post-2000

	Category Weighted Average Cohen's D
Characters	0.22
Narrative	0.16
Descriptive language	0.12
Reporting	0.1
Interactions	0.1
Emotion	0.09
Interpersonal relationships	0.07
Time	-0.05
Reasoning	-0.05
Elaboration	-0.14
Public values	-0.16
Directions	-0.16
Public language	-0.19
Academic concepts	-0.21
Personal perspective	-0.21

-1.1   -0.8   -0.5   -0.2   0.2   0.5   0.8   1.1
Category Weighted Average Cohen's D

NOTE: Positive bars identify factors more common in the post-2000 period; negative bars identify factors more common in the pre-2000 period.

tic. Comparing this with Figure 3.2, there are a few differences worth mentioning. First, in this national newspaper sample the "numbers" characteristic falls below the line of substantive significance, meaning that the difference between the pre- and post-2000 samples is too small to be meaningful. More notably, there are several new cross-period differences. In addition to being characterized by the use of imperatives, the national newspaper pre-2000 sample is also characterized by predictions of the future, immediacy, and abstract concepts. These characteristics are indicative of a more academic style and of a greater focus on time and sequencing (order of events) in news reporting in the pre-2000 period. The post-2000 period in the national newspaper sample is characterized by a heavier use of personal pronouns, reflecting a more personal tone, and the neutral attribution and use of time and date already described. Once again, it is worth emphasizing that the size of changes in the newspaper sample are fairly small. In practice, this means that the changes will be subtle and, although notable, small in size, and they should be interpreted with caution.

Figure 3.4
Detailed Metrics for Newspaper Analysis (National Newspaper Sample)

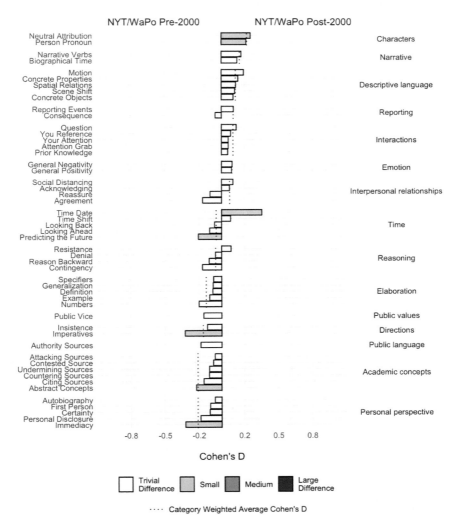

NOTE: Bars on the right identify factors more common in the post-2000 period; bars on the left identify factors more common in the pre-2000 period. Right-hand labels identify parent categories.

Table 3.5 lists the key cross-period differences with the new additions from the national newspaper analysis in bold, and it provides specific examples of each, highlighting specific words and phrases that are associated with each of the listed linguistic characteristics in each of the two periods.

We can also explore the three additional linguistic differences identified by the reduced-sample analysis in context. The following passage provides an example of the use of abstract concepts (in this case, in a discussion of changing tax policy) and of a focus on discussing the future (in this case, policy changes). Together, they provide a more academic style of exposition, grounded in data and with references to sequencing (Table 3.6).

> The bill will make subject to income tax up to 85 percent of the Social Security benefits of relatively affluent taxpayers. Calculating the tax is complicated enough; figuring out strategies to

Table 3.5
Characteristics of Newspaper Reporting, Pre- and Post-2000 (National Newspaper Sample)

Language Category	Subcategories	Example Strings
Newspaper reporting pre-2000		
Direction	Imperatives	"require;" "establish;" "encourage"
Personal perspectives	Immediacy	"right now;" "today"
Public language	Authority sources	"legal action;" "department of;" "committee"
Academic language	**Abstract concepts**	**"luxury tax;" "diagnosis;" "legislation"**
Time	**Predictions of the future**	**"next year;" "will be;" "next month;" "will never"**
Newspaper reporting 2000–2017		
Characters	Neutral attribution	"she has;" "he sees;" "she noticed"
Characters	**Personal pronouns**	**"he;" "she;" "their;" "they"**
Time	Time date	"in May;" "Dec.;" "on the day of"

NOTE: Bold characteristics are unique to the analysis of the reduced sample.

Table 3.6
Textual Examples of Pre-2000 News Presentation (National Newspaper Sample Only)

Linguistic Characteristic	Example
Abstract concepts	"Social Security beneficiaries must include in taxable income a portion of their benefits if their 'provisional income' exceeds certain thresholds." "Provisional income is defined as the sum of an individual's adjusted gross income . . ."
Predicting the future	"The bill will make subject to income . . ."

avoid it can be even trickier. Social Security beneficiaries must include in taxable income a portion of their benefits if their "provisional income" exceeds certain thresholds. Provisional income is defined as the sum of an individual's adjusted gross income, tax-exempt interest, certain foreign-source income and half of the taxpayer's Social Security benefit. Under the present law, 50 percent of the benefits are taxed at the person's ordinary rate if the provisional income is more than $25,000 for a single person, or $32,000 per couple. Under the new law, up to 85 percent can be taxed if the provisional income exceeds $34,000 for a single person, or $44,000 for a couple.[7]

The post-2000 period, based on the analysis of the national newspaper sample, appears to have somewhat heavier use of personal pronouns, largely reflective of the more narrative and subjective character of print journalism during this period (Table 3.7). Notably, the tone and style of this passage is very similar to that used earlier to characterize the same post-2000 period using the full sample.

On a warm summer night, Kristin Van Goor was jolted awake by the sound of knocking. She hurried down the wooden staircase in her pajamas. Through the windows, she saw red and blue police lights flashing, and her husband, Dave, on the doorstep.

---

[7] John Cushman, Jr., "The Budget Struggle: Wealthy or Not, Taxpayers Will Find Plenty of Surprises," *New York Times*, August 8, 1993.

Table 3.7
Textual Examples of Post-2000 News Presentation (National Newspaper Sample Only)

Linguistic Characteristic	Example
Personal pronouns	"She hurried down the wooden staircase in her pajamas. Through the windows, she saw red and blue police lights flashing, and her husband, Dave, on the doorstep."

A detective in a police cruiser shouted, "Are you all good?" Dave gave a nod and walked inside their Hill East home, just after midnight. Dave paced in the living room. The memories spilled out in jagged pieces. He remembered the black gun held to his head. Three young men, wearing black masks over their faces, surrounded him as he walked home from the Stadium-Armory Metro station about 11:30 p.m. on Aug. 20, 2015.[8]

As in the case of the full sample, the key trend in the national newspaper sample is one of stability despite various differences. About 57 percent of linguistic factors show no statistically significant difference. Areas with the least stability are the treatment of time, the use of descriptive language, use of elaboration (e.g., examples, descriptions, specifiers), and treatment of characters (e.g., attribution, personal pronouns). Areas with the greatest stability remain more or less the same as the full sample and are some of the more essential aspects of newspaper journalism: reporting, public language, public values, and use of directive language. Results at the level of the parent category appear in Table 3.8. The full list of linguistic characteristics that fails to reach statistical significance is provided in Appendix B.

Subsample Comparisons, by Paper

In addition to the two main analyses, we also conducted several additional subsample analyses, intended to assess the sensitivity of our results to alternative specifications. For each of the three newspapers in our sample, we compared pre-2000 content with post-2000 content

---

[8]   Amy Brittain, "The Crimes Against Them Were Terrifying, but the Judicial System Made It Worse," *Washington Post*, December 4, 2016.

Table 3.8
Nonstatistically Significant Language Characteristics
(National Newspaper Sample)

Language Category	Characteristics Not Significant (%)
Personal perspective	55
Time	33
Emotion	71
Descriptive language	14
Interpersonal relationships	64
Public values	75
Public language	75
Academic language	58
Reasoning	50
Interactions	62
Elaboration	38
Reporting	83
Directions	71
Narrative	50
Characters	40

for that newspaper only. We provide relevant figures in Appendix B, summarizing the results here.

The individual subsample analyses manifest both similarities and differences with each other and with the aggregate analysis. First, in all three cases, the changes over time are small in size, reinforcing the overarching observation of consistency over time for newspapers. This is especially true for the *Washington Post* sample: The effect sizes are very small, and relatively few characteristics even meet the threshold for statistical significance. However, the differences that we do see largely match those described for the aggregate sample and are similar in the aggregate across the three subsamples.

New York Times

For the *New York Times,* the pre-2000 period is more heavily characterized by appeals to authority, official titles and positions, insistence, imperatives, and the use of citations to respected sources. It is also characterized by a greater use of immediacy (i.e., references to "right now"). The pre-2000 period also shows some use of the first person and personal disclosure—instances where the journalist's own voice might come through—and a relatively higher use of contingency reasoning (if . . . then) and future prediction. In contrast, reporting from the post-2000 period was more heavily focused on characters and emotion, relying heavily on personal pronouns and references to time. At least for this outlet, then, there appears to be a shift from a pre-2000 style that is more heavily anchored in tradition and authority to a post-2000 style that is more interactive and narrative, but somewhat less academic and less referential to authority figures and sources. This pattern closely follows that described for the full sample.

Washington Post

There are very few statistically significant differences for the *Washington Post* subsample and even fewer characteristics reach the level of being substantively meaningful based on their Cohen's D. In fact, only three characteristics rise to this level. First, the pre-2000 period is most strongly characterized by more-frequent references to "public vice" (crime, immorality). Second, the post-2000 period is characterized by relatively more questions and intensity, elements of personal perspective, and interactions. The *Washington Post* seems to have experienced relatively little change in reporting style, but those changes that do occur are consistent with the narrative elsewhere in this chapter, of a shift from a more straightforward, academic style of reporting to one more heavily characterized by emotion and interactions.

St. Louis Post-Dispatch

For the *St. Louis Post-Dispatch* sample, we again see the small effect sizes and both similarities and differences with the full analysis. As a regional paper, it would not be surprising to see more-substantial differences between this subsample and the overall sample. For this outlet, the pre-2000 period was characterized by use of numbers, use of narrative verbs, retrospective analysis, and countering sources (suggestive of an argumentative style). In contrast, the post-2000 period is characterized by strong reporting language (updates, reporting events and states); is highly interactive with many questions, references to "you" and "your," and language indicative of curiosity; frequent concessions and forward reasoning; focus on immediacy ("right now");

frequent use of elaboration, examples, and comparison; metadiscourse; and time-date references. The specific linguistic characteristics for each period of this subsample differ somewhat from the overall sample, but the subsample is similar to both of the other two subsample analyses in that the post-2000 period in all cases provides a more emotive and personal text. Interpreting these changes in a more holistic way, we can say that the post-2000 reporting is more interactive and personal, features more examples and comparisons, better captures elements of time and narrative, and offers more-complex and more-sophisticated reasoning.

Summary

There are certainly differences across outlets, but the story told by each of the subsample analyses is largely consistent with the story told by the aggregate analysis. First, we see the same small effect sizes, indicating a good deal of consistency over time in the way that newspapers cover and present news. However, we do see some differences: Pre-2000 reporting across our three sources used language that was more heavily event- and context-based, with more references to time, official titles, and positions and institutions, and more-descriptive, elaborative language used to provide story details; post-2000 reporting does more storytelling, with an emphasis on interactions, personal perspective, and emotion. Our subsample analyses are important because they emphasize various key points. First, they provide support for the overall finding that newspaper content has been characterized by much consistency over time. Second, they provide support for the observation of a shift from a more academic, straightforward, event-based reporting to reporting based on personal perspective and interpersonal connections. Finally, the subsample analyses underscore the fact that these general trends manifest differently in each specific outlet, so although our overarching findings might provide some broader insights, we must be cautious about generalizations. Table 3.9 shows comparisons by newspaper.

Discussion

Our analysis of newspaper journalism before and after 2000 provides several insights. First, the dominant trend is one of consistency in this

Table 3.9
Comparisons by Paper

Sample	New York Times	Washington Post	St. Louis Post-Dispatch
Characteristics of pre-2000 reporting	• Predicting the future • Contingency reasoning • Citing sources • Authority sources • Insistence • Imperatives • First person • Immediacy • Personal disclosure	• Public vice	• Academic concepts • Public language • Reasoning • Time • Directions
Characteristics of 2000–2017 reporting	• Neutral attribution • Personal pronoun • Time date	• Question • Intensity	• Immediacy • Interactions • Characters • Narrative

case. Pre- and post-2000 newspaper journalism rely equally on the use of "reporting style" (reporting states and events) although they do so in slightly different ways and to different extents. Both rely on the use of emotion, but that emotion could manifest in different ways at different times. Both also rely on personal perspective at times and also use directive language—but, again, in somewhat different ways and at different times.

With this overarching consistency as a backdrop, there have been some subtle but meaningful changes across the two corpora, falling into several categories. The pre-2000 coverage tends to have a more academic style with the use of imperatives, appeals to authorities and institutions, and an emphasis on time and directions. The post-2000 period is more narrative in tone and style, with a heavier use of personal pronouns, an emphasis on characters and interactions, and greater use of sequencing. Both convey news, but they do so in different ways, with different points of emphasis, and with different styles of communicating with and interacting with readers. Importantly, these overarching observations extend across all the samples analyzed.

CHAPTER FOUR

Differences in Television News

Our next set of analyses assessed television news transcripts, with two comparative analyses. First, we compare broadcast television news in the pre-2000 period (ABC, NBC, and CBS) with broadcast television news in the post-2000 period. Second, we compare broadcast television news (ABC, NBC, CBS) with prime-time cable programming (MSNBC, CNN, Fox News) from 2000 to 2017.

To preview the results, change over time for broadcast television news was more pronounced than in newspaper reporting, as was the contrast between broadcast television and cable programming. The strongest change for broadcast news was a shift away from complex, detailed reporting of public problems to more conversational, personal exchanges between speakers (a change not dissimilar from that observed for newspaper reporting). That contrast was even stronger when we compared broadcast television news with prime-time cable programming: Prime-time cable programming in our sample is much more personal, conversational, interactive, and argumentative than broadcast television news—the reporting in broadcast news was more straightforward, with rich description of events and narratives but with less personal, subjective, and interactive content. As noted at the outset, we expect differences between broadcast news and prime-time cable programming because each aims at a different purpose. Broadcast news channels intend to provide primarily reporting; the prime-time cable programming that we feature is more opinion-based. Our objective is to document this difference empirically and quantitively and provide insight into the more specific nature of the differences and also possibly uncover more-subtle differences that we might not take note of otherwise.

Results

Broadcast Television News, Pre- and Post-2000

Figures 4.1 and 4.2 visualize the results of the RAND-Lex analysis comparing broadcast television pre-2000 with broadcast television post-2000 (see Chapter Three for an explanation of how to interpret these graphs). Figure 4.1 provides the overview; Figure 4.2 provides a more-detailed view of linguistic elements that differ in their use across periods. The full ANOVA results are in Appendix C. A first observation is that the effect sizes are generally much larger for this comparison than they were for our newspaper analysis. Bars that extend to the left (negative values) highlight linguistic categories that are more common in the pre-2000 period; those that extend to the right (positive values) identify characteristics more common in the post-2000 period. Here,

Figure 4.1
Significant Linguistic Factors by Group: Broadcast Television

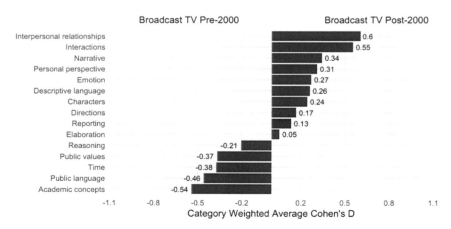

NOTE: Positive bars identify factors more common in the post-2000 period; negative bars identify factors more common in the pre-2000 period.

Figure 4.2
Detailed Metrics for Broadcast Television Analysis

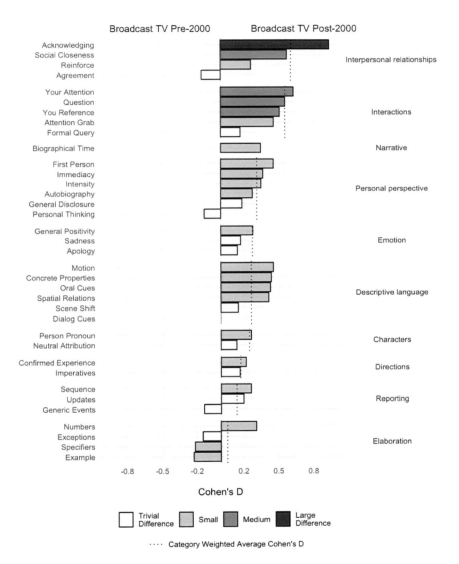

Figure 4.2—Continued

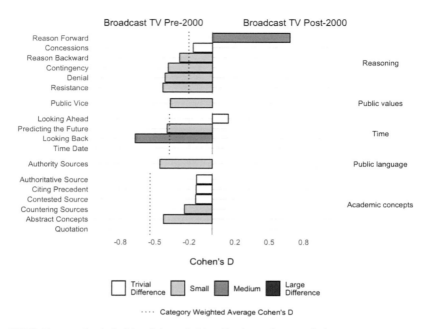

NOTE: Bars on the left side of the axis identify those characteristics more common pre-2000; bars on the right side of the axis identify factors more common post-2000.

we focus on describing the differences with the largest effect size, particularly those characteristics with a Cohen's D of ±0.2.

Our analysis of broadcast news suggests that the complexity and richness of reporting language declined over time. In the pre-2000 period, broadcast news was more likely to use academic language (including abstract concepts), complex reasoning about causality and contingencies, and argumentative reasoning (denying and resisting opposing arguments). The pre-2000 period also used more-precise language: specifiers that made clear all, some, or none of the things being discussed (in other words, the language makes clear what is and is not covered), along with examples of what was being discussed. Finally, all this was grounded in a shared public language about authority sources for public life (again, as in newspaper reporting), and about public vices, such as bribery, corruption, or violence.

After 2000, broadcast news loses much of this academic and precise tone. It becomes more conversational, with more extemporaneous speech and less preplanned speech. This also has meant more subjectivity: less straight reporting of preplanned stories, and more conversation among newscasters, between newscasters and expert guests, and between newscasters and the audience. Such conversations are interactive and feature personal perspectives; speakers interact interpersonally.[1] The use of reasoning language declined broadly, but the oral nature of later broadcast news also meant the use of additive reasoning: "John and Sue want X to happen. *And so* they will do Y. *And* that means Z. *So* we have to wait and see." Finally, this kind of talk-news in the post-2000 period features personal pronouns of the characters they describe.

Other changes to broadcast news in the post-2000 period are an increase in descriptive language and more sequencing—for example, when newscasters talk through visuals and videos. Lastly, we found increased positivity—more mentions of "love," people having "a shot at" a better life, or cases where "people are making a real difference." We can describe this increase in positive language, but we are not sure why it has occurred and cannot connect it to other features of broadcast news in the post-2000 period. It is possible that this increase is related in some ways to the increasing appeals to emotion noted in the post-2000 newspaper corpus.

Textual examples that illustrate these differences in context can help illustrate what the differences between the pre-2000 and post-2000 period looked like in practice. Table 4.1 provides a summary of the linguistic differences across the two periods with specific examples.

Considering examples and blocks of text in context is more useful. A good example of the more-complex, rich reporting observed in the pre-2000 period is the following story of medical malpractice. It contains the language of public authorities (such as licenses or the government), public vices (such as malpractice), reasoning on contin-

---

[1] In addition to a more conversational and personal style from news reporters, we also noticed that samples of broadcast news that were rich in personal perspective featured soundbites from press conferences and statements, which of course are conversational, have at least implied interactivity, and might come from a personal perspective.

Table 4.1
Characteristics of Broadcast News, Pre- and Post-2000

Language Category	Subcategories	Example Strings
Broadcast news pre-2000		
Academic register	• Abstract concepts • Countering sources	• "royalties;" "aspect;" "career" • "denied;" "he denies"
Time	• Time date • Looking back • Predicting the future	• "in May;" "Dec.;" "on the day of" • "previously;" "was;" "in the past" • "would surely;" "will"
Description	• Dialogue	• "he said;" "she added"
Elaboration	• Specifiers • Examples	• "for all;" one of;" "in which" • "in the case of;" "for example"
Reasoning	• Reasoning backward • Contingency • Denial • Resistance	• "because;" "as a result of;" "based on" • "could;" "might have;" "if she" • "not necessarily;" "not all;" "not, "can't" • "instead;" "it's just that;" refusal to"
Public values	• Public vice	• "sexual harassment;" "war criminal;" "violating a"
Public language	• Authoritative sources	• "legal action;" "department of;" "committee"

Table 4.1—Continued

Language Category	Subcategories	Example Strings
Broadcast news 2000–2017		
Interpersonal relationships	• Social closeness • Acknowledging • Reinforcing	• "we have;" "our;" "all of us" • "thanks;" "thank you;" "appreciated" • "that is exactly right;" "that's right"
Interactions	• Your attention	• "you see;" "goes to show you;" "you know"
Personal perspective	• First person • Immediacy • Intensity • Autobiography	• "my;" "I;" "me" • "this time;" "now;" "at this" • "very;" "completely;" "we plead" • "I was;" "I've;" "I started"
Narrative	• Biographical time	• "working as;" "10 year old"
Emotion	• Positivity	• "best wishes;" "recovering;" "enthusiastic"
Characters	• Personal pronouns	• "her;" "their;" "she"
Directions	• Confirming experience	• "you'll see;" "you're about to"
Description	• Motion • Concrete properties • Oral cues • Spatial relations	• "come down;" "put in" • "red;" "big;" "images;" "empty" • "uh huh." "yeah, "well" • "here;" "5 miles;" "across the Midwest"
Reporting	• Sequences	• "begin;" "after;" "second wave"
Elaboration	• Numbers	• "one;" "$;" "20;" "million"
Reasoning	• Reasoning forward	• ". And;" ". So.;" "and so"

gency and causality, and the reporting elements of time and elaboration about which exact victims are included. It also works to make concepts tangible for viewers. Table 4.2 identifies these characteristics with specific text-based examples.

> In France tonight, people are mourning a young man who died as the result of deliberate medical malpractice. During the 1980s, about 1,500 French hemophiliacs were infected with the AIDS virus because of a deliberate decision by officials to continue giving transfusions with blood they knew to be infected. One of those who received the bad blood was Stephane Gaudin. He died today. Here's ABC's Jim Bittermann. Stephane Gaudin was 13 years old when he watched his younger brother Laurent die of AIDS. He vowed he would struggle harder before death took him. So he tried to ignore that he, too, was AIDS sick and pursued his dream to get his pilot's license. The story of Stephane and his brother, videotaped by their father, is known to virtually everyone in France. The two boys, both hemophiliacs, were infected by tainted blood products distributed by French health authorities who knew they were contaminated. The public outcry over the Gaudin boys and hundreds of other victims forced the government to bring those responsible to trial last summer. Stephane and his parents attended every day of the proceedings. They said they wanted to see justice done. When Dr. Michel Garretta, the director of the French blood transfusion center, was found guilty, the Gaudins felt vindicated. But they were outraged that Garretta's sentence was just four years in jail. Just last month, as Garretta's appeal came up, Stephane, now very sick, struggled to come to court again.[2]

The post-2000 reporting, in contrast, is more subjectively personal and represents a typical conversational exchange characteristic of post-2000 broadcast television. One very apparent difference is the subjectivity: a combination of first-person pronouns, autobiographical talk, personal perspective language, and language of intensity or immediacy. There is also interpersonal language in plural pronouns and

---

[2]   Jim Bittermann, *World News Tonight with Peter Jennings*, ABC News, June 2, 1993.

Table 4.2
Textual Examples of Pre-2000 Broadcast Television

Linguistic Characteristic	Example
Public authorities	"French health authorities" "Director of the French blood transfusions"
Public vice	"Medical malpractice"
Time	"Trial last summer" "1980s"
Elaboration	"1,500 French hemophiliacs"
Reasoning (contingency and causality)	". . . were infected with the AIDS virus because of a deliberate decision by officials to continuing giving transfusions with blood they knew to be infected"

acknowledgements, along with interactional talk about "did you" and "how much you," and—even though the subject matter is challenging—positive emotion language about luck and love. More-personal, subjective content might be effective at attracting viewers, motivating people to take action, or highlighting the importance of an issue—telling the story of alcoholism and anxiety through a firsthand account invites more audience involvement and emotional engagement.[3] The following illustrative example is a rich example of positive emotion, first-person pronouns, autobiographical recollection, and intensity (e.g., "would die for," "amazing"). Table 4.3 breaks out examples of some of these distinctive characteristics.

> On television, she's the picture of calm. I'm Elizabeth Vargas in Baghdad. Traveling the world as a journalist. Return here to Jerusalem. For some of those years, Elizabeth was secretly battling a life-threatening addiction off camera. Thanks, Elizabeth, very much . . . Haunted by crushing insecurity and anxiety that began as a child, Elizabeth says a glass or two of wine fueled by that anxiety, over the years, became a dangerous addiction. There

---

[3]   Mervi Pantti, "The Value of Emotion: An Examination of Television Journalists' Notions on Emotionality," *European Journal of Communication*, Vol. 25, No. 2, 2010; Chris Peters, "Emotion Aside or Emotional Side? Crafting an 'Experience of Involvement' in the News," *Journalism*, Vol. 12, No. 3, 2011.

Table 4.3
Textual Examples of Post-2000 Broadcast Television (Vargas Excerpt)

Linguistic Characteristic	Example
Positive emotion	"I am, there's, you know, I am so lucky to have my two amazing children and to have this amazing job."
First person pronouns	"I wouldn't give a nanosecond's worth of thought to die for my children, to kill for my children. But I would die for my children, but I couldn't stop drinking for my children."
Autobiographical recollection	"And I do vividly remember, that one afternoon, Sam standing by the, my head in the bed, saying, Mommy, when are you gonna get up? And I remember I could smell the sunscreen and I could feel the heat from his little body, because he had just come in from the beach"
Intensity/immediacy	"I don't know if I will ever forgive myself for hurting them with my drinking, ever."

are millions of men and women battling this across the country. And this statistic, more than 60 percent of women that struggle with alcohol also struggle with anxiety. Good evening. We begin tonight with two rescue efforts. To watch Elizabeth anchor live television in moments of crisis, you'd have no idea she was forcing herself to suppress deep anxiety. If you watch carefully at the beginning of every newscast, you will see me lean in and I grip the desk with my right hand. And then on my left hand, which is I'm holding my pen, I'm taking my engagement ring and I'm digging the edge of it into my thumb. Why did you go into this business if it was going to torment you? I loved it. I still love it. I love telling people stories. But, I mean, people can look at you and say you're so lucky, really. I am lucky. It's easy to say that on the outside looking in. And first of all, yes, I am, there's, you know, I am so lucky to have my two amazing children and to have this amazing job. It doesn't matter how much you have or how little you have, it didn't matter, it leveled me. And Elizabeth remembers a moment on vacation with her boys. The sun was out, the boys were up and she was in bed. I was drinking and sleeping. And I do vividly remember, that one afternoon, Sam standing by the, my head in the bed, saying, Mommy, when are you gonna get up? And I remember I could smell the sunscreen and I could feel the heat from his little body, because he had just come in from the beach. And I would die for my children, Diane. I wouldn't give a nanosecond's worth of thought to die for my children, to kill for my children. But I would die for my children, but I couldn't stop drinking for my children. I don't know if I will ever forgive myself for hurting them with my drinking, ever.[4]

Both the pre-2000 and post-2000 pieces clearly have emotional content and each tells the story of one family or one individual. But there are differences in the way each story is told. The pre-2000 piece makes multiple references to authority—institutions and individuals—and uses clear specifiers interwoven with the broader facts of the story—who else was affected and how. It also features backward reasoning and retrospective analysis, all hallmarks of the pre-2000 period. The post-2000 text, however, is highly subjective, with fewer appeals to authority sources, makes reference to family and other relationships, and is told in the first person, all distinct from the previous era. Notably, the more-personal and conversational language used in the post-2000 period and the use of anecdotes and emotion in reporting is not unlike what we observed in the post-2000 newspaper analysis; in that, we saw a similar, though more subtle, shift away from a more-formal, factual reporting style and toward a more-interactive and personal one. Of course, there are similarities as well. Both tell the human side of a pervasive public health issue and both rely on storytelling to increase emotional appeal. In addition, some of the differences between these two examples might simply be driven by the two different formats— one a news report, the other an interview. We do not seek to make the argument that there has been a wholesale shift in news reporting to the subjective. Rather we use these two examples to illustrate what the changes in language and representation that emerge from our qualitative analysis look like in practice.

Although the pre-2000 and post-2000 samples manifest more differences in this case, there are still many ways in which the two samples are more similar than different. In the aggregate, only 54 percent of the

---

[4] "Elizabeth's Story: Talks About Battle with Addiction and Anxiety," *World News Tonight with David Muir*, ABC, September 9, 2016.

linguistic characteristics in our statistical analysis fall below the level of statistical significance, suggesting some degree of consistency across the two periods (see Table 4.4). This consistency appears greatest in those linguistic characteristic categories with the lowest percentage of statistically significant characteristics, such as use of narrative, directive language, use of reporting style, and use of personal perspective. In other words, on these dimensions, there has not been much change in television reporting over time. On the other hand, areas where the two are more clearly distinct are character references, reasoning style, and use of descriptive language. These results are consistent with the more specific analysis just described. The full list of linguistic characteristics that fails to reach statistical significance is provided in Appendix B.

Analysis of Broadcast Television News Versus Prime-Time Cable Programming (2000–2017)

In the previous section, we discussed how broadcast news became more conversational and subjectively personal: in very broad strokes, a kind of

Table 4.4
Nonstatistically Significant Language Characteristics: Broadcast Television (Pre- and Post-2000)

Language Category	Characteristics Not Significant (%)
Personal perspective	45
Time	44
Emotion	57
Descriptive language	64
Interpersonal relationships	75
Public values	75
Public language	58
Academic language	25
Reasoning	75
Interactions	71
Elaboration	50
Reporting	75
Directions	71
Narrative	100
Characters	20

shift from a retrospective journalism told in the context of public authority and public virtue to a subjective form of journalism based on first-person stories and interactions. The difference between broadcast news and prime-time cable programming is similar but perhaps even starker.

Figures 4.3 and 4.4 visually show the results of the RAND-Lex analysis comparing cable programming with broadcast television news in the 2000–2017 period. Figure 4.3 provides the higher-level, aggregated view consolidated by linguistic category. This figure compares broadcast news with prime-time cable programming—negative bars identify characteristics more common in prime-time cable programming and positive bars identify elements more common in broadcast news. Directive language, references to interactions, use of personal perspective, and reasoning are all more common in prime-time cable programming. Descriptive language, elaboration, emotional appeals, references to relevant characters and important temporal factors, and (to a lesser extent) narrative storytelling and public language are all more common in broadcast news. Broadcast news is more narrative than cable programming and is focused on telling the story and using emotional appeals (in the post-2000 period) to pull the audience in. In

Figure 4.3
Significant Linguistic Factors by Group: Broadcast Versus Cable

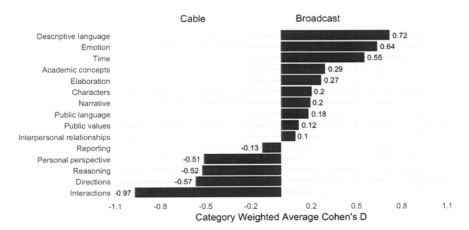

NOTE: Positive bars identify factors more common in broadcast television news; negative bars identify factors more common in prime-time cable programming.

Figure 4.4
Detailed Metrics: Broadcast Versus Prime-Time Cable Programming Analysis

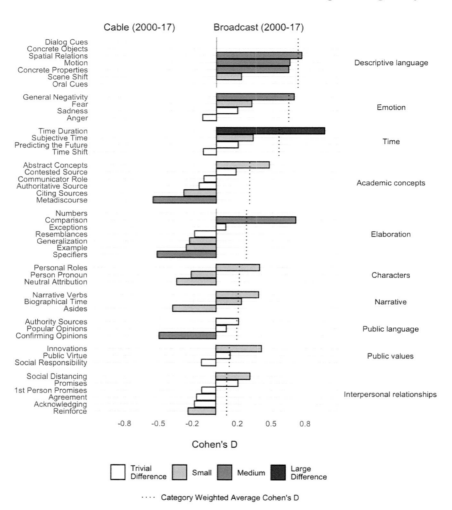

Figure 4.4—Continued

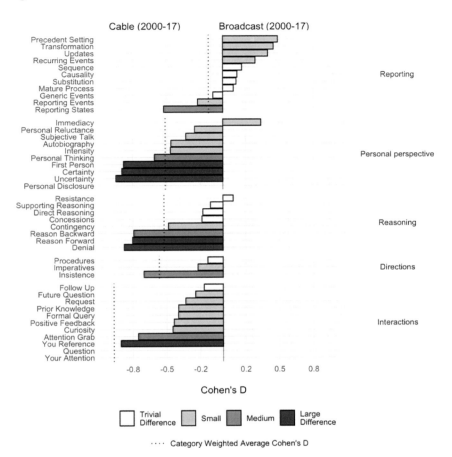

NOTE: Bars on the left side of the axis identify those characteristics in prime-time cable programming; bars on the right side of the axis identify factors more common in broadcast television news.

contrast, cable programming appears more directive in nature, more based on opinion and argumentation. This difference is consistent with our expectations based on the goals and motives of cable versus broadcast television as defined in Chapter One.

Figure 4.4 identifies the specific linguistic elements that are distinct between prime-time cable programming and broadcast journalism. Bars on the right of the graph indicate features that are more common in broadcast news than in prime-time cable programming—references to concrete objects and properties, comparisons, spatial relationships, precedent-setting, and general negativity. More generally, broadcast television news is distinctive when compared with prime-time cable programming in four ways: reporting, negativity, innovation, and urgency. Even in its more-personal reporting since 2000, broadcast television news has multiple dimensions of what we would characterize as traditional reporting: detailed description of people as they speak, act, and move about the material world; contextualizing those descriptions in time (both calendar and subjectively experienced time); and sharing updates and changing events with viewers. Negativity (e.g., misery, bitterness, and cruelty) and the language of social distance (e.g., stories about divorce, attacks, "sticking it to" someone) also distinguish broadcast news from cable programming—both are more common in broadcast than in cable. Finally, broadcast news more often reports on innovations (e.g., new drugs or technology), and grounds all of this in the urgency of "right now."

Bars on the left identify elements that are more common in prime-time cable programming in the 2000–2017 period—first-person narratives, elements of both certainty and uncertainty (often in the expression of opinions and the use of ambiguity), metadiscourse, denial, personal disclosure, insistence, reasoning, attention-grabbing language, questioning, and references to or talk directed at the viewing audience ("you reference"). Prime-time cable programming, therefore, is much more strongly interactive among multiple speakers, features extemporaneous speech, and comes much more often from a personal perspective. Even the language of public matters and interpersonal talk is subjective, revolving less around a reporting of facts and more around agreement with and confirmation of opinions. Reasoning is also much more strongly present, particularly the argumentative dimensions of reasoning, such as denial. Closely related to this argumentative style is direction language, in which speakers insist on what must be done or has to happen, and imperative language of orders. Taken together, our analysis suggests that, compared with broadcast television news, prime-time cable programming is characterized by more-argumentative language, more-personal and subjective exposition of topics, more use of opinion and personal interaction, and more-dogmatic positions for and against specific positions. As noted, this difference is not surprising, given that prime-time cable shows tend to be more opinion-based intentionally (as their business strategy and even raison d'etre) than broadcast television news.

There are also other fine-grained differences between the two kinds of news coverage. Broadcast news is richer in the academic language of abstract concepts; prime-time cable programming has the academic language of metadiscourse, a feature linked to orality ("basically," and "I find" types of oral prestaging of one's position). Broadcast news elaborates on numbers and makes comparisons; cable television more often uses a single anecdote for the purpose of generalizations.

Table 4.5 summarizes the differences between broadcast television and prime-time cable programming and provides specific example strings to contextualize what these differences mean in practice.

These differences can be more easily interpreted when they are presented and analyzed in context. The most distinctive features of broadcast television news in contrast to cable are its use of descriptive language, references to the concrete world, time, elaboration, and appeals to emotion. The following excerpt is a good example, rich with descriptions of objects, places, and movement in the concrete world; elaboration through counts and comparisons within daily, weekly, or seasonal time duration; and touching on negative emotions (consistent with our analysis of the evolution of broadcast journalism over time). This sample has some of the emotional, personal, and subjective features highlighted in the post-2000 sample of broadcast television ("I wouldn't give up my cellphone"), and it is also closer to what we might call "straight reporting" in the topics covered and its use of descriptive language to illustrate the context of the event. Table 4.6 breaks out examples of these unique characteristics.

> Environmental group concerned about cell phone radiation with Brian Williams, brought to you in part by . . . We mentioned this a minute ago, a story out today about cell phones getting a lot of attention. Researchers have been debating whether the radiation from cell phones poses any kind of a health risk. Now there's a new list out that is intensifying this debate. Our report from NBC's Rehema Ellis. Almost everywhere you turn, someone's on

Table 4.5
Characteristics of Broadcast News Versus Prime-Time Cable Programming

Language Category	Subcategories	Example Strings
Broadcast television news 2000–2017		
Description	• Dialogue	• "he said;" "she added"
	• Concrete objects	• "the fire;" "pictures;" "the highway"
	• Spatial relations	• "here;" "5 miles;" "across the Midwest"
	• Motion	• "back over;" "sprinting;" "close"
	• Concrete properties	• "reddish;" "shiny;" "young"
	• Scene shifts	• "right there;" "headed to;" "comes from"
Time	• Time duration	• "through September;" "evening;"
	• Subject time	• "fast;" "in just;" "late"
Emotion	• General negativity	• "a chilling;" "beheaded"
	• Fear	• "nervous;" "watch out for;" "afraid of"
Elaboration	• Numbers	• "one;" "$;" "20;" "million;"
	• Comparisons	• "the same;" "less;" more"
Narrative	• Narrative verbs	• "called her;" "killed his;" "met him"
	• Biographical time	• "working as;" "10 year old"
Characters	• Personal roles	• "veteran;" "husband;" "police lieutenant"
Academic register	• Abstract concepts	• "mental health;" "aspect;" "surveillance"
Interpersonal relationships	• Social distance	• "feud;" "hostage;" "burglar"
Public values	• Innovation	• "brand new;" "cutting edge;" "something new"
Reporting	• Precedent setting	• "for the first time;" "make history"
	• Transformation	• "increasingly;" "turns out;" "converted to"
	• Updates	• "just days ago;" "the news;" "we have"
	• Recurring events	• "routine;" "a wave of;" "every hour"
Personal perspective	• Immediacy	• "this time;" "now;" "at this"

Table 4.5—Continued

Language Category	Subcategories	Example Strings
Prime-time cable programming 2000–2017		
Interactions	• Future question	"would he;" "who will;" "who would"
	• Request	"asked for;" "will you;" "asked them to"
	• Prior knowledge	"of course;" "as you can imagine"
	• Curiosity	"how to;" "of what;" "how can"
	• Positive feedback	"that is correct;" "go ahead"
	• Attention grab	"now;" "let's talk about"
	• Question	"?;" "how did;" "who is"
	• Your attention	"you see;" "goes to show you;" "you know"
Reasoning	• Concessions	"having said that;" "but;" "true"
	• Reasoning forward	". And;" ". So;" "and so"
	• Reasoning backward	"because;" "as a result of;" "based on"
	• Contingency	"could;" "might have;" "if she"
	• Denial	"not necessarily;" "not all;" "not;" "can't"
Directions	• Imperatives	"take;" "require;" ". Stop"
	• Insistence	"should;" "you have to"
Personal perspective	• First person	"my;" "I;" "me"
	• Personal disclosure	"I want to;" "I just;" "I am"
	• Uncertainty	"Guessed;" "something;" "somebody"
	• Certainty	"I know;" "sure;" "that's it"
	• Personal thinking	"understand;" "believe;" "imagine"
	• Intensity	"very;" "so much;" "the most"
	• Autobiography	"I was;" "I've;" "I started"
	• Subjective talk	"opinion;" "almost;" "a little"
	• Personal reluctance	"I have to;" "I had to"
Descriptive language	• Oral cues	"uh huh;" "yeah;" "well,"
Reporting	• Reporting events	"open a;" "use the;" "composing"
	• Reporting states	"is a;" "they are;" "it's"
Public language	• Confirming opinions	"I agree;" "advocating;" "endorse"

Table 4.5—Continued

Language Category	Subcategories	Example Strings
Prime-time cable programming 2000–2017—continued		
Characters	• Personal pronouns • Neutral attribution	• "her;" "their;" "she" • "she has;" "he sees;" "she noticed"
Interpersonal relationships	• Reinforce	• "that's right;" "that's exactly right"
Academic	• Metadiscourse • Citing sources	• "so to speak;" "basically;" "I find" • "said;" "bragging about;" "suggest that"
Elaboration	• Specifiers • Examples • Generalization	• "for all;" one of;" "in which" • "in the case of;" ", for example," • "everybody;" "all the time;" "everyone"

a cell phone. I wouldn't give up my cell phone. There are about 270 million cell phones nationwide. For years, some people have been concerned about what comes with this convenience, concern because each one emits some level of nonionizing radiation, the same type that comes from microwave ovens. It's a less intense form of energy than the kind from radiation in X-rays. Now, an advocacy organization called the Environmental Working Group is pushing for more federal regulation. It has compiled data from cell phone manufacturers about radiation levels and posted it on its Web site. The group says it usually gets about 300,000 visitors a month to the site. After posting the list, they say traffic spiked to 100,000 visitors in just one day. I think that speaks to the fact that consumers are obviously very interested in whether or not their cell phones are safe. A spokesman for the wireless industry says the industry complies with all safety guidelines. We are not scientists. And so that's why we rely on the conclusions of groups such as the American Cancer Society. The majority of scientific studies do not show any link between cell phone use and health hazards. The word radiation strikes fear into people's hearts, but the reality is that this kind of radiation is the kind that, based on the physics, would not be thought to cause cancer.[5]

In contrast, the following excerpt is a good example of the more conversational, interactive, argumentative, and even confrontational language of prime-time cable programming. This type of language

Table 4.6
Textual Examples of Post-2000 Broadcast Television (Cell Phone Excerpt)

Linguistic Characteristic	Example
Subjectivity/personal perspective	"I wouldn't give up my cell phone"
Negative emotions	"people have been concerned;" "strikes fear"
Time duration	"a month;" "just one day;" "for years"
Elaboration through numbers, counts	"270 million cell phones nationwide" "300,000 visitors;" "100,000 visitors"

---

[5]   Brian Williams, "Environmental Group Concerned About Cell Phone Radiation," *NBC Nightly News*, NBC, September 10, 2009.

often appears on prime-time cable programming in the form of live interviews or videotaped coverage with an ordinary person or people thrust into the spotlight through tragedy. These exchanges are intensely personal, subjective, and have the oral hallmarks of unplanned speech. This sample has all these language features, and we have highlighted examples of the rich combination of orality ("you know," " I was like,") with personal, subjective talk in examples in Table 4.7.

> I spoke with her exclusively just days after her release. Here's what she tells about why she killed her son. I was in an abusive relationship. It just triggered all of this paranoia. I knew that people were there trying to harm me. My abuser tried to set me on fire. I had a mental breakdown because I thought people were after me. I got very paranoid. They had me diagnosed as paranoid schizophrenic. I started taking medication, took it for six months, quit taking the medication. I started getting paranoid again. So, tell me what happened. My kids—two of my kids were asleep in the bedroom. My daughter was asleep on the couch because she had just had surgery and my other son was watching TV in the living room. And I stayed up all night long. And—You're paranoid, you're worried that somebody was coming in? Yes. I—at about 7:30 in the morning, I tried to call my sister on her cell phone and the cell phone did this really wonky thing and it then gave me a busy signal on a cell phone and I was like, they've, you know, they've got my sister, they've got my mom, they're killing them. And I ran in the kitchen and I got a knife and was going to go kill myself because my abuser had told me that I was safe as long as I stayed with them, you know. And I thought at first I was like, if I kill myself then they won't have no reason to come. And I was going down the hallway toward the bathroom and I was like, my kids, you know, they're going to rape my kids, they're going to torture my kids, they're going to mutilate my kids.[6]

This intensely subjective, conversational style is also visible in an argumentative approach to reporting that is characteristic of prime-

---

[6] Drew Pinsky, "Possible Reasons for Charlie Bothuell's 11 Day Disappearance; Story Behind the Woman Who Killed Her Own Son in the Midst of a Psychiatric Break; Oldest Daughter Held Little Patrick in Her Arms as He Died," *Dr. Drew*, CNN, July 2, 2014.

Table 4.7
Textual Examples of Post-2000 Prime-Time Cable Programming

Linguistic Characteristic	Example
Personal perspective/first person reference	"I stayed up all night long;" "I knew people were trying to harm me"
Orality	"I was like," "you know"
Personal pronouns	"they've got my sister, they've got my mom"
Intensity	"very paranoid"
You reference	"You're paranoid, you're worried that somebody was coming in?"

time cable programming as compared with broadcast television. The following text provides one illustrative example of this type of reporting. There is strong argumentative reasoning: argument concessions, denial, causal reasoning backward, and contingency reasoning. In the following example, these language elements are not directly commingled, but come in sequence as the interviewer and speaker argue back and forth. We highlight linguistic elements characteristic of this style in Table 4.8.

> We were not threatening anybody. We're not—I'm not saying what you did is illegal. I am saying it is awful. I'm saying it's, look—No, it's not awful. In fact, we did the same thing to Tom Wheeler when he was the FCC chair. And it helped to finally convince them to do the right thing. Because you are threatening at home. I mean, why not go to his office? Why not write a piece for the *New York Times*? Why not come out on this show? Because Ajit Pai is not listening to people. He's always made his decision. He is in a repeal net neutrality so people cannot choose where they want to go, when they want to go. They will let Comcast—you just agree with the policy. I get it. You disagree with the policy. No, you don't get it. No. I disagree with the approach. Because he is going to start in a room that can proceed on Thursday. He decides an issue. He is going to exchange—How do you know? Because he said it. He's made public speeches saying—So, he's got opinions, you've got opinions. But the point is, you were going to his house, that is a threat. He is no longer a Verizon lawyer. Okay. Again, I am not here to defend

Table 4.8
Textual Examples of Post-2000 Prime-Time Cable Programming:
Argumentation and Reasoning

Linguistic Characteristic	Example
Argumentative reasoning	"It also requires an administrative process in order to make decisions. And you have to allow people to make their comments. You have to evaluate their comments fairly. You can't go on a biased opinion. Ajit Pai comes in as a Verizon lawyer. Okay. He is still acting like a Verizon lawyer. We want him to hear us."
Contingency reasoning	"The reason I will go to his house is because he will not listen to people."
Concessions	"Again, I am not here to defend his views of network neutrality. I am here to defend the idea you can have a reasonable conversation without threatening someone."

his views of network neutrality. I am here to defend the idea you can have a reasonable conversation without threatening someone. The reason I will go to his house is because he will not listen to people. He has shown that over and over again. Who is the people? How do you know you represent the people more than he does? He had more comments ever in the last campaign—Comments on some like web or something? On the FCC comment page, 3.7 million comments in the last campaign to get that neutrality. Now, when Tom Wheeler didn't listen to those people, we went to his house, too. Well, hold on! Because we have to have these people—His candidate won a presidential election, are you kidding me? It doesn't matter. Of course it does. That is our system. No? It also requires an administrative process in order to make decisions. And you have to allow people to make their comments. You have to evaluate their comments fairly. You can't go on a biased opinion. Ajit Pai comes in as a Verizon lawyer. Okay. He is still acting like a Verizon lawyer. We want him to hear us. What I am saying is—We want him to hear us. Why not just hit him in the face then? Because that is not going to work. But if it did work, would you?[7]

---

7   Tucker Carlson, "Report: Trump Revealed Classified Info to Russians; Dems and Media Melt Down over Trump Presidency; Leftists Protest Gay Conservative Journalist; Cyberattack Impacted 200,000 Computers in 150 Countries," *Tucker Carlson Tonight*, Fox News

Another characteristic of cable programming that emerges from these examples and our RAND-Lex analysis is a less direct and more-filtered presentation of news. Rather than being presented directly through a host, news is instead presented indirectly, through the subject and course of the interview or discussion. For example, in the sample text, substantive information about the topic (net neutrality) and the process for changing that policy emerge through the interview rather than being presented directly by the host.

Unlike the comparisons for newspapers and broadcast TV, the differences between prime-time cable programming and broadcast television for the 2000–2017 period are fairly significant and far-reaching, and similarities are relatively fewer. Only 25 percent of the linguistic characteristics in our stance dictionary fall below the threshold of statistical significance (although many others fail to reach the level of substantive importance). Table 4.9 shows the percentage of factors in each linguistic category that fall below the level of statistical significance. Each of the linguistic characteristics in the descriptive language, reasoning style, narrative, and characters are statistically significant. Changes in reporting style and use of personal perspective are also extensive, as indicated by this table. There does appear to be more consistency in a few areas, such as use of directive and academic language. These results confirm our expectation that prime-time cable programming and broadcast news actually look very different because of their different orientation and objectives, but the results also give some insight into how they are similar. The full list of linguistic characteristics that fail to reach statistical significance is provided in Appendix B.

Discussion

This chapter considered the difference in broadcast television journalism before and after 2000 and the difference between broadcast televi-

---

Network, May 15, 2017. We present this data as RAND-Lex would see it, which is devoid of paragraphs or breaks between speakers.

Table 4.9
Nonstatistically Significant Language Characteristics:
Broadcast Versus Cable

Language Category	Characteristics Not Significant (%)
Personal perspective	9
Time	44
Emotion	43
Descriptive language	0
Interpersonal relationships	45
Public values	25
Public language	25
Academic language	58
Reasoning	0
Interactions	15
Elaboration	13
Reporting	8
Directions	57
Narrative	0
Characters	0

sion news and prime-time cable programming in the period from 2000 to 2017.

Broadcast journalism in the post-2000 period does differ from that before 2000 in ways that are largely consistent with the newspaper observations in Chapter Three. In the period prior to 2000, broadcast television journalism was characterized by a stronger use of precise academic language, complex reasoning, and references to public life and authority figures and institutions. Coverage of key issues focused on events and sequences and exploited examples to specify what was and what was not included. After 2000, however, broadcast journalism loses some of this academic tone, becoming more conversational, more personal, and more interactive. The language of post-2000 broadcast journalism became more descriptive, with more-frequent use of first-person language, oral cues, spatial relations, and personal pronouns. There also appears to have been an increase in elaboration (use of specifiers and numbers) and a reliance on biographical time to describe events and experiences. However, there continued to be some similarities. First, both the pre- and post-2000 corpora rely on a more narrative style, though this shifts from narration of events in the pre-2000 period to personal narration in the post-2000 period. Second, both have elements of reporting style, underscoring the point that both are, first and foremost, journalistic efforts. Third, both demonstrate complex reasoning (though in different ways) and are anchored in a common frame of public values and public language. The difference between the periods, then, is largely one of emphasis, from academic to descriptive, within a common framework.

We found many more differences when comparing broadcast news with cable programming. Broadcast journalism differs from cable programming in at least three ways: references to urgency, innovation, and reporting style. It also has multiple dimensions of what we would consider "traditional reporting," such as references to concrete objective facts, spatial relationships, detailed descriptions of what people said when speaking, comparisons, and references to time. In other words, it is heavily grounded in the here and now—what people said and did, when it happened, and how they were related in space and time to others. In contrast, cable programming was characterized by meta-discourse, orality, and argumentation; by questioning and reasoning; and by interactions between people. It was less about reporting events and more about exposition of and debate about opinions, directions and imperatives, and generalizations. There are a few areas of commonality—they are less distinct in their use of academic language and directive language—although even here, each incorporates these characteristics in slightly different ways. As noted previously, the greater difference between cable programming and broadcast television news is to be expected based on the very different objectives and business models of the two platforms. Cable programming, particularly during prime time, is geared toward a narrower audience and uses opinions and provocative material to attract attention; broadcast television aims at a wider audience and sticks closer to traditional forms of reporting. Notably, neither type of media is inherently better than the other. Rather, they complement each other and fulfill different functions for both the individual and for the media ecosystem.

CHAPTER FIVE

Comparing Print and Online Journalism

Our final comparative analysis looked at differences and similarities between more-conventional print journalism and online journalism (i.e., publications that are only online) for the period 2012–2017. The sample of publications for online journalism was described in Chapter Two. It is worth reiterating that although the sample was chosen to provide some ideological diversity and to include the most-trafficked online journalism sites, it excludes a large number of other online journalism outlets. As a result, we are limited in our ability to generalize across the entire field of online journalism.

We describe two analyses in this chapter. First, we compare the full set of six online journalism outlets defined in Chapter Two (Breitbart News, TheBlaze, Buzzfeed Politics, Daily Caller, Huffington Post, and Politico) with the full sample of three newspapers (the *New York Times, Washington Post, St. Louis Post-Dispatch*) for the period 2012–2017. Next, we consider a limited analysis that compares only four of the online sources (Breitbart News, Daily Caller, Huffington Post, Politico) with the sample of national newspapers (*New York Times, Washington Post*) for the period 2012–2017. In this second analysis, we dropped the outlet with a smaller user base from our sample of left- and right-leaning online journalism and from our newspaper sample. We use this analysis to assess the robustness of our analysis to small changes to our textual corpora.

To preview the results, we found when comparing newspaper with online journalism in our sample of highly trafficked sites that online journalism was significantly more personal and subjective, more interactive, and more focused on arguing for specific positions. In contrast, the conventional print newspapers we studied were more strongly characterized by more use of characters, time, and descriptive language and by their more narrative context. Our analysis suggests large effect sizes, indicating large differences across the two samples. These results hold across both samples.

Results

Analysis of Full Newspaper Sample Compared with Full Online Journalism (2012–2017)

Figures 5.1 and 5.2 provide visual summaries of our analysis and results. (Full ANOVA results are provided in Appendix C.) Figure 5.1 illustrates differences between the digital and print journalism samples in terms of linguistic categories and gives some sense of relative effect sizes. Negative bars indicate features more characteristic of online journalism; positive bars highlight factors that are more common for conventional newspapers. In Figure 5.2, bars on the left side of the graph identify linguistic features that are more common in the online journalism sample; bars on the right side identify those elements that are more common in newspapers.

Similar to our analysis of broadcast news and prime-time cable programming, we found that, compared with the newspaper journalism sample, the online journalism in our sample of highly trafficked sites is more personal and subjective, more interactive, and more focused on arguing for specific positions. Our online journalism sample is more strongly characterized by the use of directive language (sometimes of advocacy), references to personal interactions or interpersonal relationships, a strong personal presence, references to public values and authorities, and references to self. The result is a journalism that remains heavily anchored in key policy and social issues but that reports on these issues through personal frames and experiences—for example, analysis of the health care costs of opioid addiction through first-person narratives or analysis of proposed policy changes through the use of personal experiences and anecdotes. We provide additional

Figure 5.1
Significant Linguistic Factors by Group: Newspapers Versus Online Journalism (Full Sample)

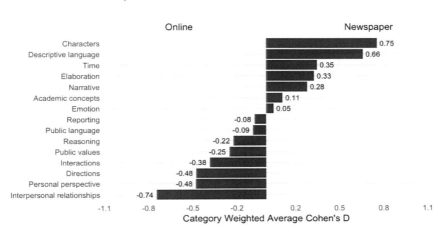

NOTE: Bars on the left side of the axis identify those characteristics more common in the online sample; bars on the right side of the axis identify factors more common in the newspaper sample.

details of this framing later in this chapter. Other distinctive characteristics of the online journalism sample are social closeness, subjective perspective, immediacy, certainty, insistence, and argumentation. Most often, these characteristics combine to argue for a particular viewpoint or perspective or are used in a context of agenda-setting. We also found that the academic language of sourcing and citing was more common in online reporting, as was a focus on public virtues and goods: reforms, improved access, and progress. Online journalism on these highly trafficked sites has some elements of traditional reporting; some elements of the newer, more subjective reporting style; and some unique characteristics, such as advocacy-oriented language. It is worth noting that the effect sizes for the newspapers and online journalism comparison are some of the largest of any analysis discussed in this report.

In contrast, the conventional print newspapers we studied are more strongly characterized by greater use of characters, time, and descriptive language (to describe events or issues) and by a more narra-

Figure 5.2
Detailed Metrics: Newspapers Versus Online Journalism Analysis

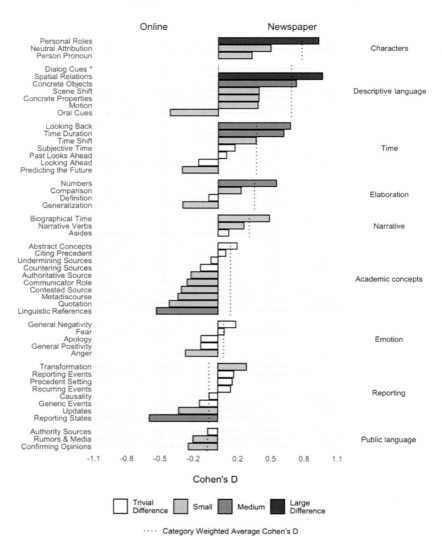

Figure 5.2—Continued

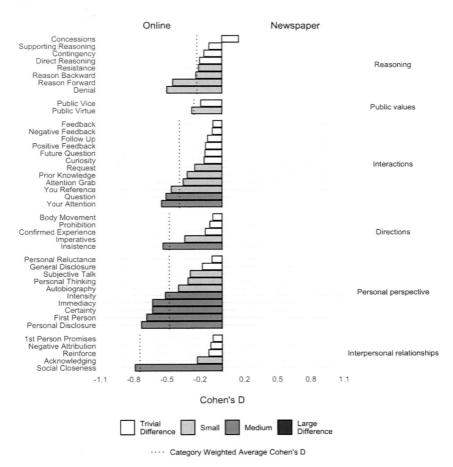

NOTE: Bars on the left side of the axis identify those characteristics more common in the online sample; bars on the right side of the axis identify factors more common in the newspaper sample.

tive context. The print journalism sample appears to be more strongly characterized by the use of concrete objects, numbers, references to duration, connections to individual roles, spatial relationships, and retrospective reasoning. Newspaper reporting in the 2012–2017 period features characters and narrative, contextualized with descriptions of the material world, and dated in time. That set of features is very much a "who, what, where, when" style of reporting, even as it incorporates emotional appeals (patterns largely consistent with the characterization of post-2000 print reporting described previously). Similar to what we found when comparing broadcast television with cable, newspaper reporting in our sample is also marked by the complexity of abstract concept language and by elaboration through enumeration and comparisons.

We can also explore these differences using examples from the text data. Table 5.1 summarizes the differences between newspaper and online journalism in the 2012–2017 period and provides words and phrases that more clearly illustrate the language differences just described.

Illustrative contextual examples also demonstrate the difference between online and print journalism. First, we provide an example that shows how online journalism leverages personal, subjective perspectives to argue about public goods, in this case access to birth control. The following example contains autobiographical and subjective register talk, combined with argumentative reasoning, along with language about social virtues, such as education and health access. This text is explicitly personal in nature, giving readers a direct window into the inner experiences of the writer. It is also conversational, almost an appeal to the reader and an invitation to engage. Sometimes this subjective perspective might emerge in confessional-type talk from ordinary people sharing their stories.

> I started using the birth control pill when I was 17. I had a boyfriend and thought we were ready for all that stuff, but I didn't want babies. I'm from a really small town and knew education was the only way to get out, so I wanted to go to college, get my PhD, and I knew having a baby would slow that down. My husband and I stopped using birth control in 2011 and had a baby in 2012, and now I'm back on the pill because I don't want any more kids [laughs]. I have a lot of friends who went off birth control after having a kid and now they've got two, three, four, five kids—and while that's okay for them, that's not what I

Table 5.1
Characteristics of Newspapers and Online Journalism, 2012–2017

Language Category	Subcategories	Example Strings
Newspapers 2012–2017		
Characters	• Personal roles • Neutral attribution	• "veteran;" "husband;" "police lieutenant" • "she has;" "he sees;" "she noticed,"
Description	• Spatial relations • Concrete objects • Motion • Scene shifts	• "here;" "5 miles;" "across the Midwest" • "the fire;" "pictures;" "the highway" • "back over;" "sprinting;" "close" • "right there;" "headed to;" "comes from"
Time	• Time duration • Looking back	• "through September;" "evening" • "who had;" "was;" "there were"
Emotion	• General negativity • Fear	• "a chilling;" "beheaded" • "nervous;" "watch out for;" "afraid of"
Elaboration	• Numbers • Comparisons	• "one;" "$;" "20;" "million" • "the same;" "less;" more"
Narrative	• Narrative verbs	• "called her;" "killed his;" "met him"
Academic register	• Abstract concepts	• "mental health;" "aspect;" "surveillance"
Reporting	• Transformation	• "increasingly;" "turns out;" "converted to"

Table 5.1—Continued

Language Category	Subcategories	Example Strings
Online journalism 2012–2017		
Descriptive language	• Dialogue	• "he said;" "she added"
Academic	• Quotation • Metadiscourse • Citing sources • Linguistic reference • Contested source • Communicator role • Authoritative source	• [""] • "so to speak;" "basically;" "I find" • "said;" "bragging about;" "suggest that" • "titled;" "speeches;" "report" • "arguing;" "claiming;" "arguing on" • "audience;" "speaker;" "the audience" • "ruled that;" explains that;" "confirms that"
Elaboration	• Generalization	• "everybody;" "all the time;" "everyone"
Reporting	• Updates • Reporting states	• "just days ago;" "the news;" "we have" • "is a;" "they are;" "it's"
Public language	• Confirming opinions	• "I agree;" "advocating;" "endorse"
Public values	• Public virtue	• "much good;" "rising star," "advancement of"
Interactions	• Request • Prior knowledge • You reference • Attention grab • Question • Your attention	• "asked for;" "will you;" "asked them to" • "of course;" "as you can imagine" • "you;" "your;" "you're" • "now;" "let's talk about" • "?;" "how did" "who is" • "you see;" "goes to show you;" "you know"

Table 5.1—Continued

Language Category	Subcategories	Example Strings
Online journalism 2012–2017—continued		
Reasoning	• Reasoning forward • Reasoning backward • Resistance • Denial	• ". And;" ". So." "and so" • "because;" "as a result of;" "based on" • "instead;" "it's just that;" refusal to" • "not necessarily;" "not all;" "not;" "can't"
Directions	• Imperatives • Insistence	• "take;" "require;" ". Stop" • "should;" "you have to"
Personal perspective	• First person • Personal disclosure • Certainty • Personal thinking • Intensity • Immediacy • Autobiography • Subjective talk	• "my;" "I;" "me" • "I want to;" "I just;" "I am" • "I know;" "sure;" "that's it" • "understand;" "believe;" "imagine" • "very;" "so much;" "the most" • "this time;" "now;" "at this" • "I was;" "I've;" "I started" • "opinion;" "almost;" "a little"
Interpersonal relationships	• Social closeness	• "we have;" our;" "all of us"

wanted to do. One kid is plenty! I've still got time to dedicate to him, and to my career.—Sarah, 29, Maryland[1]

But that same subjectivity and personal disclosure or autobiographical style could be mixed with social closeness, generalizations, and personal thinking to describe political and social problems and their implications in a direct and accessible way. Table 5.2 illustrates some specific examples of this narrative style in context.

> I began to feel that Chavez had cleverly duped the revolutionaries in Venezuela. He basically appointed all of the various guerrilla leaders to low-level government positions, like he had "Mao." He threw some bones at them and the rest of their revolutionaries fell in line. Most of the core government decision-makers were of European descent not indigenous at all. I began to look at Chavez with great skepticism. I didn't share my concerns with my newfound friends . . . , but I did start traveling to various barrios to meet with those who had criticisms of the way the Bolivarian revolution was playing out. I began to realize that Venezuela was a country in the process of revolution and that various camps existed in the government none of which trusted the others. All of them would inquire as to what another group said to me. All of them would press me to find out if another group criticized "the process." I began to see that all of them were worried that everyone else was either CIA [Central Intelligence Agency] or somehow against the revolution.[2]

Newspaper journalism, in contrast, is characterized by event- and context-based reporting that emphasizes personal roles ("reporters," "the police," and "the nurse"), verbs to indicate what the characters did, the material objects ("gun," "popcorn bag," "the floor") and spatial relations ("nearby," "in the chest") describing where events occurred, and the time sequencing ("were," "was," "had been"). This event- and context-based

---

[1]   Catherine Pearson, "Proof Birth Control Access Is a Very, Very Big Deal to Women," Huffington Post, July 1, 2014.

[2]   Brandon Darby, "How I Spent My Time in Hugo Chávez's Venezuela," Breitbart News, March 6, 2013.

Table 5.2
Textual Examples of Online Journalism: Personal Disclosure and Thinking, Social Closeness

Linguistic Characteristic	Example
Personal disclosure	"I began to look at Chavez with great skepticism. I didn't share my concerns with my newfound friends . . . , but I did start traveling to various barrios to meet with those who had criticisms of the way the Bolivarian revolution was playing out."
Subjectivity	"All of them would inquire as to what another group said to me. All of them would press me to find out if another group criticized 'the process.' I began to see that all of them were worried that everyone else was either CIA or somehow against the revolution."
Social closeness	"my newfound friends"
Generalizations	"All of them;" "everyone else"
Personal thinking	"began to see;" "began to feel"

reporting provides a more objective accounting than the examples from online journalism already presented. These features are spread throughout the following passage, as the writer lays out a scene and tells a story (Table 5.3 highlights some specific examples):

That's when Mr. Oulson made what would turn out to be a fatal move. This was a boutique theater with rows of large seats that are elevated from one another, with a foot and a half of legroom between them. Mr. Oulson turned to face Mr. Reeves and swung the popcorn bag at his side; kernels struck Mr. Reeves' face. Mr. Reeves, a co-founder of the Tampa Police Department's first tactical response team, reacted. Struck in the face by what he told police was a "dark object," he reached for his .380 and fired, just as his son Matthew, also a police officer, entered the theater. Mr. Oulson's wife, Nicole, had placed her hand on her husband's chest and was struck in the finger. Mr. Oulson was hit once in the chest. The people nearby laid him down on the floor and rested his head on Mr. Cummings's foot. Mr. Cummings's son called for help while the nurse in the audience rendered aid. Police said Mr. Reeves sat down calmly, put the gun on his lap and stared ahead. A sheriff's deputy from

Table 5.3
Textual Examples of Newspaper Journalism: Characters, Action, Motion, and Spatial Relations

Linguistic Characteristic	Example
Characters, personal roles	"Police officer;" "sheriff's deputy;" "reporters;" "nurse"
Action, motion	"entered the theater;" "placed her hand;" "turned to face"
Material objects	"The gun;" "popcorn bag"
Spatial relations/locations	"in the chest;" "nearby;" "in the finger"

nearby Sumter County who saw the muzzle flash snatched the weapon from him. Police said Mr. Reeves resisted at first and then acquiesced. The gun was jammed. At 1:30, a call came over the police radio that someone had been shot at the theater. The police feared the worst and prepared to respond to mass casualties. "When you hear this come over the radio, I can tell you, your heart drops," Sheriff Chris Nocco told reporters. Mr. Reeves's clothes were taken for evidence, and he was taken to jail in a hazmat suit. TV cameras showed him walking up to the police cruiser as if it were his own, with no officer escorting him close behind. His lawyer, Richard Escobar, said Mr. Reeves, who is charged with second-degree murder, acted in self-defense.[3]

Next, we provide another example of newspaper reporting from the 2012–2017 period that highlights the linguistic differences between the online and print samples. This example shows these linguistic differences in the context of addressing key policy issues—in this case, school performance—with a heavy emphasis on numbers, comparisons, time, and duration. Abstract concepts for assessment, such as "scales" and "measures," are combined with educational abstractions,

---

[3] Frances Robles, "A Movie Date, a Text Message and a Fatal Shot," *New York Times*, January 22, 2014.

such as "social studies."[4] The article elaborates on the issue through the use of enumeration language (numbers), duration, and comparisons ("less than," "most," "compared to"). The sample features these elements and we break out specific examples in Table 5.4.

> Based on the results to be released today, 18 districts across the state would be demoted from accredited to provisional if the state board were to immediately judge them. That includes two in St. Louis County: Ferguson-Florissant and University City. Provisionally accredited is considered less than 70 percent on the new scale, while unaccredited is less than 50 percent. Ferguson-Florissant may be on the cusp, but it has climbed the scale compared to data from 2012. The district saw growth in individual students' math scores in the latest results. Superintendent Art McCoy says there are new plans for improvement in social studies, an area of weakness, as well as attendance and ACT scores. Every junior in the district will take the college-entrance exam this year. "We're expecting some huge gains," McCoy said. The state does not accredit charter schools, but for the first time, the system gives a look at charter school performance that goes beyond test scores. Charter schools in the city continue to improve, with two, City Garden Montessori and North Side Community School, receiving a perfect rating. Statewide, 11 of 520 school districts are cur-

Table 5.4
Textual Examples of Newspaper Journalism: Abstract Concepts, Elaboration, Time

Linguistic Characteristic	Example
Abstract concepts	"Criteria;" "measures;" "scales;" "scores;" "social studies;" "accredited"
Comparisons	"More than;" "greater;" "less than"
Numbers	"14-point;" "90 percent;" "13 standards"
Time duration	"Five years;" "this year;" "in 2011"

---

4 Such terms as *standards, criteria, measures,* and *scales* are considered abstract in that they refer to concepts and not things.

rently classified as provisionally accredited. Since first beginning the school improvement system decades ago, Missouri's education department has updated its measures every five years or so. The state Board of Education adopted the new standards in 2011, basing them on what it would take for Missouri to rank among the top 10 states for student achievement by 2020. Most districts are judged on 140 possible points. Districts can be "accredited with distinction" if they earn 90 percent or greater of the points available, and satisfy other criteria that have not yet been set. Under the previous 14-point scale system, more than 80 percent of districts met at least 13 standards for K-12 districts. But even amid those high ratings, more than half of Missouri students overall were not passing the state's tests for communication arts and math.[5]

In analyses of other media, we were able to find significant areas of similarity. In the comparison of online journalism and newspapers, we found relatively few areas of overlap. Table 5.5 identifies the percentage of linguistic characteristics in each of the higher categories that fail to reach statistical significance. In the aggregate, 22 percent of all characteristics fail to meet this threshold. For most individual categories, this percentage is even lower, staying at zero in many cases. This underscores just how different newspaper and online journalism are on many dimensions. Areas of greatest similarities fall into two main categories: references to interpersonal relationships and references to public values. These two elements appear to be more similar in nature across the two samples. In Appendix B, we present this same analysis at the level of linguistic characteristic rather than higher language category.

Reduced Sample (*New York Times* and *Washington Post* Versus Breitbart, Huffington Post, Daily Caller, Politico)

As noted in this chapter's introduction, to assess the robustness of our analyses to changes in the text corpora, we conducted a secondary analysis that limited the newspaper sample to national newspapers

---

5   Jessica Bock, "The Grades Are In: New System Makes Finer Distinctions Among Districts; 'Perfect' Districts Lose Ranking with New Standards Education," *St. Louis Post-Dispatch*, August 23, 2013.

Table 5.5
Nonstatistically Significant Language Characteristics:
Online Versus Newspapers (Full Sample)

Language Category	Characteristics Not Significant (%)
Personal perspective	9
Time	11
Emotion	29
Descriptive language	0
Interpersonal relationships	55
Public values	50
Public language	35
Academic language	25
Reasoning	0
Interactions	8
Elaboration	50
Reporting	33
Directions	29
Narrative	0
Characters	0

and the online sample to four sources, two left-leaning and two right-leaning (dropping the least-trafficked left- and right-leaning sources).

Figures 5.3 and 5.4 show the results of this analysis at the parent category and linguistic characteristic level, respectively. Rather than directly interpreting these graphs, however, we focus on differences that emerge between this analysis and the analysis of the full newspaper-versus-online comparison already described. Table 5.6 compares the results of the two analyses. All characteristics present in one analysis and not in the other are in bold text. The first key observation is that there are relatively few significant differences between the two samples. Although there are slight differences, the online samples in each analysis appear similar in terms of linguistic characteristics, and the same is true of the newspaper samples. This provides some confidence in the stability of these results, at least for our set of sources. Full ANOVA results are provided in Appendix C. Appendix B presents a comparative graph that shows the result of both online-versus-newspaper comparisons on a single chart, underscoring the similarity of the two analyses.

Figure 5.3
Significant Linguistic Factors by Group: Newspapers Versus Online Journalism (Reduced Sample)

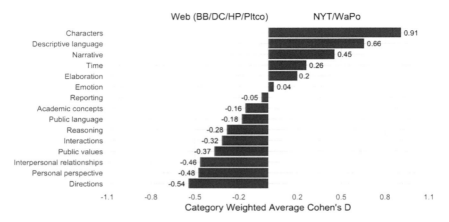

NOTE: Bars on the left side of the axis identify those characteristics more common in the online sample; bars on the right side of the axis identify factors more common in the newspaper sample.

Turning to the cross-sample differences, there are three linguistic characteristics that appear in the full analysis and not the analysis of the reduced sample. In the full sample, but not in the reduced sample, newspaper journalism is characterized by "transformation" language that emphasizes change and discontinuity ("broke off," "came to"). In addition, the online sample is characterized by references to author-itative sources and by references to rumors and media. In all three cases, the difference is one of effect size—the effect size falls below the 0.2 threshold for the reduced-sample analysis.

The reduced online-versus-newspaper sample also has three new meaningful differences. First, there is more citing of sources (a more academic style) in the newspaper journalism of this sample than in the online journalism of this sample. Second, online journalism in the reduced sample contains more emotion (specifically, general positiv-ity, which does not appear in the newspaper journalism sample in this case) and more references to public virtue (e.g., happiness, fairness, human rights). Together, these differences suggest a somewhat more

Figure 5.4
Detailed Metrics: National Newspapers and Reduced Online Sample

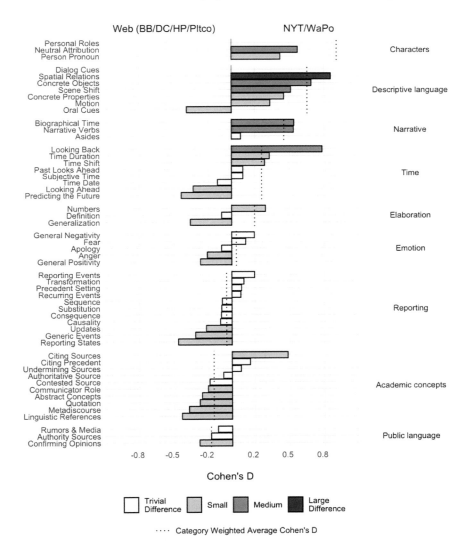

Figure 5.4—Continued

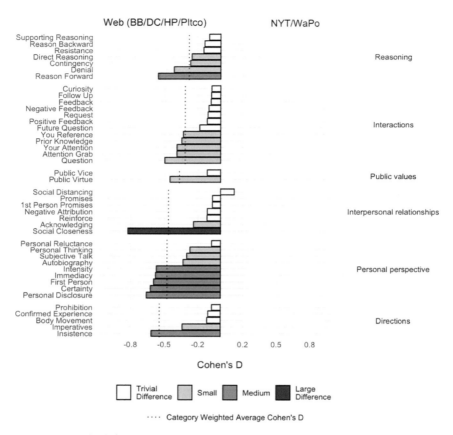

NOTE: Bars on the left side of the axis identify those characteristics more common in the online sample; bars on the right side of the axis identify factors more common in the newspaper sample.

positive tone in online journalism than in newspaper journalism for this reduced sample, a trend that we did not find as strongly in the full-sample comparison.

We can explore these changes in more detail by considering what they look like in context. Table 5.7 provides some example strings for each of the three linguistic characteristics that appear in the reduced-sample analysis and not in the full analysis.

Table 5.6
Newspapers Versus Online Journalism, Both Samples

Sample	Full Newspaper/Full Online Sample Analysis	National Newspaper/Reduced Online Sample
Newspapers	• Characters (e.g., personal roles, neutral attribution, personal pronoun) • Descriptive language (e.g., spatial relations, concrete objects, concrete properties, motion) • Time (e.g., looking back, time duration and shift) • Numbers • Narrative (e.g., biographical time, narrative verbs) • **Transformation**	• Characters (e.g., personal roles, neutral attribution) • Descriptive language (e.g., spatial relations, concrete objects, concrete properties, motion) • Time (e.g., looking back, time duration and shift) • Numbers • Narrative (e.g., biographical time, narrative verbs) • **Citing sources**
Online sources	• Oral cues • Predicting the future • Generalization • Emotion (anger) • Updates, reporting states • Academic concepts (e.g., linguistic references, quotations, metadiscourse, **authoritative sources**, contested sources) • **Rumors and media** • Confirming opinions • Reasoning (e.g., forward, backward, denial, resistance) • Interactions (you references, attention grab, prior knowledge, questions) • Interpersonal relations (social closeness) • Personal perspective (e.g., personal disclosure, first person, immediacy, autobiography, personal thinking, intensity, certainty, subjective talk) • Directions (insistence, imperatives)	• Oral cues • Predicting the future • Generalization • Emotion (anger, **general positivity**) • Updates, reporting states • Academic concepts (e.g., linguistic references, quotations, metadiscourse, contested sources) • Confirming opinions • Reasoning (e.g., forward, backward, denial, resistance) • Interactions (you references, attention grab, prior knowledge, questions) • **Public virtue** • Interpersonal relations (social closeness) • Personal perspective (e.g., personal disclosure, first person, autobiography, personal thinking, intensity, certainty, subjective talk) • Directions (insistence, Imperatives)

NOTE: All characteristics present in one analysis and not in the other are in bold text.

Table 5.7
Characteristics of Newspaper and Online Journalism, 2012–2017 (Reduced Sample's Unique Characteristics)

Language Category	Subcategories	Example Strings
Newspapers 2012–2017		
Academic concepts	Citing sources	"according to;" "commented;" "he said;" "in an interview"
Online 2012–2017		
Emotion	General positivity	"with the help of;" "celebrate;" "tender;" "embraces;" "intimate;" "strongly support"
Public values	Public virtues	"reform;" "achievement;" "dedicated;" "safer;" "right direction"

We can also explore these differences in context. The following block of text provides a clear example of general positivity, combined with references to public virtue. The passage also contains other elements and characteristics mentioned elsewhere, but we emphasize these two to highlight what seems to be unique about online journalism in the reduced sample and provide specific examples in Table 5.8.

And there's another risk: By casting terrorists as masterminds, we overestimate them, and this overestimation boosts their reputations, inadvertently increasing their global status and recruiting power. Overestimation also makes the West swing wildly in response (see the invasion of Iraq). Casting terrorists as masterminds also tends to under-estimate the capacity of the West to confront, if not defeat, terrorism with its prestigious resources and military might. If there is any real genius to the terrorist method, it's the ongoing ability of its commanders to persuade individuals to lay down their lives in suicide operations. That idea may be genius, of an evil kind, but the implementation is not. The designer of a suicide operation is no more a mastermind than is the pilot of a US drone, and he's much more vulnerable to a counterstrike.[6]

---

6   Jack Shafer, "The Myth of the Terrorist Mastermind," Politico, November 16, 2015.

Table 5.8
Textual Examples of Online Journalism (Reduced Sample): General Positivity and Public Virtue

Linguistic Characteristic	Example
General positivity	"boosts their reputations;" "increasing their global status"
Public virtue	"its prestigious resources;" "genius;" "ability"

Finally, we consider areas of similarity between the online and newspaper journalism in the reduced sample. As with the full sample, we see very few overlaps or areas of consistency. In the aggregate, as shown in Table 5.9, 20 percent of characteristics fail to meet the statistical significance threshold (though others might fall below the substantive importance threshold). There are only two areas for which there is evidence of some substantial consistency—public values and elaboration. There seems to be evidence that these two dimensions are represented in both online and print journalism, but the same is less true of other linguistic categories, many of which have no characteristics that meet traditional levels of statistical significance (or only one such characteristic). In Appendix B, we provide the full list of nonsignificant linguistic characteristics.

Discussion

The analysis and examples in this chapter identify the linguistic differences that surfaced in our comparison of online and newspaper journalism over the 2012–2017 period. There are some similarities across the two platforms. The greatest areas of similarity occur in the use of and references to public values, the use of elaboration (numbers, examples, descriptors), and references to personal interactions.

There are, however, many more areas of difference. Compared with the online sample, the print journalism sample remained far more anchored in what we might consider to be traditional reporting: the presentation of a narrative, time sequencing, reporting about characters and their specific actions, enumeration, and comparison. In contrast,

Table 5.9
Nonstatistically Significant Language Characteristics:
Online Versus Newspapers (Reduced Sample)

Language Category	Characteristics Not Significant (%)
Personal perspective	18
Time	0
Emotion	29
Descriptive language	0
Interpersonal relationships	36
Public values	50
Public language	25
Academic language	25
Reasoning	13
Interactions	8
Elaboration	63
Reporting	8
Directions	29
Narrative	0
Characters	0

the online journalism sample is more conversational, with more emphasis on interpersonal interactions, personal perspectives, and opinions. Appeals are less narrative and more argumentative, with an eye toward persuasion. The emphasis is less on personal roles and more on assessments of social and public virtues and concerns. As noted elsewhere, at least a part of this difference might be driven by characteristics of the media ecosystem itself and the different evolution and business model of print and online news. Newspaper journalism has remained more traditional in many ways, continuing its efforts to appeal to a wide audience; online journalism outlets often work to build niches and use a more interactive style to engage with their readers.

Both types of journalism provide information to consumers, but they are very different in how they present that information and how they encourage readers to interact with it. Our examples capture only a handful of the thousands of texts that we looked at, but they do indicate how the online material reads differently and provides different kinds of information. The information in print journalism is more straightforward, even where it features personal perspective and subjectivity; news in online journalism is conveyed in an innately personal way by the journalist, one that is heavily dependent on context and experience.

CHAPTER SIX

Summary and Conclusions

This study is one of the first to empirically assess differences in the ways that news is presented over time and across platforms, using both quantitative and qualitative approaches. We must be careful about generalizing too far from the specific sources that we analyzed, but we do observe some broad trends consistently across our different analyses. As we move from news coverage prior to 2000 to news coverage after 2000, and as we move from conventional media to "newer" media (e.g., cable and online), our analysis suggests that news coverage has shifted away from a more traditional style characterized by complex, detailed reporting that emphasizes events, context, public figures, time, and numbers toward a more personal, subjective form of reporting that emphasizes anecdotes, argumentation, advocacy, and emotion. Observed shifts have not been wholesale, however, and there is much that has remained the same over time and across media. For example, journalism across platforms is often characterized by continued adherence to reporting styles (e.g., sequencing, events, dialogue, motion) and often a similar anchoring in common public values. In this chapter, we take a step back, discussing key insights from each analysis and drawing parallels across the different comparisons to build a more holistic sense of what has changed, what has stayed the same, and why these factors could be important. Key findings from our analysis are summarized in Table 6.1.

In our temporal analyses of broadcast news and newspapers, we observed a shift in reporting from event-based reporting rich with contextual details and description to a reporting style that is more subjective and oriented toward advocacy, interpersonal interaction, and

Table 6.1
Summary of Key Results

Sample	Variables	
Newspaper journalism	Prior to 2000	After 2000
	Context- and event-based reporting, relies on directives, use of titles and official positions, appeals to authority	Narrative style with more storytelling and appeals to emotion
Broadcast television	Prior to 2000	After 2000
	Academic style, use of numbers, abstract reasoning and argument, more precise language	Conversational tone, more personal perspective and subjectivity
Broadcast versus cable television, 2000–2017	Broadcast	Cable
	Detailed descriptions of the present, of people speaking, of the material world; Social distance	Highly interactive and subjective, argumentation and imperatives aimed at persuasion and debates
Print versus online journalism 2012–2017	Print	Online
	Emphasizes character and narrative, more emphasis on context, sequences, and events	Personal and subjective, interactive, emphasizing argument and advocacy, urgent language, generalizations

argumentation. In addition, the use of emotional appeals, subjective reporting, and argument have increased over time in the sources that we explored. The specifics of these shifts have differed somewhat across platforms. Changes have been least notable in print journalism; they are more visible in our empirical analysis when comparing changes in television broadcast journalism over time.

Print Journalism: Modest Shifts Toward More-Subjective Reporting

For our print journalism sample, many of the linguistic features found to be characteristic of the pre-2000 period were frequently used together to describe key political, social, and policy issues. This meant laying out the counts involved (costs, demographics, and statistical descriptions), the shared public basis for authority on the issues (the courts, Congress, even "the public" itself), and the directive nature of policy (their approvals, prohibitions, and requirements). In the post-2000 sample, there has been a meaningful shift away from such language and toward unpacking social and policy issues through character-centered stories: homeless children as a way to discuss homelessness or soldiers' lives as a way to discuss war and foreign policy. On the one hand, this greater use of emotion might reflect efforts by journalists to reach their audiences in new ways and engage them more personally and directly. On the other, it might reflect a shift in response to the changing economic dynamics of the media industry and the increasingly intense competition among media outlets for readers and advertisers. As noted in the introduction, the changing economic and market conditions of the media industry can shape decisions about how to present news, and we might be seeing some of that here. Most likely, it is a combination of these factors and others.

Television News: Stronger Shifts to Subjectivity, Conversation, and Argument

Turning to television, we found two very important threads in our analysis. First, we observed the rise of a more subjective, conversational, argumentative style of news presentation, in contrast to a more conventional kind of straight reporting that deals with complexity and grounds news in the abstract concepts and values of shared public matters. In the area of broadcast journalism, we see a gradual shift from the pre-2000 period, in which more-conventional reporting used precise and concrete language with appeals to public sources of authority, to the post-2000 period, in which journalism is more subjective with a decrease in the use of concrete language and an increase in unplanned speech, expression of opinions, interviews, and arguments. When comparing broadcast news with prime-time cable programming in the period after 2000, we see an even more dramatic difference, with prime-time cable programming being more subjective, abstract, and directive. Cable programming is also more likely to feature argumentative language and content, content that is based more on the expression of opinion than it is on the provision of facts, and advocacy for those same opinions rather than a balanced description of context or events.

A second thread is the relationship between broadcast news and cable programming. Changes over time in the linguistic style of broadcast television (pre- and post-2000) generally mirror the contrast between broadcast news and prime-time cable programming: a shift to a more subjective, more conversational, and more deliberative approach to providing news. The style of the post-2000 broadcast television news, in the end, is somewhere between broadcast journalism in the pre-2000 period and cable programming in the post-2000 period. As discussed earlier, this might reflect a response to market and competitive pressures and a shift by broadcast television news to retain its viewership in the competition with cable programming.

The stark differences between prime-time cable programming and broadcast news are likely driven largely by a difference in the intention of the programming and the different business models and market objectives of the different platforms. In other words, the characteristics of prime-time cable programming might be different because they are *intended* to be more opinion-oriented than broadcast news in order to appeal to specific niche audiences and to pursue other important objectives. Broadcast journalism and cable programming do not appear to be interchangeable; instead, they seem to be very distinct forms of news and very different ways of communicating with the public.

Online Journalism: Toward a Subjective Kind of Advocacy

Finally, the contrast between our samples of newspaper and online journalism mimics the other "new media" trends we have observed when analyzing changes in print journalism over time and when comparing broadcast news with prime-time cable programming. Online journalism is more personal and direct, narrating key social and policy issues through very personal frames and subjective references. Online journalism often uses directive language, immediacy, and certainty to set an agenda or advocate a particular viewpoint, but this is not universally true. Finally, online journalism in our sample is also characterized by several elements of a more academic style, such as the use of citations and references. In contrast, print journalism over this same period is seemingly more traditional, characterized by the presentation of a narrative, time sequencing, reporting about characters and their specific actions, enumeration, and comparison. Compared with online journalism in the 2012–2017 period, then, newspaper journalism is characterized by a "who, what, where, when" style of reporting, even as it incorporates emotional appeals and personal perspectives.

Across all three sets of analyses, the general journalistic trend in our data appears to be one that is shifting away from more traditional reporting, with an emphasis on concrete objects, sequences, characters and events, narration, and storytelling, and toward a style characterized by very subjective and personal appeals, advocacy for specific positions, overt arguments, and urgency. Of course, the shifts described have not been complete or wholesale, even within our sample of data. It is not the case that the prime-time cable programming or the online journalism in our sample are entirely devoid of detailed, contextual, and event-based reporting or that print journalism in the pre-2000 period lacked any emotional appeals or advocacy-oriented language in news coverage. In fact, there are areas where our comparisons turned up no large differences fairly consistently. For instance, although different platforms used them differently, news presentation across platforms tended to share some use of elaboration (e.g., details, examples, numbers), some use of public language and the frame of public values, and some characteristics of a "reporting style" (e.g., sequencing, events, dialogue).

However, our analysis does suggest that the balance between these different linguistic styles has shifted over time and differs across platforms. Linguistic styles also are combined in different ways. In aggregate, then, we are left with a more narrative journalism that features more subjective and interactive coverage and with less of the detailed event- or context-based reporting that used to characterize news coverage. We cannot attach a normative value to this shift in and of itself. As noted elsewhere, a more personal style might be more effective in engaging a wider audience or helping readers relate to a story, but it also could replace objective reporting of context- or event-based details that are also necessary for the reader.

We wish to emphasize that our analysis considered only a selected sample of news sources. Our analysis of changes in television and prime-time cable programming is broadly representative of those two forms of media; our newspaper analysis and exploration of online journalism might be less generalizable. The additional subsample analyses provide us some confidence in the robustness of our results, but future work should seek to replicate the analysis here for other sources as a way to determine whether the patterns and trends we surfaced do indeed apply to the fields of newspaper and online journalism writ large.

In the next section, we explore some of the broader implications of these changes for Truth Decay as a phenomenon, and we explore questions raised by this research that we might be able to address with our newly collected empirical data.

Implications for Truth Decay

Our analysis suggests three key insights for our ongoing study of Truth Decay: One is directly connected to our motivating question while the other two provide insights with broader relevance to the Truth Decay research agenda, which is focused generally on changes and dynamics in the media ecosystem.

Is News Presentation Today More or Less Reliant on Opinions Than in the Past?

As noted in the introduction, this report was motivated by a desire to collect and study empirical data relevant to two of Truth Decay's four trends: the blurring of the line between fact and opinion and the increasing relative volume of opinion over fact. RAND-Lex does not directly measure use of fact and opinion, but it does capture such things as authoritative language, reporting of events, time, and authority figures, subjectivity, and use of emotion. We cannot directly answer the question of whether use of facts has become more or less common in news presentation, but our results have provided insight into the prevalence of subjective or opinion-based content over time and across platforms.

The general trends observed in our analysis do seem to provide some initial evidence of a gradual and subtle shift—both over time and between old and new media—toward a more subjective form of journalism that is grounded less in precedent than in personal perspective. In each of the analyses that consider changes over time, we find some evidence of a shift from a journalistic style based on the use of public language, academic register, references to authority, and event-based reporting to a style of journalism based more heavily on personal perspective, narration, and subjectivity. We see this trend in broadcast news and to a lesser extent in newspapers. We can also compare the characteristics of "new" and "old" media using the RAND-Lex results (these comparisons should be considered informal, however, because we did not do them within the RAND-Lex tool; they are extrapolations). For example, we found that cable programming is highly interactive and subjective and relies on arguments and opinions to persuade and debate, a stark contrast from the more academic style and precise language employed in broadcast television in the pre-2000 period. Similarly, our online journalism sample was characterized by a personal and subjective style that in many cases emphasizes argument and advocacy; this was very different from the pre-2000 print journalism sample, which relied more heavily on event-based reporting, often with references to authoritative institutions or sources.

Therefore, we do find evidence of a more widespread use of opinion and subjectivity in the presentation of news than in the past. This is consistent with the Truth Decay framework, but three important caveats are necessary. First, as noted throughout, we must be cautious about generalizing from our results, especially for the online and newspaper sources. Our results and observations about trends in the apparent use of authoritative versus subjective language and personal sources apply to the specific outlets and time periods considered in this report. We cannot make a broader argument about news presentation writ large without additional research. Second, although we can identify RAND-Lex categories that are reasonable proxies for the types of changes in news presentation suggested by the Truth Decay framework, these will provide only indirect and imperfect measures for such concepts as "reliance on fact or evidence" and "reliance on opinion." Finally, we remind the reader that some of the effect sizes are relatively small and that changes observed over time and differences across platforms are subtle in many cases. Future research, ideas for which are described later, can help build the robustness of the insights produced by this analysis.

Different Platforms Work as Complements, Not Replacements

Our analysis also provides evidence that different sources provide news in different ways and with different linguistic characteristics. News sources are not interchangeable, then, but each provides unique content and information to the media ecosystem (although there certainly is overlap). Our findings are related to the broader literature on media complementarity, which argues that individuals tend to rely on many sources of information to meet different needs.[1] Given our finding

---

[1]   Mohan J. Dutta-Bergman, "Complementarity in Consumption of News Types Across Traditional and New Media," *Journal of Broadcasting & Electronic Media*, Vol. 48, No. 1, 2004; Oscar Westlund and Mathias A. Färdigh, "Accessing the News in an Age of Mobile Media: Tracing Displacing and Complementary Effects of Mobile News on Newspapers and Online News," *Mobile Media & Communication*, Vol. 3, No. 1, 2015; Trevor Diehl, Matthew Barnidge, and Homero Gil de Zúñiga, "Multi-Platform News Use and Political Participation Across Age Groups: Toward a Valid Metric of Platform Diversity and Its Effects," *Journalism & Mass Communication Quarterly*, September 20, 2018.

that different types of media present news in different ways, it makes sense that people might turn to multiple platforms because they are getting slightly different types of information and different frames in each case. From this perspective, trends toward an increasing number and diversity of types of news presentation appear beneficial for users and might not mean the eventual elimination of traditional forms of media.[2]

That each platform or medium might provide news in a slightly different way also echoes McLuhan's argument that "the medium is the message." As information consumers, we are affected not only by the information that we consume, but also by the technologies or platforms through which we consume it.[3] The notion of *affordances* suggests that the effects of a medium depend on the interaction between the characteristics of the technology and the people using it.[4] In other words, it is the relationship and interaction between the user and the technology that influences the meaning and importance of a given medium within the information ecosystem and within society.[5] Applied to social media, for example, this would mean that the role and importance of social media in our media ecosystem (and our interpersonal relationships) are shaped by the interaction between the

---

[2] The alternative, *displacement theory*, suggests that individuals have a fixed amount of attention for information and media, so the addition of new sources crowds out older ones. See Joseph M. Kayany and Paul Yelsma, "Displacement Effects of Online Media in the Socio-Technical Contexts of Households," *Journal of Broadcasting & Electronic Media*, Vol. 44, No. 2, 2000; and Stan J. Liebowitz and Alejandro Zentner, "Clash of the Titans: Does Internet Use Reduce Television Viewing?" *Review of Economics and Statistics*, Vol. 94, No. 1, 2012.

[3] Marshall McLuhan, *Understanding Media*, Cambridge, Mass.: MIT Press, reprint edition, 1994.

[4] The term affordances was coined by psychologist James Gibson, who developed the concept over many years. James J. Gibson, *The Ecological Approach to Visual Perception*, London: Psychology Press and Routledge Classic Editions, reprint edition, 2014.

[5] Samer Faraj and Bijan Azad, "The Materiality of Technology: An Affordance Perspective," in Paul M. Leonardi, Bonnie A. Nardi, and Jannis Kallinikos, eds., *Materiality and Organizing*, Oxford, England: Oxford University Press, 2012; Paul M. Leonardi, "Theoretical Foundations for the Study of Sociomateriality," *Information and Organization*, Vol. 23, No. 2, 2013.

characteristics of the technology (e.g., speed and ease of access) and the ways in which information consumers use that technology. From this perspective, different approaches to news presentation across types of media also might be caused, at least in part, by this interaction among the technology, the user, and society. Understanding this complex relationship seems central to developing a better understanding of Truth Decay and deserves additional attention.

News Presentation and Trust in the Media

Finally, our results raise an important question about how changes in news presentation could influence the relationship between news consumers and the media more generally. Data show that trust in media institutions has fallen dramatically over the past decade, and we define it as one of the four trends that make up Truth Decay. This decline in trust has extended across platforms, and although newspapers and television experienced a slight uptick in 2017, this seems to have been a one-year increase only, and the current level remains well below historical averages. In 2018, 45 percent of respondents reported a great deal or a fair amount of trust in the media to report information fairly and accurately. However, the same survey reported that trust declined back toward lower 2016 levels for newspapers (with 23 percent reporting a great deal or quite a lot of confidence) and for television news (with 20 percent reporting a great deal or quite a lot of confidence).[6]

There are many reasons why people might have low trust in media. Some recent surveys suggest that it is concern over false information that drives distrust. In one survey, more than 50 percent of consumers reported that media companies play a role in the problem of disinformation by what they choose to print and by spreading false information, both intentionally and unintentionally.[7] In fact, about 70 percent of news consumers say they believe publication of false information is

[6]   Gallup, "Confidence in Institutions", webpage, undated; Jeffrey Jones, "U.S. Media Trust Continues to Recover From 2016 Low," Gallup, October 12, 2018.

[7]   Christine Schmidt, "Planted Stories? Fake News as Editorial Decisions? Trump or CNN? A Poll Examines the Public's Trust of Mainstream Media," Neiman Lab, April 3, 2018.

intentional sometimes or often, although this number is significantly higher for Republicans (92 percent) than Democrats (53 percent).[8] An increasing number of sources might confuse consumers seeking fact-based information, eroding their trust in media more generally.[9]

Trust in media varies across media platforms. As noted, trust in broadcast and newspaper journalism has been similar over time.[10] Trust in online sources is much more variable: Some studies find that online news is viewed as more credible than television or newspapers;[11] others report that it is less so.[12] Different platforms also can be judged based on different criteria. For example, trust in television newscasts might be based on sources of news, such as the anchors delivering the information, while newspapers are judged more generally as an institution.[13]

Trust in media also might be driven by partisanship. Past research clearly shows that attitudes toward the media are heavily affected by

---

[8] Sara Fischer, "92% of Republicans Think Media Intentionally Reports Fake News," Axios, June 27, 2018.

[9] Knight Foundation, "10 Reasons Why American Trust in the Media Is at an All-Time Low," Medium.com, January 15, 2018a.

[10] Bruce H. Westley and Werner J. Severin, "Some Correlates of Media Credibility," *Journalism Quarterly*, Vol. 41, Summer 1964; Richard F. Carter and Bradley S. Greenberg, "Newspaper or Television: Which Do You Believe?" *Journalism Quarterly*, Vol. 42, Winter 1965; Cecile Gaziano and Kristin McGrath, "Measuring the Concept of Credibility," *Journalism Quarterly*, Vol. 63, Autumn 1986; Matthias Kohring and Jörg Matthes, "Trust in News Media: Development and Validation of a Multidimensional Scale," *Communication Research*, Vol. 34, No. 2, 2007.

[11] Thomas J. Johnson and Barbara K. Kaye, "Cruising Is Believing? Comparing Internet and Traditional Sources on Media Credibility Measures," *Journalism & Mass Communication Quarterly*, Vol. 75, No. 2, 1998; Eun Go, Kyung Han You, Eun Hwa Jung, and Hongjin Shim, "Why Do We Use Different Types of Websites and Assign Them Different Levels of Credibility? Structural Relations Among Users' Motives, Types of Websites, Information Credibility, and Trust in the Press," *Computers in Human Behavior*, Vol. 54, January 2016.

[12] Pew Research Center, *One-in-Ten Voters Online for Campaign '96*, 1996.; Spiro Kiousis, "Public Trust of Mistrust? Perceptions of Media Credibility in the Information Age," *Mass Communication and Society*, Vol. 4, No. 4, 2001; Thomas J. Johnson and Barbara K. Kaye, "Some Like It Lots: The Influence of Interactivity and Reliance on Credibility," *Computers in Human Behavior*, Vol. 61, August 1, 2016.

[13] John Newhagen and Clifford Nass, "Differential Criteria for Evaluating Credibility of Newspapers and TV News," *Journalism Quarterly*, Vol. 66, No. 2, 1989.

political beliefs and partisanship in the United States.[14] In one recent study, respondents significantly alter their expression of perceived trust based on the source, expressing substantially higher trust in sources that share their perspective and partisan preference than in sources from across the political aisle (e.g., less trust for Fox News among Democrats or for MSNBC among Republicans).[15]

Finally, past research has shown that trust is correlated with consumption. News consumers tend to trust most what they consume and to consume what they trust, especially when choosing among platforms and among outlets.[16] Looking at cable news, for example, Stroud and Lee show that the relationship between political attitudes and cable news consumption choices is mediated by perceived credibility.[17] However, it is unclear from past research whether perceptions of overall news media credibility are related in a direct way to frequency of news consumption.[18]

This brings us back to the question posed at the start of this section: Do changes in news presentation affect the relationship (and specifically trust) between news consumers and media institutions? By

---

[14] Albert C. Gunther, "Biased Press or Biased Public?" *Public Opinion Quarterly*, Vol. 56, No. 2, 1992; David A. Jones, "Why Americans Don't Trust the Media: A Preliminary Analysis," *Harvard International Journal of Press/Politics*, Vol. 9, No. 2, 2004; Tien-Tsung Lee, "Why They Don't Trust the Media: An Examination of Factors Predicting Trust," *American Behavioral Scientist*, Vol. 54, No. 1, 2010.

[15] Knight Foundation, "An Online Experimental Platform to Assess Trust in the Media," webpage, July 18, 2018b.

[16] Robert P. Hawkins, Suzanne Pingree, Jacqueline Hitchon, Bradley W. Gorham, Prathana Kannaovakun, Eileen Gilligan, Barry Radler, Gudbjorg H. Kolbeins, and Toni Schmidt, "Predicting Selection and Activity in Television Genre Viewing," *Media Psychology*, Vol. 3, No. 3, 2001; Yariv Tsfati and Joseph N. Cappella, "Do People Watch What They Do Not Trust? Exploring the Association Between News Media Skepticism and Exposure," *Communication Research*, Vol. 30, No. 5, 2003; Nikolaus G. E. Jakob, "No Alternatives? The Relationship Between Perceived Media Dependency, Use of Alternative Information Sources, and General Trust in Mass Media," *International Journal of Communication*, Vol. 4, 2010.

[17] Natalie Jomini Stroud and Jae Kook Lee, "Perceptions of Cable News Credibility," *Mass Communication and Society*, Vol. 16, No. 1, 2013.

[18] Wayne Wanta and Yu-Wei Hu, "The Effects of Credibility, Reliance, and Exposure on Media Agenda-Setting: A Path Analysis Model," *Journalism Quarterly*, Vol. 71, No. 1, 1994.

considering the results of the analysis in this report alongside past and recent research on trust and the news media, we can use the changes in news presentation that we observed to make some inferences about what they might mean for trust in the media more generally. Past research suggests that the way information is presented can shape perceived credibility of news.[19] In this report, we have described evidence showing that news presentation has changed over time and differs across platforms. A set of survey experiments conducted by the Knight Foundation and Gallup in 2018 provides some insight into what these specific changes could mean for trust in media. For example, when asked to provide reasons why they distrusted certain media sources, concern about news coverage that relies too heavily on opinion and emotions was the second most common response, following inaccuracy in news coverage. In addition, when asked to rank how important various factors were to their willingness to trust news organizations, 91 percent reported that it was very important or important that the source clearly label commentary and opinion as such and distinguish it from fact.[20]

We cannot definitively describe the relationship between trust and changes in news presentation, but we do have evidence that the types of changes in news presentation that we identified in this report are relevant to individual news consumer decisions about which media organizations to trust. Specifically, trends toward subjective journalism that features more personal perspective and more emotion might influence trust in the news media. This relationship deserves additional attention.

Limitations

We have alluded throughout this report to limitations of our analysis, but it is worth repeating them here. First, we consider only a limited

---

[19] Lee, 2010; Knight Foundation, 2018b.

[20] Knight Foundation and Gallup Polling, *Indicators of News Media Trust*, Washington, D.C., September 11, 2018.

set of sources, and our samples (with the exception of the television samples) are not generalizable to all newspapers or all online outlets. We have conducted several additional analyses to assess the robustness of our results to different specifications, and our results have held up to this scrutiny, but we still must be careful not to overgeneralize the results. In the next section, we provide some discussion of how future analyses could work toward generalizability. We also only consider newspapers, television, and online journalism. A more comprehensive analysis of how news presentation changes over time and across platforms would need to explore radio, social media, images, and other forms of news.

Second, RAND-Lex itself has some limitations. For example, although its taxonomy is extensive, we are limited to considering changes that fall within its bounds. This means that the analysis we have presented captures only some aspects of evolving linguistic styles. In addition, the tool can deal only with data sets of a certain size. To address this, we cut the corpora in half or quarters, but obviously the ideal would have been to use all stories and articles for each source. Along those lines, although we aimed to use primarily news stories, we know that our sample likely included some entertainment, sports, and other stories. This means that a small portion of our data did not focus on news per se. This is not optimal but also not likely to have a real effect on our results because of the overall sample size. Furthermore, if these items are featured in the front section of a newspaper or covered prominently on television and online, then these stories might be important enough or have some societal connection to warrant inclusion in our analysis.

A third limitation focuses on what questions this report cannot answer. We focus on measuring changes in news presentation. Our analysis cannot tell us why these changes occur or whether they affect the way that consumers interpret or share information. We do not attach normative values to observed differences and changes, we do not make recommendations for how to "change things back," and we do not identify "problems." Instead we use the results to better understand changes in the media ecosystem and to further investigate Truth Decay as a phenomenon.

Next Steps: What Other Research Is Needed?

This report has provided empirical evidence of the ways in which the linguistic tone and style of several different types and sources of news reporting have changed over time and differ across platforms. It also has raised a variety of questions that warrant further investigation. Here, we discuss the ways in which our analysis can be supplemented and expanded.

Replication of Results

As noted throughout, our analysis is limited in terms of generalizability. To assess the robustness of our results and the extent to which they can be applied more broadly, the analyses here should be replicated using samples consisting of different news outlets. This is of particular concern for the print and online journalism analysis, which can be replicated using more-diverse samples and samples that simply contain different sets of outlets. This could be a wider set of national newspapers, a sample of only regional outlets, or a sample of local and community papers. In addition to analyzing each of these sources independently, comparisons could also be conducted to assess how the linguistic style used in national, regional, local, and community journalism (newspapers and other sources) might vary.

It would also be valuable to explore the use of other stance dictionaries and other analytical tools in a similar methodology to assess changes in news presentations. There are other taxonomies available for stance analysis,[21] and RAND-Lex's modular structure treats the dictionaries within a taxonomy as plug-and-play resources. However, it is worth noting that each of these stance taxonomies has a slightly different orientation and asks a slightly different question. Analyzing textual data using these alternative taxonomies would supplement but not replicate the analysis presented here.

---

[21] We distinguish between *semantic analysis* (focused on content) and *stance analysis* (focused on perspectives and attitudes). Because content changes over time, semantic analysis tools were not appropriate for our project.

As one example, we could use one of several semantic analysis systems, such as the University Centre for Computer Corpus Research on Language's Semantic Analysis System or WordNet (e.g., affect or appraisal).[22] Semantic analyses focus specifically on affect and appraisal—that is, the emotional content of text—and so are more limited in nature than the RAND-Lex taxonomy, but they still could provide useful insights. The other very broad, general-purpose stance taxonomy available is Tausczik and Pennebaker's Linguistic Inquiry Word Count (LIWC).[23] LIWC has been used alongside the CMU stance taxonomy in a large open-ended survey to analyze attitudes around opening special operations to women.[24] LIWC is an explicitly psychometric tool, aimed at detecting the psychological states of writers and speakers behind their language use. This made it less appropriate for the specific analysis that we conducted, but the use of LIWC could provide useful supplementary analysis in the future. These additional analyses would allow us to make more-general statements about differences in news presentation across sources and over time and to dig deeply into specific aspects of stance.

In addition to this validation, our analyses could be expanded in several other ways as well. First, we did not consider several very important types of media. We did not explore news magazines (e.g., *Time, Newsweek, The Week*),[25] radio reporting, or social media. The method used here could be replicated for these forms of media. It would be

---

[22] Susan Broomhall, ed., *Early Modern Emotions: An Introduction*, Abingdon, England: Routledge, 2016.

[23] Yla R. Tausczik and James W. Pennebaker, "The Psychological Meaning of Words: LIWC and Computerized Text Analysis Methods," *Journal of Language and Social Psychology*, Vol. 29, No. 1, 2010.

[24] Thomas S. Szayna, Eric V. Larson, Angela O'Mahony, Sean Robson, Agnes Gereben Schaefer, Miriam Matthews, J. Michael Polich, Lynsay Ayer, Derek Eaton, William Marcellino, Lisa Miyashiro, Marek Posard, James Syme, Zev Winkelman, Cameron Wright, Megan Zander-Cotugno, and William Welser IV, *Considerations for Integrating Women into Closed Occupations in U.S. Special Operations Forces: Appendixes*, Santa Monica, Calif.: RAND Corporation, RR-1058/1-USSOCOM, 2015.

[25] This could be online or print news magazines. News magazines are typically considered as their own type of platform.

particularly interesting to observe the extent to which social media and online journalism vary and even how the language used by mainstream papers differs when promoting stories on social media (e.g., tweets) compared with the stories themselves as they appear in print.

Second, we could also expand the analysis to consider other types of journalism, such as advocacy or participatory journalism, and how the presentation of these types of information have changed over time or vary across platforms. This would provide a more holistic picture of changes in media presentation generally than the narrower focus on news we have presented here. Third, we could expand our analysis to assess changes in news presentation outside of the United States. Right now, we are limited by the number of languages that RAND-Lex can work in, but as new languages are added and as we explore other stance taxonomies, this cross-cultural comparison could become possible.

Another extension of the analysis presented here would be to identify news articles and broadcasts about a single topic (e.g., homelessness or education)—or, where possible, a single event—from across outlets, types of media, or over time and to use RAND-Lex or another tool to explore the extent to which presentation of news differs within a specific domain or about a specific issue. This type of analysis would be similar to some of the previous work described in Chapter One. However, an analysis using RAND-Lex could consist of a much larger corpora of text, increasing the robustness and generalizability of any findings. Using some mix of responses across outlets, across platforms, and over time to a single issue, event, or set of related events would provide additional and diverse insights into differences in news presentation.

Finally, we focused our analysis here on textual data. However, news is communicated through many other forms of media—especially graphics, photos, and videos—that play an increasingly important role in how people consume and interpret information. An important question is how the use, content, style, and other characteristics of these different forms of visual media have changed over time and how they differ across platforms. This type of analysis would require different tools (RAND-Lex is a text-based tool), but there are many tools available for image analysis that would support such an effort. When completed, it would be useful to compare an image-based analysis with a text-based analysis and observe the ways that the patterns are both similar and different.

Implications of Changes in News Presentation

This report has documented differences in the way news is presented across types of media and how print and broadcast journalism have changed over time. A natural next step is to explore the effects that such differences have on information consumers and, more broadly, on the role that media plays in society.

For example, one important next question is whether different ways of presenting news—e.g., the style of print journalism compared with the style of cable television—affect how individuals process and respond to that information. Existing research considers how such factors as word choice, framing, and partisan bias influence the way in which consumers interpret and respond to news. However, the majority of existing work does not consider the specific linguistic changes and differences that we identified in our empirical analysis. Future research could take the empirical changes documented in this report and use survey experiments to understand how changes in such things as argumentative language, use of descriptive language, use of subjective language, and language of urgency and immediacy affect people's ability to interpret and understand news, their ability to identify and distinguish between facts and opinions, and their susceptibility to false and misleading information.

A second possibility would be to focus on content creators. One important line of inquiry would be to understand how journalists view and interpret the changes in news presentation. This could be accomplished through interviews with experienced journalists and through primary source research using the memoirs of leading journalists in previous eras. An alternative research direction would be to conduct an in-depth analysis of publicly funded journalism (e.g., the Public Broadcasting Service or National Public Radio) compared with content produced by for-profit entities. If it is the case that economics is a significant driver of content decisions, then it is possible that publicly funded journalism might not manifest the same changes in news presentation as sources with a profit motive, such as those used in our analysis.

Insight into how different models of news production shape news presentation over time would be valuable as we consider the future of our information ecosystem.

These are only some of the many possible analyses that could be conducted to explore the broader implications of changes over time in the presentation of news and of cross-platform differences. Our ultimate objective is to develop a better understanding of the Truth Decay phenomenon, how it has affected the media ecosystem, and how it could continue to do so in the future. The documenting of empirical differences in news presentation over time and across platforms in the U.S. context is an essential first step toward these objectives.

About RAND-Lex

RAND-Lex is RAND's proprietary suite of text analytic tools designed to analyze large text data sets through rigorous text analytics. RAND-Lex has built-in statistical testing, expert workflows, and tool-tips to assist in answering policy questions through empirical analysis of text collections (or corpora) that are too large for human labor to read. Here are some examples of operationally relevant questions and problems that RAND analysts have addressed using RAND-Lex:

- In the wider Islamic world, who supports or opposes ISIS on social media platforms, such as Twitter? What other issues and concerns do these supporting or opposing groups care about? What are the likely paths of engagement and the most-influential communities?
- How effective has Russian propaganda been in shaping the terms of debate in the near abroad?
- How can combatant commands measure their effectiveness in combating extremist messaging?

Capabilities of RAND-Lex

RAND-Lex is a human-in-the-loop solution for analyzing large collections of unstructured or semistructured text. It is meant not to replace human analysis but to leverage it. Think of RAND-Lex as a prosthetic for human reading that can offer an analyst potential handfuls of needles from enormous fields of haystacks but also recognize kinds of needles that are different from the ones that humans tend to notice. In the end, human attention is required to decide what needles are relevant and what they mean.

RAND-Lex has four modules, and each module provides a different function.

- **Lexical Analysis:** This module helps with understanding what a text collection is about through the use of word counts, inductively pulling out keywords and connected word pairs or triplets from text. The Lexical Analysis module draws from theory and methods in corpus linguistics and uses statistical tests for unusual word frequencies and word associations to analyze any large text collection. For example, if one were to look at a large collection of Arabic language social media data from a particular group arguing about ISIS, one might find words for Egypt, ISIS, oil, constitution, and the Sinai, along with word pairs for Egyptian Presidents, Egyptian newspapers, and the Muslim brotherhood. This would help the analyst understand this is an Egyptian community with concerns about Egyptian sovereignty and governance. The Lexical Analysis module is language agnostic.
- **Stance Comparison:** This module deploys an expert dictionary-based approach that helps identify attitudes and beliefs through categories of words—such as affect, certainty/uncertainty, values, social closeness/distance—to help with understanding how the world is being represented in text. For example, if one were to analyze a corpus of public outreach from an extremist group, one might find that the favored argument strategy appeals to a sense of community and a willingness to join and take risks to protect those that the group feels are endangered. Two or more corpora can be compared to see if the mean amounts of any language category—e.g., mean amounts of anger, sadness, certainty, uncertainty, or past or future orientation—are significantly different. Currently, RAND has English, Arabic, and Russian dictionaries for Stance Comparison.
- **Topic Modeling:** This module can be used to discover the top-level themes that make up a large text collection and to explore

how words are used in context. For example, one might look at all Marine Corps doctrinal publications and find such major topics as the enemy, war, military operations, and logistics. This is a top-level view of a text collection that helps to clarify the actual topics at issue and can help make clear disconnects between what is being discussed or written about and what people think is being discussed or written about.

- **Text Classifier:** This is a supervised machine-learning module that lets analysts code and tag text by giving an algorithm human coding to mimic. For example, a goal can be to classify hundreds of thousands of tweets into categories of hostile, neutral, and friendly. Instead of trying a sampling strategy, one might hand-code 1,000 tweets and then have the machine "learn" the coding criteria and code the rest automatically. The accuracy could be good, and depending on the goals, this module might provide a useful labor trade-off.

RAND-Lex requires text data: This text can come from tweets or other social media platforms, from blogs or webscrapes, from interviews, or from open-form survey responses—basically any pile of documents too large for humans to read and process. RAND-Lex cannot read this material the way a human can (with contextual and cultural knowledge), but it can pull out what is unusual or structured in a pile of unstructured talk.

Stance Analysis Taxonomies

RAND-Lex's stance analysis uses the DocuScope stance thesaurus developed by David Kaufer and Suguru Ishizaki at CMU:[1] a very large-scale expert dictionary of approximately 40 million word and phrase strings within a linguistic taxonomy of 121 variables. These linguistic characteristics cover a variety of functional, pragmatic goals

---

[1]   David Kaufer, Suguru Ishizaki, Jeff Collins, and Pantelis Vlachos, "Teaching Language Awareness in Rhetorical Choice: Using IText and Visualization in Classroom Genre Assignments," *Journal of Business and Technical Communication*, Vol. 18, No. 3, 2004.

in language use.[2] Examples of variables are certainty and uncertainty, social distance and closeness, affect, describing the material and spatial dimensions of the world, and indexing such public matters as social virtues and vices.

The CMU dictionary has been found useful across a variety of text analytic tasks and problems. In linguistic forensics, variable counts were combined with most-frequent-word counts for valid and highly accurate (70–90 percent) authorship identification of unattributed Ronald Reagan speeches.[3] The dictionary has also been found to be accurate in a wide range of automatic text classification tasks.[4] The underlying linguistic taxonomy has been useful in cross-cultural English as a second language instruction, allowing rural Chinese students to write in U.S. English genres without U.S. cultural experience or prior English genre instruction.[5] Finally, in sentiment analysis, the various dictionary counts were combined with n-grams to produce highly accurate predictions of consumer sentiment in online unstructured texts, retaining a 92-percent accuracy rate while increasing parsimony in the number of features needed for analysis by an order of magnitude.[6]

---

[2] An important distinction in linguistics is between semantics (the informational content of an utterance) and pragmatics (the social or practical goal of an utterance). Marcellino, 2014; William M. Marcellino, "Revisioning Strategic Communication Through Rhetoric and Discourse Analysis," *Joint Forces Quarterly*, No. 76, 2015.

[3] Edoardo M. Airoldi, Annelise G. Anderson, Stephen E. Fienberg, and Kiron K. Skinner, "Who Wrote Ronald Reagan's Radio Addresses?" *Bayesian Analysis*, Vol. 1, No. 2, 2006; Edoardo M. Airoldi, Annelise G. Anderson, Stephen E. Fienberg, and Kiron K. Skinner, "Whose Ideas? Whose Words? Authorship of the Ronald Reagan Radio Addresses," *Political Science & Politics*, Vol. 40, No. 3, 2007.

[4] Jeffrey A. Collins, *Variations in Written English*, Washington, D.C.: U.S. Department of the Air Force, CI02-1189, 2003; Jonathan Hope and Michael Witmore, "The Hundredth Psalm to the Tune of 'Green Sleeves': Digital Approaches to Shakespeare's Language of Genre," *Shakespeare Quarterly*, Vol. 61, No. 3, 2010.

[5] Yongmei Hu, David Kaufer, and Suguru Ishizaki, "Genre and Instinct," in "Genre and Instinct," in Yang Cai, ed., *Computing with Instinct: Rediscovering Artificial Intelligence*, Berlin: Springer Science and Business Media, 2011.

[6] Xue Bai, "Predicting Consumer Sentiments from Online Text," *Decision Support Systems*, Vol. 50, No. 4, 2011.

Caveats Regarding the CMU Stance Model

We note that the CMU stance model is just that: a model. For example, the taxonomy makes a distinction between "concrete objects" and "abstract concepts"; that is, between material objects in the physical world and cognitive and linguistic abstractions. The metaphysical correctness of that distinction is less important to us than the fact that the CMU stance model has wide utility and is relevant to our question about how news is being reported (rather than the content of reporting)—and, as noted, it is the only available stance taxonomy that would allow us to conduct the type of analysis that we sought to accomplish. Ideally, we would compare the results using RAND-Lex with results using a different taxonomy to see how they differ. As the fields of textual analysis and machine-based coding evolve and new taxonomies emerge, this sort of comparative analysis will be possible.

We also note that the coding of word and phrase strings is robust at the aggregate level of large numbers but not at the micro-level of individual codings, where we expect the contextual nature of language to lead to a certain level of noise.[7] So, for example, a particular coding such as "afraid of" might have meant the reverse in context: i.e., "I'm not afraid of him." The utility of the expert dictionary and its underlying model of how speakers use language to accomplish pragmatics tasks is whether coding such strings as "afraid of," "nervous," and "watch out for" in aggregate usefully captures something meaningful.[8]

Finally, we point out that whatever the value of any single set of codings—e.g., reasoning backward to causes, contingency reasoning, or denial of another's position—automated approaches to text are reli-

---

[7] Ishizaki, Suguru, and David Kaufer, "Computer-Aided Rhetorical Analysis," in Philip M. McCarthy and Chutima Boonthum-Denecke, eds., *Applied Natural Language Processing: Identification, Investigation and Resolution*, Hershey, Pa.: IGI Global, 2012.

[8] An example of specific contextual use that was systematically distinct enough to require adjustment was the variable for "Rumors and Media," in which the proper name "The Buzz" was being coded in the sense of gossip or hype. RAND-Lex allows for by-exception recoding of strings in such cases.

able: They are consistent and replicable.[9] Because this is a machine approach, coding is 100 percent the same each time it is applied and to each data set. It might or might not be helpful to see that the collection of newspapers from before 2000 and the collection from after 2000 differ greatly in how often such phrases as "he said," "she said," and "he went on to say" appear. Descriptively, however, the coding can be trusted because the method is consistent and repeatable.

Table A.1 defines the full stance dictionary, both parent categories and linguistic characteristics.

---

[9]   Chong Ho Yu, Angel Jannasch-Pennell, and Samuel DiGangi, "Compatibility Between Text Mining and Qualitative Research in the Perspectives of Grounded Theory, Content Analysis, and Reliability," *Qualitative Report*, Vol. 16, No. 3, 2011.

Table A.1
Definitions of Stance Variables and Categories

Name	Definition
Personal perspective	Language from a subjective perspective, including our personal certainty, intensity, and temporal experience
First person	Self-reference (e.g., I, me, my, myself)
Personal disclosure	Self-reference (e.g., I, me, my) combined with personal thought or feeling verbs (e.g., I think, I feel, I believe
Personal reluctance	First-person resistance in decisionmaking (e.g., I am sorry that, I'm afraid that)
Autobiography	Self-reference (e.g., I, me, my) combined with have or used-to, signaling personal past (e.g., I have always, I used to)
Personal thinking	The use of words indicating the unshared contents of an individual mind (e.g., believe, feel, conjecture, speculate, pray for, hallucinate); a front-row seat into someone else's mind
General disclosure	Disclosing private information (e.g., confess, acknowledge that, admit, let on that, let it slip that)
Certainty	"for sure;" "definitely"
Uncertainty	"maybe;" "perhaps"
Intensity	Involved and committed to the ideas being expressed (e.g., very, fabulously, really, torrid, amazingly)
Immediacy	"right now;" "now;" "just then"
Subjective talk	Acknowledging that a perception is subjective/tentative (e.g., "it seems," "appears to be")
Time	Temporality, including temporal perspective
Subjective time	Experiencing time from the inside ("Seems like only yesterday")
Looking ahead	The use of words indicating the future (e.g., in order to, look forward to, will be in New York)
Predicting the future	Confident predictions, often using epistemic modals ("we will," "there will be")
Looking back	Mental leap to the past (e.g., "used to," "have been," "had always wanted")
Past looks ahead	Presents what the future looked like from the vantage of the past (e.g., "Lincoln was to look for the general who could win the war for him")
Time shift	"next week;" "next month"
Time duration	Temporal intervals (e.g., "for two years," "over the last month")
Biographical time	Life milestones (e.g., "in her youth," "it would be the last time")
Time date	E.g., "June 5, 2000"

Table A.1—Continued

Name	Definition
Emotion	Affective language
General positivity	Covers all positive emotion language ("joy," "wonderful")
General negativity	Negative language that doesn't fall into categories of anger, fear, sadness, reluctance, or apology ("that sucks," "suicidal")
Anger	Use of words referencing anger
Fear	Use of words referencing fear
Sadness	Sadness (negative emotion)
Reluctance	Resistance within the mind (e.g., regret that, sorry that, afraid that)
Apology	E.g., "I'm sorry," "I have failed"
Descriptive language	Descriptions of the world
Dialogue	Dialogue cues (e.g., quote marks, "she said")
Oral talk	Oral register (e.g., "well," "uh . . . um")
Concrete properties	Use of words indicating concrete properties (e.g., pink, velvety) revealed by the five senses
Concrete objects	Concrete nouns (e.g., table, chair)
Spatial relations	E.g., "nearby," "away from"
Scene shift	Shifts in spatial location (e.g., "left the room," "went outdoors")
Motion	E.g., run, skip, jump
Interpersonal relationships	Text about/constructing the social world
Promises	Words indicating a promise being made (e.g., promise, promised that)
First-person promises	First-person promises (e.g., "I promise," "we promised that")
Reassure	Reassuring words (e.g., don't worry, it's okay)
Reinforce	Positive social reinforcement (e.g., "congratulations," "good going")
Acknowledging	Use of words that give public notice of gratitude to persons (e.g., I acknowledge your help, thank you) (Acknowledgments without gratitude are in apology and concessions categories.)
Agreement	Public notice of acceptance or agreement (e.g., I accept, I agree)
Social closeness	Language of social belonging, fellow feeling, or like-mindedness
Positive attribution	Positive attributions to people "given credit for," or "ability to"
Social distancing	Negative/distant social relations (e.g., condemn, denounce, criticize)

Table A.1—Continued

Name	Definition
Negative attribution	Negative attributions to people (e.g., "be unqualified for," "oafish," "psycho")
Confront	To confront or threaten the addressee (e.g., "Let's face it," "how dare you")
Public values	**Language about the public good**
Public virtue	Positive, publicly endorsed values and standards of the culture (e.g., justice, happiness, fairness, "human rights")
Innovations	Significant discovery (e.g., breakthrough, cutting-edge, state-of-the-art)
Public vice	Standards and behavior publicly rejected by the culture (e.g., injustice, unhappiness, unfairness, "civil rights violations")
Social responsibility	Language of public accountability (e.g., to "take care of" our vets, or to "take on" Wall Street)
Public language	**Public sharing of talk**
Rumors and media	Words circulating over formal or informal media channels; includes institutional networks but also rumor, gossip, buzz, and memes (distinct from authority sources category)
Authority sources	Public or institutional authorities, already familiar and respected in the culture (e.g., "founding fathers," "the courts," "the Prophet," "duly authorized")
Popular opinions	Beliefs, ideas, and approaches circulating in the culture and well known (e.g., "some hold that," "others believe that," "in the history of")
Confirming opinions	Agreeing with and supporting ideas that are already out in the culture and well known (e.g., "I recognize that," "I agree with")
Academic language	**Academic register**
Abstract concepts	E.g., "gross amount, "money," "evolutionary theory"; includes Latinate/Hellenic (tion, sion, ment, ogy, logy) suffixes and other patterns indicating abstract general concepts
Communicator role	Formal communication situation (e.g., "speaker," "listener," "audience")
Linguistic references	References to language (e.g., noun, verb, adjective, play, novel, poem, prose)
Citing precedent	Referencing a chain of historical decisions to which you can link your own ideas (e.g., has long been; has a long history)
Citing sources	External sources (e.g., "according to," "sources say," "point out that")
Undermining sources	A citation that hints at a biased or deficient source
Countering sources	A citation used to counter a previous statement
Speculative sources	A citation of a source that is guessing

Table A.1—Continued

Name	Definition
Authoritative source	A citation of a source that knows (e.g., "support that")
Contested source	A citation of a source in a debate ("argue for," "content that")
Attacking sources	A citation attacking a previous source
Quotation	Use of quotations
Metadiscourse	Navigational guides through the stream of language (e.g., to clarify, just to be brief, this paper will argue, my purpose is)
Reasoning	**Logic and argument language**
Reason forward	Chain of thought moving forward from premise to conclusion, cause to effect (e.g., thus, therefore)
Reason backward	Use of words indicating a chain of thought moving backward from conclusion to premise, effect to cause (e.g., because, owing to the fact, on the grounds that)
Direct reasoning	Words that initiate and direct another's reasoning (e.g., suppose that, imagine that)
Supporting reasoning	Use of words indicating support or evidence for a reasoning process that you or someone you are citing has
Contingency	Words indicating contingency (e.g., if, possibly)
Denial	"Not" or other negative elements in front of an assertion, denying what a listener or reader might believe (e.g., "not what you think")
Concessions	Acknowledging weaknesses in one's own position or the strengths in the position of an opponent (e.g., although, even if, it must be acknowledged)
Resistance	Opposition or struggle between competing ideas, events, forces, or groups (e.g., "veto," "counterargument," "military operations against")
Interactions	**Linguistic interactions**
Curiosity	Involving the audience in a common line of thinking (e.g., what then shall we make of?)
Question	Use of questions
Future question	Use of questions that start with the epistemic modal "will" to indicate the question pertains to a future state
Formal query	Use of survey-type queries ("if so, when," or "do you know")
Attention grab	Summoning another's attention (e.g., let us, I advise you, I urge)
Your attention	Summoning the attention of a second person "you" (e.g., "look, you")
You reference	Use of words referencing a second person "you" (you see it's good)
Request	Use of words that make requests (e.g., I request)

Table A.1—Continued

Name	Definition
Follow up	Referencing a previous interaction (e.g., in response to your, per your last message)
Feedback	Use of words indicating generic feedback to another (e.g., "okay")
Positive feedback	Words indicating positive feedback (e.g., that's very good, very nice)
Negative feedback	Use of words indicating negative feedback (e.g., that's awful, that's crummy)
Prior knowledge	Indicating that ideas under discussion are already public and familiar (e.g., "as you know")
Elaboration	Adding details or explication to talk
Generalization	Indicating generalizations to members of a class (e.g., all, every)
Example	Indicating an example (e.g., "for example")
Exceptions	Exception to general states (e.g., "an exception," "the only one to")
Comparison	Indicating conceptual similarity and difference, such as "more" or "fewer"
Resemblances	Use of words indicating perceptual similarity (e.g., resembles, looks like)
Specifiers	Indicating more specific or restricted information is to come (e.g., in particular, more specifically)
Definition	Indicating definitions (e.g., is defined as, the meaning of the term)
Numbers	Use of words indicating numbers
Reporting	Reporting states, events, changes, and causal sequences
Reporting states	Using verbs "is," "are," and "be" to report constant states of information, along with other reporting verbs (e.g., is carried by, is housed in)
Reporting events	Reporting event information, usually with verbs (e.g., established, instituted, influenced)
Recurring events	Use of words reporting event recurrence over time (e.g., again, recurred)
Generic events	Reporting events that repeat over time through processes of biology, culture, and convention (e.g., sleeping, playing, working, relaxing)
Sequence	Sequential processes unfolding over time (e.g., first, second)

Table A.1—Continued

Name	Definition
Mature process	Mature sequential processes, now in its late or advanced stages of development (e.g., "so thoroughly," "well into")
Causality	Causes of sequences unfolding over time (e.g., "the aftereffects," "because of," "by means of")
Consequence	Consequences in sequences unfolding over time (e.g., "resulting in," "significant effects")
Transformation	E.g., "broke off, "came true," "metamorphize"
Substitution	E.g., "in exchange for," "in place of"
Updates	Reporting an update (e.g., "have now," "announced that")
Precedent setting	Use of words reporting historical "firsts"
Directions	**Directions and guidance**
Imperatives	Imperative verbs (usually beginning a sentence (e.g., "need to respond by" ". Stop" ". Take your")
Procedures	Procedures to perform (e.g., "go back to step" "use only")
Body movement	Physical directions to the body (e.g., clasp, grab, twist, lift up)
Confirmed experience	Confirmation of a just-taken instructional step (e.g., "as you see," "now you will")
Error recovery	How to recover from error (e.g., "should you get lost," "if that doesn't work")
Insistence	Insistence, either on action (e.g., you need to come) or on reasoning (e.g., you need to consider); hallmarks of insistence language are the modals "must," "should," "need," and "ought"
Prohibition	E.g., "ought not," "should never"
Narrative	**Storytelling**
Narrative verbs	Use of past -ed verbs indicating the action of a story (e.g., came, saw, conquered)
Asides	Side comments or return from one (e.g., "by the way," "anyway")
Characters	**Characters in the social and physical world**
Person pronoun	Pronouns (e.g., he, she) indicating persistent topical reference to people, especially in narrative
Neutral attribution	She/he/they attributions without positive or negative assessment (e.g., "he works," "she testified," "they vanished")
Personal roles	Referencing a person's formal occupational and identity roles (e.g., "butcher," "African American," "veteran")
Dialog cues	E.g., "', he added" "piped up"
Oral cues	"you guys" "ROFL"

Graphs from Subsample Analyses

Newspapers

This section presents the detailed linguistic characteristic graphs for the three single outlet analyses discussed in Chapter Three (the *New York Times*, *Washington Post*, and *St. Louis Post-Dispatch*).

In Figures B.1–B.3, the bars represent the size of differences between the pre-2000 and post-2000 periods (the bars reflect *Cohen's D*, a standardized measure of effect size) for the linguistic elements listed. The negative columns identify characteristics that are more common in the post-2000 period; the positive columns identify characteristics that are more common in the pre-2000 period.

Figure B.1
***New York Times*, Pre- and Post-2000 Comparison**

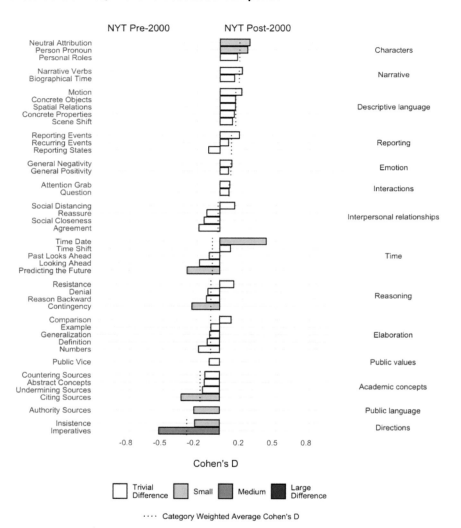

Figure B.1—Continued

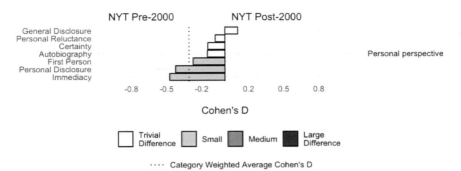

NOTE: For our analysis of the *New York Times* sample, we found that the pre-2000 period appeared to have a higher incidence of personal perspective than the post-2000 period. This was an unexpected result, so we wanted to dig deeper. We found that this result was driven largely by one linguistic characteristic in the pre-2000 period—immediacy or the references to "right now." This characteristic, although a measure of personal perspective, is different from others within this category that are more subjective in nature and that characterize our sample of online journalism and prime-time cable programming more heavily. Finally, we note that the effect sizes across the board for this analysis are small, as is the case for all our newspaper analyses.

Figure B.2
Washington Post, Pre- and Post-2000 Comparison

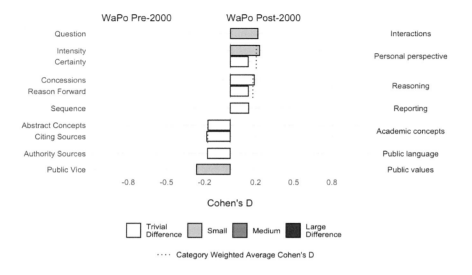

Figure B.3
St. Louis Post-Dispatch, **Pre- and Post-2000 Comparison**

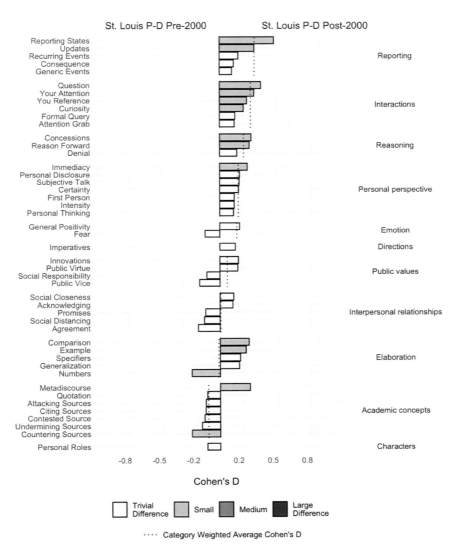

Figure B.3—Continued

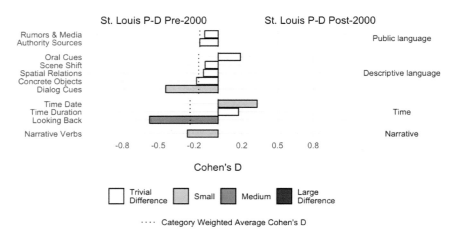

The following is a full list of linguistic characteristics that failed to reach statistical significance for the full-sample newspaper analysis presented in Chapter Three.

Anger
Apology
Aside
Authoritative citation
Autobiography
Cause
Communicator role
Confidence
Confirmed thought
Confirm experience
Confront
Consequence
Deny disclaim
Direct reasoning
Disclosure
Error recovery
Example
Exceptions
Fear
Feedback
Followup

Future question
Generalization
Generic events
In media
Inclusive
Language reference
Mature process
Move body
Negative attribution
Negative feedback
Open query
Person property
Positive feedback
Positive attribution
Precedent defending
Precedent setting
Private thinking
Procedures
Prohibitive
Quotation
Reason forward
Received point of view (POV)

Reinforce
Reluctance
Request
Resemblances
Responsibility
Sad
Self-promise
Self-reluctance
Sense object
Sequence
Specifiers
Speculative citation
Subjective perception
Subjective time
Substitution
Support
Transformation
Uncertainty
Updates

The following is a full list of linguistic characteristics that failed to reach statistical significance for the reduced-sample newspaper analysis presented in Chapter Three.

Anger
Apology
Aside
Authoritative citation
Cause
Communicator role
Comparison
Concessive
Confirmed thought
Confirm experience
Confront
Curiosity
Direct reasoning
Disclosure
Error recovery
Exceptions
Fear
Feedback
Followup
Future in past
Future question
Generic events
In media

Inclusive
Innovations
Intensity
Language reference
Mature process
Metadiscourse
Move body
Negative attribution
Negative feedback
Open query
Oral cues
Person property
Positive feedback
Positive attribution
Precedent defending
Precedent setting
Private thinking
Procedures
Prohibitive
Promise
Quotation
Reason forward
Received POV

Recurring events
Reinforce
Reluctance
Reporting states
Request
Resemblances
Responsibility
Sad
Self-promise
Self-reluctance
Sequence
Speculative citation
Standards positive
Subjective percept
Subjective time
Substitution
Support
Time duration
Transformation
Uncertainty
Updates

Broadcast Television and Cable Programming

Here, we provide a full list of linguistic characteristics that failed to reach statistical significance for the pre-and post-2000 broadcast news analysis presented in Chapter Four.

Anger

Aside

Attack citation

Cause

Citations

Communicator role

Comparison

Confidence

Confirmed thought

Confront

Consequence

Curiosity

Definition

Direct reasoning

Error recovery

Fear

Feedback

Followup

Future in past

Future question

Generalization

In media

Innovations

Insist

Language reference

Mature process

Metadiscourse

Movebody

Narrative verbs

Negative citation

Negative attribution

Negative relation

Negativity

Negative feedback

Person property

Positive feedback

Positive attribution

Precedent setting

Prior knowledge

Procedures

Prohibitive

Promise

Reassure

Received POV

Recurring events

Reluctance

Reporting events

Reporting states

Request

Resemblances

Responsibility

Self-promise

Self-disclosure

Self-reluctance

Sense object

Speculative citation

Standards positive

Subjective percept

Subjective time

Substitution

Support

Time duration

Time shift

Transformation

Uncertainty

Here, we provide a full list of linguistic characteristics that failed to reach statistical significance for the analysis comparing broadcast news and cable prime-time programming presented in Chapter Four.

Attack citation	Language reference	Quotation
Confirm experience	Move body	Reassure
Confront	Negative citation	Reluctance
Consequence	Negative attribution	Repair citation
Definition	Negative feedback	Speculative citation
Disclosure	Positive attribution	Negative standards
Error recovery	Positivity	Time date
Feedback	Precedent defending	
Future in past	Prohibitive	
In media	Project ahead	
Inclusive	Project back	

Online Journalism

Figure B.4 compares the results of the two analyses described in Chapter Five (online versus newspaper journalism) in a visual graphic. The red dots indicate the results of the full analysis; the blue dots show the results of the analysis of the reduced sample. The key observation is the closeness of the results (small distances separating the two results). In most cases, these differences are trivial. This suggests that our results are at least somewhat robust to changes made to the sample.

Figure B.4
Online Versus Newspaper Journalism Analysis Comparison

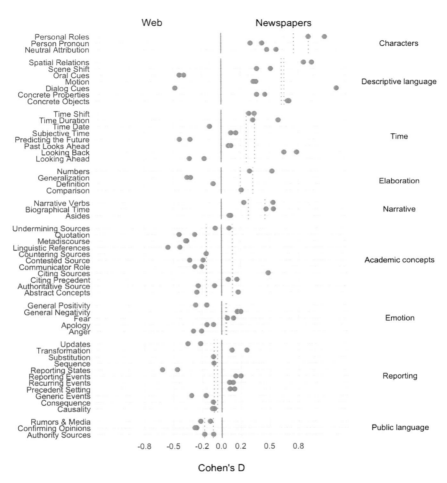

Red dots: online versus newspapers (full sample); blue dots: online versus newspapers (reduced sample)

Figure B.4—Continued

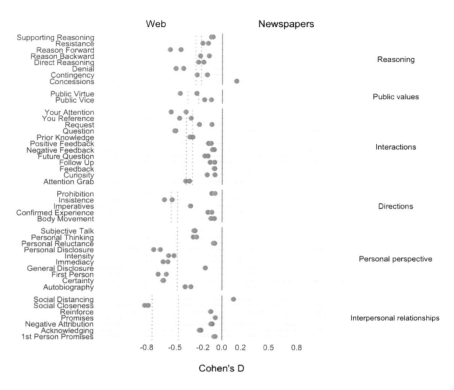

Red dots: online versus newspapers (full sample); blue dots: online versus newspapers (reduced sample)

This is a full list of linguistic characteristics that failed to reach statistical significance for full-sample online-versus-newspaper journalism comparisons presented in Chapter Five.

Accept agree	Mature process	Resemblances
Attack citation	Negative relation	Responsibility
Citations	Open query	Sad
Confront	Positive attribution	Sequence
Consequence	Procedures	Specifiers
Error recovery	Promise	Speculative citation
Example	Reassure	Substitution
Exceptions	Received POV	Time date
Innovations	Reluctance	Uncertainty

This is a full list of linguistic characteristics that failed to reach statistical significance for reduced-sample online-versus-newspaper journalism comparisons presented in Chapter Five.

Accept agree	Exceptions	Reluctance
Attack citation	Innovations	Repair citation
Comparison	Mature process	Resemblances
Concessive	Open query	Responsibility
Confront	Positive attribution	Sad
Disclosure	Procedures	Specifiers
Error recovery	Reassure	Speculative citation
Example	Received POV	Uncertainty

ANOVA Results

This appendix contains the ANOVA results from our RAND-Lex analyses, organized by chapter. Each table provides the linguistic characteristic and category, the Cohen's distance (measure of effect size), and the p-value for the ANOVA comparison. We consider the result statistically significant when the p-value is less than 0.05 (indicated by a 1 in the ANOVA significant column in Table C.1).

Newspaper Comparisons (Chapter Three and Appendix B)

Table C.1
Full Newspaper Sample, Pre- and Post-2000

Language Characteristic	Language Category	Cohen's Distance	ANOVA Significant	P-Value
AbstractConcepts	Academic concepts	−0.12432	1	0.00000085
Attack_Citation	Academic concepts	0.00000	0	0.02208617
Authoritative_Citation	Academic concepts	0.00000	0	0.08919639
Citations	Academic concepts	−0.11670	1	0.00000401
CommunicatorRole	Academic concepts	0.00000	0	0.21842025
Contested_Citation	Academic concepts	−0.06823	1	0.00777222
LangRef	Academic concepts	0.00000	0	0.39817778
Metadiscourse	Academic concepts	0.08495	1	0.00089197
Neg_Citation	Academic concepts	−0.11534	1	0.00000522
Precedent_Defending	Academic concepts	0.00000	0	0.16767554
Quotation	Academic concepts	0.00000	0	0.03276399
Repair_Citation	Academic concepts	−0.11646	1	0.00000420
Speculative_Citation	Academic concepts	0.00000	0	0.18756665
Neutral_Attribution	Characters	0.21672	1	0.00000000
PersonPronoun	Characters	0.14251	1	0.00000001
PersonProperty	Characters	0.00000	0	0.20769977
DialogCues	Descriptive language	−0.11634	1	0.00000430
Motions	Descriptive language	0.12745	1	0.00000044
OralCues	Descriptive language	0.00000	0	0.01602863
SceneShift	Descriptive language	0.00000	0	0.16289161
SenseObject	Descriptive language	0.00000	0	0.38034868
SenseProperty	Descriptive language	0.08031	1	0.00170501
SpaceRelation	Descriptive language	0.00000	0	0.16421632
ConfirmExperience	Directions	0.00000	0	0.39849313

Table C.1—Continued

Language Characteristic	Language Category	Cohen's Distance	ANOVA Significant	P-Value
ErrorRecovery	Directions	0.00000	0	0.39892816
Imperative	Directions	−0.25775	1	0.00000000
Insist	Directions	−0.10002	1	0.00008468
MoveBody	Directions	0.00000	0	0.13632013
Procedures	Directions	0.00000	0	0.31909260
Prohibitive	Directions	0.00000	0	0.12746881
Comparison	Elaboration	0.10628	1	0.00002846
Definition	Elaboration	−0.07350	1	0.00413040
Example	Elaboration	0.00000	0	0.20322898
Exceptions	Elaboration	0.00000	0	0.36285423
Generalization	Elaboration	0.00000	0	0.17578508
Numbers	Elaboration	−0.21097	1	0.00000000
Resemblances	Elaboration	0.00000	0	0.10807721
Specifiers	Elaboration	0.00000	0	0.24790206
Anger	Emotion	0.00000	0	0.36939592
Apology	Emotion	0.00000	0	0.29344041
Fear	Emotion	0.00000	0	0.04983769
Negativity	Emotion	0.00000	0	0.08511972
Positivity	Emotion	0.10076	1	0.00007462
Reluctance	Emotion	0.00000	0	0.39892816
Sad	Emotion	0.00000	0	0.06880148
Attention_Grabber	Interactions	0.08541	1	0.00083483
Curiosity	Interactions	0.00000	0	0.02988862
Feedback	Interactions	0.00000	0	0.39701816
FollowUp	Interactions	0.00000	0	0.38389058
Future_Question	Interactions	0.00000	0	0.18067809
NegFeedback	Interactions	0.00000	0	0.26759399
OpenQuery	Interactions	0.00000	0	0.12674330
PosFeedback	Interactions	0.00000	0	0.34641941
PriorKnowledge	Interactions	0.00000	0	0.19645924
Question	Interactions	0.17383	1	0.00000000

Table C.1—Continued

Language Characteristic	Language Category	Cohen's Distance	ANOVA Significant	P-Value
Request	Interactions	0.00000	0	0.17693106
You_Attention	Interactions	0.14077	1	0.00000002
You_Reference	Interactions	0.14810	1	0.00000000
Accept_Agree	Interpersonal relationships	−0.16393	1	0.00000000
Acknowledge	Interpersonal relationships	0.09005	1	0.00041986
Confront	Interpersonal relationships	0.00000	0	0.39390481
Inclusive	Interpersonal relationships	0.00000	0	0.39169066
Negative_Attribution	Interpersonal relationships	0.00000	0	0.09830098
Negative_Relation	Interpersonal relationships	0.00000	0	0.22413222
Positive_Attribution	Interpersonal relationships	0.00000	0	0.13972285
Promise	Interpersonal relationships	0.00000	0	0.04776769
Reassure	Interpersonal relationships	−0.08753	1	0.00061206
Reinforce	Interpersonal relationships	0.00000	0	0.18515079
Self_Promise	Interpersonal relationships	0.00000	0	0.38469517
Aside	Narrative	0.00000	0	0.05705734
Biographical_Time	Narrative	0.09881	1	0.00010371
Narrative_Verbs	Narrative	0.00000	0	0.01251971
Autobio	Personal perspective	0.00000	0	0.25351917
Confidence	Personal perspective	0.00000	0	0.28590225
Disclosure	Personal perspective	0.00000	0	0.26334921
FirstPer	Personal perspective	0.00000	0	0.09781167
Immediacy	Personal perspective	−0.19444	1	0.00000000
Intensity	Personal perspective	0.06823	1	0.00776800

Table C.1—Continued

Language Characteristic	Language Category	Cohen's Distance	ANOVA Significant	P-Value
PrivateThinking	Personal perspective	0.00000	0	0.09986707
SelfDisclosure	Personal perspective	−0.09899	1	0.00010060
SelfReluctance	Personal perspective	0.00000	0	0.28795664
SubjectivePercept	Personal perspective	0.00000	0	0.24969549
Uncertainty	Personal perspective	0.00000	0	0.36545797
CommonAuthorities	Public language	−0.18980	1	0.00000000
ConfirmedThght	Public language	0.00000	0	0.19205576
In_Media	Public language	0.00000	0	0.03046122
ReceivedPOV	Public language	0.00000	0	0.29809730
Innovations	Public values	0.00000	0	0.02066240
Responsibility	Public values	0.00000	0	0.33372115
StandardsNeg	Public values	−0.14777	1	0.00000000
StandardsPos	Public values	0.08272	1	0.00122312
Concessive	Reasoning	0.00000	0	0.02875316
Contingency	Reasoning	−0.16374	1	0.00000000
DenyDisclaim	Reasoning	0.00000	0	0.34207600
DirectReasoning	Reasoning	0.00000	0	0.32913645
ReasonBackward	Reasoning	−0.09555	1	0.00017709
ReasonForward	Reasoning	0.00000	0	0.14423046
Resistance	Reasoning	0.07457	1	0.00361675
Support	Reasoning	0.00000	0	0.39891850
Cause	Reporting	0.00000	0	0.39479339
Consequence	Reporting	0.00000	0	0.38845280
GenericEvents	Reporting	0.00000	0	0.26236019
MatureProcess	Reporting	0.00000	0	0.10807806
Precedent_Setting	Reporting	0.00000	0	0.34737862
RecurringEvents	Reporting	0.00000	0	0.04594238
ReportingEvents	Reporting	0.08640	1	0.00072327
ReportingStates	Reporting	0.12022	1	0.00000198

Table C.1—Continued

Language Characteristic	Language Category	Cohen's Distance	ANOVA Significant	P-Value
Sequence	Reporting	0.00000	0	0.24312530
Substitution	Reporting	0.00000	0	0.34506068
Transformation	Reporting	0.00000	0	0.34131965
Updates	Reporting	0.08741	1	0.00062321
Future_in_Past	Time	0.00000	0	0.06442278
PredictedFuture	Time	−0.13617	1	0.00000006
ProjectAhead	Time	−0.07443	1	0.00367957
ProjectBack	Time	−0.17738	1	0.00000000
SubjectiveTime	Time	0.00000	0	0.14994159
TimeDate	Time	0.30142	1	0.00000000
TimeDuration	Time	0.07365	1	0.00405773
TimeShift	Time	0.08979	1	0.00043655

Table C.2
National Newspaper Sample, Pre- and Post-2000

Language Characteristic	Language Category	Cohen's Distance	ANOVA Significant	P-Value
AbstractConcepts	Academic concepts	−0.22452	1	0.00000000
Attack_Citation	Academic concepts	−0.05894	1	0.00401792
Authoritative_Citation	Academic concepts	0.00000	0	0.11346517
Citations	Academic concepts	−0.15770	1	0.00000000
CommunicatorRole	Academic concepts	0.00000	0	0.30048265
Contested_Citation	Academic concepts	−0.07380	1	0.00029623
LangRef	Academic concepts	0.00000	0	0.39881859
Metadiscourse	Academic concepts	0.00000	0	0.30918012
Neg_Citation	Academic concepts	−0.10862	1	0.00000007
Precedent_Defending	Academic concepts	0.00000	0	0.36469610
Quotation	Academic concepts	0.00000	0	0.38587509
Repair_Citation	Academic concepts	−0.10994	1	0.00000005
Speculative_Citation	Academic concepts	0.00000	0	0.38958704
Neutral_Attribution	Characters	0.25619	1	0.00000000

Table C.2—Continued

Language Characteristic	Language Category	Cohen's Distance	ANOVA Significant	P-Value
PersonPronoun	Characters	0.21794	1	0.00000000
PersonProperty	Characters	0.00000	0	0.04295905
DialogCues	Descriptive language	0.00000	0	0.35120416
Motions	Descriptive language	0.19568	1	0.00000000
OralCues	Descriptive language	0.00000	0	0.07039804
SceneShift	Descriptive language	0.11796	1	0.00000000
SenseObject	Descriptive language	0.10380	1	0.00000026
SenseProperty	Descriptive language	0.14641	1	0.00000000
SpaceRelation	Descriptive language	0.12611	1	0.00000000
ConfirmExperience	Directions	0.00000	0	0.30697758
ErrorRecovery	Directions	0.00000	0	0.04632573
Imperative	Directions	−0.32528	1	0.00000000
Insist	Directions	−0.12650	1	0.00000000
MoveBody	Directions	0.00000	0	0.08288522
Procedures	Directions	0.00000	0	0.31993733
Prohibitive	Directions	0.00000	0	0.08855585
Comparison	Elaboration	0.00000	0	0.01296637
Definition	Elaboration	−0.07852	1	0.00011432
Example	Elaboration	−0.10622	1	0.00000013
Exceptions	Elaboration	0.00000	0	0.32075776
Generalization	Elaboration	−0.07543	1	0.00021471
Numbers	Elaboration	−0.19972	1	0.00000000
Resemblances	Elaboration	0.00000	0	0.17800955
Specifiers	Elaboration	−0.07150	1	0.00046043
Anger	Emotion	0.00000	0	0.35053960
Apology	Emotion	0.00000	0	0.15068865
Fear	Emotion	0.00000	0	0.14266426
Negativity	Emotion	0.09402	1	0.00000334

Table C.2—Continued

Language Characteristic	Language Category	Cohen's Distance	ANOVA Significant	P-Value
Positivity	Emotion	0.08884	1	0.00001167
Reluctance	Emotion	0.00000	0	0.39893330
Sad	Emotion	0.00000	0	0.20273257
Attention_Grabber	Interactions	0.05995	1	0.00342802
Curiosity	Interactions	0.00000	0	0.38388548
Feedback	Interactions	0.00000	0	0.05705480
FollowUp	Interactions	0.00000	0	0.20125457
Future_Question	Interactions	0.00000	0	0.39470171
NegFeedback	Interactions	0.00000	0	0.10387594
OpenQuery	Interactions	0.00000	0	0.23883101
PosFeedback	Interactions	0.00000	0	0.34804150
PriorKnowledge	Interactions	0.05515	1	0.00711925
Question	Interactions	0.13062	1	0.00000000
Request	Interactions	0.00000	0	0.32941450
You_Attention	Interactions	0.05996	1	0.00342196
You_Reference	Interactions	0.08097	1	0.00006818
Accept_Agree	Interpersonal relationships	−0.16686	1	0.00000000
Acknowledge	Interpersonal relationships	0.06980	1	0.00063301
Confront	Interpersonal relationships	0.00000	0	0.34667345
Inclusive	Interpersonal relationships	0.00000	0	0.01356450
Negative_Attribution	Interpersonal relationships	0.00000	0	0.03267008
Negative_Relation	Interpersonal relationships	0.10032	1	0.00000066
Positive_Attribution	Interpersonal relationships	0.00000	0	0.18427110
Promise	Interpersonal relationships	0.00000	0	0.07537876
Reassure	Interpersonal relationships	−0.10048	1	0.00000063
Reinforce	Interpersonal relationships	0.00000	0	0.30565029

Table C.2—Continued

Language Characteristic	Language Category	Cohen's Distance	ANOVA Significant	P-Value
Self_Promise	Interpersonal relationships	0.00000	0	0.39884414
Aside	Narrative	0.00000	0	0.01711544
Biographical_Time	Narrative	0.13830	1	0.00000000
Narrative_Verbs	Narrative	0.17413	1	0.00000000
Autobio	Personal perspective	−0.05945	1	0.00371033
Confidence	Personal perspective	−0.10472	1	0.00000020
Disclosure	Personal perspective	0.00000	0	0.01299798
FirstPer	Personal perspective	−0.10070	1	0.00000060
Immediacy	Personal perspective	−0.32134	1	0.00000000
Intensity	Personal perspective	0.00000	0	0.23682948
PrivateThinking	Personal perspective	0.00000	0	0.25240972
SelfDisclosure	Personal perspective	−0.18623	1	0.00000000
SelfReluctance	Personal perspective	0.00000	0	0.10310150
SubjectivePercept	Personal perspective	0.00000	0	0.39320642
Uncertainty	Personal perspective	0.00000	0	0.24277821
CommonAuthorities	Public language	−0.18547	1	0.00000000
ConfirmedThght	Public language	0.00000	0	0.06433421
In_Media	Public language	0.00000	0	0.39846425
ReceivedPOV	Public language	0.00000	0	0.30522730
Innovations	Public values	0.00000	0	0.08918008
Responsibility	Public values	0.00000	0	0.23785645
StandardsNeg	Public values	−0.15875	1	0.00000000
StandardsPos	Public values	0.00000	0	0.25977040
Concessive	Reasoning	0.00000	0	0.39192381
Contingency	Reasoning	−0.16957	1	0.00000000
DenyDisclaim	Reasoning	−0.05463	1	0.00767981

Table C.2—Continued

Language Characteristic	Language Category	Cohen's Distance	ANOVA Significant	*P*-Value
DirectReasoning	Reasoning	0.00000	0	0.14334780
ReasonBackward	Reasoning	−0.10962	1	0.00000005
ReasonForward	Reasoning	0.00000	0	0.24279185
Resistance	Reasoning	0.08261	1	0.00004785
Support	Reasoning	0.00000	0	0.32308152
Cause	Reporting	0.00000	0	0.37251842
Consequence	Reporting	−0.05448	1	0.00785128
GenericEvents	Reporting	0.00000	0	0.32809298
MatureProcess	Reporting	0.00000	0	0.16157431
Precedent_Setting	Reporting	0.00000	0	0.38941013
RecurringEvents	Reporting	0.00000	0	0.19051912
ReportingEvents	Reporting	0.10622	1	0.00000013
ReportingStates	Reporting	0.00000	0	0.21722361
Sequence	Reporting	0.00000	0	0.03428320
Substitution	Reporting	0.00000	0	0.05882761
Transformation	Reporting	0.00000	0	0.17797185
Updates	Reporting	0.00000	0	0.07131135
Future_in_Past	Time	0.00000	0	0.01504546
PredictedFuture	Time	−0.20499	1	0.00000000
ProjectAhead	Time	−0.10504	1	0.00000018
ProjectBack	Time	−0.06209	1	0.00242788
SubjectiveTime	Time	0.00000	0	0.36846866
TimeDate	Time	0.35374	1	0.00000000
TimeDuration	Time	0.00000	0	0.20130488
TimeShift	Time	0.07920	1	0.00009923

Table C.3
New York Times, Pre- and Post-2000

Language Characteristic	Language Category	Cohen's Distance	ANOVA Significant	P-Value
AbstractConcepts	Academic concepts	−0.13445	1	0.00000095
Attack_Citation	Academic concepts	0.00000	0	0.05792925
Authoritative_Citation	Academic concepts	0.00000	0	0.04359250
Citations	Academic concepts	−0.34075	1	0.00000000
CommunicatorRole	Academic concepts	0.00000	0	0.30093739
Contested_Citation	Academic concepts	0.00000	0	0.01234073
LangRef	Academic concepts	0.00000	0	0.34957046
Metadiscourse	Academic concepts	0.00000	0	0.37466397
Neg_Citation	Academic concepts	−0.14996	1	0.00000004
Precedent_Defending	Academic concepts	0.00000	0	0.28799194
Quotation	Academic concepts	0.00000	0	0.34346694
Repair_Citation	Academic concepts	−0.12916	1	0.00000259
Speculative_Citation	Academic concepts	0.00000	0	0.37756503
Neutral_Attribution	Characters	0.26374	1	0.00000000
PersonPronoun	Characters	0.24462	1	0.00000000
PersonProperty	Characters	0.15363	1	0.00000002
DialogCues	Descriptive language	0.00000	0	0.08136690
Motions	Descriptive language	0.19200	1	0.00000000
OralCues	Descriptive language	0.00000	0	0.39499643
SceneShift	Descriptive language	0.11003	1	0.00006813
SenseObject	Descriptive language	0.13666	1	0.00000062
SenseProperty	Descriptive language	0.12624	1	0.00000441
SpaceRelation	Descriptive language	0.13644	1	0.00000065
ConfirmExperience	Directions	0.00000	0	0.19572825
ErrorRecovery	Directions	0.00000	0	0.01606641
Imperative	Directions	−0.53887	1	0.00000000
Insist	Directions	−0.21985	1	0.00000000
MoveBody	Directions	0.00000	0	0.35699945
Procedures	Directions	0.00000	0	0.12606061
Prohibitive	Directions	0.00000	0	0.30766092

Table C.3—Continued

Language Characteristic	Language Category	Cohen's Distance	ANOVA Significant	P-Value
Comparison	Elaboration	0.10192	1	0.00023312
Definition	Elaboration	−0.10895	1	0.00008064
Example	Elaboration	−0.07685	1	0.00577456
Exceptions	Elaboration	0.00000	0	0.34021261
Generalization	Elaboration	−0.08832	1	0.00148615
Numbers	Elaboration	−0.18611	1	0.00000000
Resemblances	Elaboration	0.00000	0	0.17159960
Specifiers	Elaboration	0.00000	0	0.17189630
Anger	Emotion	0.00000	0	0.39673132
Apology	Emotion	0.00000	0	0.19907414
Fear	Emotion	0.00000	0	0.06182636
Negativity	Emotion	0.10474	1	0.00015370
Positivity	Emotion	0.07541	1	0.00675677
Reluctance	Emotion	0.00000	0	0.39892584
Sad	Emotion	0.00000	0	0.38634893
Attention_Grabber	Interactions	0.08728	1	0.00169471
Curiosity	Interactions	0.00000	0	0.33690272
Feedback	Interactions	0.00000	0	0.26887972
FollowUp	Interactions	0.00000	0	0.24592793
Future_Question	Interactions	0.00000	0	0.24226053
NegFeedback	Interactions	0.00000	0	0.23565829
OpenQuery	Interactions	0.00000	0	0.22204821
PosFeedback	Interactions	0.00000	0	0.39592384
PriorKnowledge	Interactions	0.00000	0	0.04978944
Question	Interactions	0.07982	1	0.00413810
Request	Interactions	0.00000	0	0.35131813
You_Attention	Interactions	0.00000	0	0.36845500
You_Reference	Interactions	0.00000	0	0.11168417
Accept_Agree	Interpersonal relationships	−0.18548	1	0.00000000
Acknowledge	Interpersonal relationships	0.00000	0	0.01328808

Table C.3—Continued

Language Characteristic	Language Category	Cohen's Distance	ANOVA Significant	P-Value
Confront	Interpersonal relationships	0.00000	0	0.39069193
Inclusive	Interpersonal relationships	−0.13989	1	0.00000033
Negative_Attribution	Interpersonal relationships	0.00000	0	0.34974702
Negative_Relation	Interpersonal relationships	0.13113	1	0.00000179
Positive_Attribution	Interpersonal relationships	0.00000	0	0.11911857
Promise	Interpersonal relationships	0.00000	0	0.04404195
Reassure	Interpersonal relationships	−0.11577	1	0.00002696
Reinforce	Interpersonal relationships	0.00000	0	0.21722507
Self_Promise	Interpersonal relationships	0.00000	0	0.04488728
Aside	Narrative	0.00000	0	0.11568901
Biographical_Time	Narrative	0.12860	1	0.00000286
Narrative_Verbs	Narrative	0.19686	1	0.00000000
Autobio	Personal perspective	−0.14972	1	0.00000004
Confidence	Personal perspective	−0.14607	1	0.00000009
Disclosure	Personal perspective	0.10833	1	0.00008892
FirstPer	Personal perspective	−0.27390	1	0.00000000
Immediacy	Personal perspective	−0.47361	1	0.00000000
Intensity	Personal perspective	0.00000	0	0.20710349
PrivateThinking	Personal perspective	0.00000	0	0.39533655
SelfDisclosure	Personal perspective	−0.42291	1	0.00000000
SelfReluctance	Personal perspective	−0.08278	1	0.00293078
SubjectivePercept	Personal perspective	0.00000	0	0.04170569
Uncertainty	Personal perspective	0.00000	0	0.37233022
CommonAuthorities	Public language	−0.22802	1	0.00000000
ConfirmedThght	Public language	0.00000	0	0.36426480
In_Media	Public language	0.00000	0	0.38873208
ReceivedPOV	Public language	0.00000	0	0.16966840
Innovations	Public values	0.00000	0	0.07929392

Table C.3—Continued

Language Characteristic	Language Category	Cohen's Distance	ANOVA Significant	P-Value
Responsibility	Public values	0.00000	0	0.34183819
StandardsNeg	Public values	−0.09126	1	0.00101902
StandardsPos	Public values	0.00000	0	0.38606514
Concessive	Reasoning	0.00000	0	0.18559666
Contingency	Reasoning	−0.24665	1	0.00000000
DenyDisclaim	Reasoning	−0.10361	1	0.00018192
DirectReasoning	Reasoning	0.00000	0	0.18818148
ReasonBackward	Reasoning	−0.11749	1	0.00002024
ReasonForward	Reasoning	0.00000	0	0.01659522
Resistance	Reasoning	0.12527	1	0.00000524
Support	Reasoning	0.00000	0	0.39892191
Cause	Reporting	0.00000	0	0.39807767
Consequence	Reporting	0.00000	0	0.05465498
GenericEvents	Reporting	0.00000	0	0.18609663
MatureProcess	Reporting	0.00000	0	0.11017299
Precedent_Setting	Reporting	0.00000	0	0.03684179
RecurringEvents	Reporting	0.07574	1	0.00652413
ReportingEvents	Reporting	0.17118	1	0.00000000
ReportingStates	Reporting	−0.10092	1	0.00026969
Sequence	Reporting	0.00000	0	0.37964682
Substitution	Reporting	0.00000	0	0.13740477
Transformation	Reporting	0.00000	0	0.07361475
Updates	Reporting	0.00000	0	0.03370906
Future_in_Past	Time	−0.09335	1	0.00077232
PredictedFuture	Time	−0.29013	1	0.00000000
ProjectAhead	Time	−0.17985	1	0.00000000
ProjectBack	Time	0.00000	0	0.03148811
SubjectiveTime	Time	0.00000	0	0.29227083
TimeDate	Time	0.41322	1	0.00000000
TimeDuration	Time	0.00000	0	0.01774230
TimeShift	Time	0.09504	1	0.00061509

Table C.4
Washington Post, Pre- and Post-2000

Language Characteristic	Language Category	Cohen's Distance	ANOVA Significant	*P*-Value
AbstractConcepts	Academic concepts	−0.17400	1	0.00187107
Attack_Citation	Academic concepts	0.00000	0	0.33484351
Authoritative_Citation	Academic concepts	0.00000	0	0.05668583
Citations	Academic concepts	−0.18352	1	0.00102547
CommunicatorRole	Academic concepts	0.00000	0	0.12008136
Contested_Citation	Academic concepts	0.00000	0	0.07963708
LangRef	Academic concepts	0.00000	0	0.39547102
Metadiscourse	Academic concepts	0.00000	0	0.09668531
Neg_Citation	Academic concepts	0.00000	0	0.10913974
Precedent_Defending	Academic concepts	0.00000	0	0.31221683
Quotation	Academic concepts	0.00000	0	0.12671837
Repair_Citation	Academic concepts	0.00000	0	0.20800010
Speculative_Citation	Academic concepts	0.00000	0	0.03760188
Neutral_Attribution	Characters	0.00000	0	0.07281155
PersonPronoun	Characters	0.00000	0	0.09435883
PersonProperty	Characters	0.00000	0	0.37912802
DialogCues	Descriptive language	0.00000	0	0.07237639
Motions	Descriptive language	0.00000	0	0.10027106
OralCues	Descriptive language	0.00000	0	0.24517577
SceneShift	Descriptive language	0.00000	0	0.04656109
SenseObject	Descriptive language	0.00000	0	0.02761348
SenseProperty	Descriptive language	0.00000	0	0.03144303
SpaceRelation	Descriptive language	0.00000	0	0.29131142
ConfirmExperience	Directions	0.00000	0	0.12007786
ErrorRecovery	Directions	0.00000	0	0.09321672
Imperative	Directions	0.00000	0	0.24823583
Insist	Directions	0.00000	0	0.29212061

Table C.4—Continued

Language Characteristic	Language Category	Cohen's Distance	ANOVA Significant	P-Value
MoveBody	Directions	0.00000	0	0.29857100
Procedures	Directions	0.00000	0	0.31260431
Prohibitive	Directions	0.00000	0	0.28079391
Comparison	Elaboration	0.00000	0	0.22704229
Definition	Elaboration	0.00000	0	0.13602627
Example	Elaboration	0.00000	0	0.35024318
Exceptions	Elaboration	0.00000	0	0.18288872
Generalization	Elaboration	0.00000	0	0.39554264
Numbers	Elaboration	0.00000	0	0.25933663
Resemblances	Elaboration	0.00000	0	0.36217323
Specifiers	Elaboration	0.00000	0	0.38077184
Anger	Emotion	0.00000	0	0.03388154
Apology	Emotion	0.00000	0	0.14328468
Fear	Emotion	0.00000	0	0.19733321
Negativity	Emotion	0.00000	0	0.04477771
Positivity	Emotion	0.00000	0	0.01607602
Reluctance	Emotion	0.00000	0	0.39890174
Sad	Emotion	0.00000	0	0.24296642
Attention_Grabber	Interactions	0.00000	0	0.37131893
Curiosity	Interactions	0.00000	0	0.19631723
Feedback	Interactions	0.00000	0	0.39544517
FollowUp	Interactions	0.00000	0	0.22590063
Future_Question	Interactions	0.00000	0	0.37862186
NegFeedback	Interactions	0.00000	0	0.39154094
OpenQuery	Interactions	0.00000	0	0.26185483
PosFeedback	Interactions	0.00000	0	0.35921806
PriorKnowledge	Interactions	0.00000	0	0.31535764
Question	Interactions	0.21554	1	0.00010752
Request	Interactions	0.00000	0	0.39875289
You_Attention	Interactions	0.00000	0	0.34415331
You_Reference	Interactions	0.00000	0	0.02905102

Table C.4—Continued

Language Characteristic	Language Category	Cohen's Distance	ANOVA Significant	P-Value
Accept_Agree	Interpersonal relationships	0.00000	0	0.24083471
Acknowledge	Interpersonal relationships	0.00000	0	0.14294786
Confront	Interpersonal relationships	0.00000	0	0.33943187
Inclusive	Interpersonal relationships	0.00000	0	0.37019314
Negative_Attribution	Interpersonal relationships	0.00000	0	0.39378532
Negative_Relation	Interpersonal relationships	0.00000	0	0.26743025
Positive_Attribution	Interpersonal relationships	0.00000	0	0.04306237
Promise	Interpersonal relationships	0.00000	0	0.35589236
Reassure	Interpersonal relationships	0.00000	0	0.29357789
Reinforce	Interpersonal relationships	0.00000	0	0.25824600
Self_Promise	Interpersonal relationships	0.00000	0	0.07054726
Aside	Narrative	0.00000	0	0.20283975
Biographical_Time	Narrative	0.00000	0	0.39016719
Narrative_Verbs	Narrative	0.00000	0	0.23587330
Autobio	Personal perspective	0.00000	0	0.24927482
Confidence	Personal perspective	0.14038	1	0.01212713
Disclosure	Personal perspective	0.00000	0	0.38137488
FirstPer	Personal perspective	0.00000	0	0.39428480
Immediacy	Personal perspective	0.00000	0	0.04105847
Intensity	Personal perspective	0.22976	1	0.00003523
PrivateThinking	Personal perspective	0.00000	0	0.18020746
SelfDisclosure	Personal perspective	0.00000	0	0.37540678
SelfReluctance	Personal perspective	0.00000	0	0.27689170

Table C.4—Continued

Language Characteristic	Language Category	Cohen's Distance	ANOVA Significant	P-Value
SubjectivePercept	Personal perspective	0.00000	0	0.22646717
Uncertainty	Personal perspective	0.00000	0	0.32096893
CommonAuthorities	Public language	−0.17729	1	0.00152522
ConfirmedThght	Public language	0.00000	0	0.23893553
In_Media	Public language	0.00000	0	0.37189764
ReceivedPOV	Public language	0.00000	0	0.39863466
Innovations	Public values	0.00000	0	0.27549541
Responsibility	Public values	0.00000	0	0.31621399
StandardsNeg	Public values	−0.26467	1	0.00000169
StandardsPos	Public values	0.00000	0	0.27193852
Concessive	Reasoning	0.18804	1	0.00076188
Contingency	Reasoning	0.00000	0	0.34552158
DenyDisclaim	Reasoning	0.00000	0	0.18805584
DirectReasoning	Reasoning	0.00000	0	0.09181554
ReasonBackward	Reasoning	0.00000	0	0.20790327
ReasonForward	Reasoning	0.14179	1	0.01130220
Resistance	Reasoning	0.00000	0	0.02666839
Support	Reasoning	0.00000	0	0.06964943
Cause	Reporting	0.00000	0	0.38819895
Consequence	Reporting	0.00000	0	0.39227167
GenericEvents	Reporting	0.00000	0	0.15889380
MatureProcess	Reporting	0.00000	0	0.31242551
Precedent_Setting	Reporting	0.00000	0	0.38716516
RecurringEvents	Reporting	0.00000	0	0.08793664
ReportingEvents	Reporting	0.00000	0	0.39885552
ReportingStates	Reporting	0.00000	0	0.07865830
Sequence	Reporting	0.14427	1	0.00997049
Substitution	Reporting	0.00000	0	0.32085771
Transformation	Reporting	0.00000	0	0.22218988
Updates	Reporting	0.00000	0	0.37497956

Table C.4—Continued

Language Characteristic	Language Category	Cohen's Distance	ANOVA Significant	P-Value
Future_in_Past	Time	0.00000	0	0.39186170
PredictedFuture	Time	0.00000	0	0.39838842
ProjectAhead	Time	0.00000	0	0.27799992
ProjectBack	Time	0.00000	0	0.30714420
SubjectiveTime	Time	0.00000	0	0.24244556
TimeDate	Time	0.00000	0	0.09945407
TimeDuration	Time	0.00000	0	0.39594561
TimeShift	Time	0.00000	0	0.21246304

Table C.5
St. Louis Post-Dispatch, Pre- and Post-2000

Language Characteristic	Language Category	Cohen's Distance	ANOVA Significant	P-Value
AbstractConcepts	Academic concepts	0.00000	0	0.01261854
Attack_Citation	Academic concepts	−0.12527	1	0.00129222
Authoritative_Citation	Academic concepts	0.00000	0	0.38711054
Citations	Academic concepts	−0.12684	1	0.00111787
CommunicatorRole	Academic concepts	0.00000	0	0.34224135
Contested_Citation	Academic concepts	−0.13692	1	0.00042436
LangRef	Academic concepts	0.00000	0	0.33833576
Metadiscourse	Academic concepts	0.26197	1	0.00000000
Neg_Citation	Academic concepts	−0.16001	1	0.00003498
Precedent_Defending	Academic concepts	0.00000	0	0.22502040
Quotation	Academic concepts	−0.11253	1	0.00389980
Repair_Citation	Academic concepts	−0.25054	1	0.00000000
Speculative_Citation	Academic concepts	0.00000	0	0.39890893

Table C.5—Continued

Language Characteristic	Language Category	Cohen's Distance	ANOVA Significant	P-Value
Neutral_Attribution	Characters	0.00000	0	0.22269327
PersonPronoun	Characters	0.00000	0	0.01219434
PersonProperty	Characters	−0.11313	1	0.00371299
DialogCues	Descriptive language	−0.43974	1	0.00000000
Motions	Descriptive language	0.00000	0	0.25992406
OralCues	Descriptive language	0.18604	1	0.00000133
SceneShift	Descriptive language	−0.10856	1	0.00537479
SenseObject	Descriptive language	−0.18029	1	0.00000285
SenseProperty	Descriptive language	0.00000	0	0.08048997
SpaceRelation	Descriptive language	−0.12259	1	0.00164549
ConfirmExperience	Directions	0.00000	0	0.35594053
ErrorRecovery	Directions	0.00000	0	0.08981010
Imperative	Directions	0.13623	1	0.00045451
Insist	Directions	0.00000	0	0.34577328
MoveBody	Directions	0.00000	0	0.07822317
Procedures	Directions	0.00000	0	0.18443718
Prohibitive	Directions	0.00000	0	0.39820732
Comparison	Elaboration	0.25315	1	0.00000000
Definition	Elaboration	0.00000	0	0.34285291
Example	Elaboration	0.22633	1	0.00000000
Exceptions	Elaboration	0.00000	0	0.30188806
Generalization	Elaboration	0.16791	1	0.00001363
Numbers	Elaboration	−0.25002	1	0.00000000
Resemblances	Elaboration	0.00000	0	0.07333006
Specifiers	Elaboration	0.17720	1	0.00000425
Anger	Emotion	0.00000	0	0.15671099
Apology	Emotion	0.00000	0	0.04698399
Fear	Emotion	−0.12951	1	0.00087093

Table C.5—Continued

Language Characteristic	Language Category	Cohen's Distance	ANOVA Significant	P-Value
Negativity	Emotion	0.00000	0	0.04775762
Positivity	Emotion	0.17339	1	0.00000691
Reluctance	Emotion	0.00000	0	0.39890893
Sad	Emotion	0.00000	0	0.05439378
Attention_Grabber	Interactions	0.12909	1	0.00090629
Curiosity	Interactions	0.20916	1	0.00000005
Feedback	Interactions	0.00000	0	0.03254744
FollowUp	Interactions	0.00000	0	0.34484801
Future_Question	Interactions	0.00000	0	0.01067865
NegFeedback	Interactions	0.00000	0	0.37765995
OpenQuery	Interactions	0.13515	1	0.00050550
PosFeedback	Interactions	0.00000	0	0.22824010
PriorKnowledge	Interactions	0.00000	0	0.39780503
Question	Interactions	0.36177	1	0.00000000
Request	Interactions	0.00000	0	0.39627085
You_Attention	Interactions	0.30184	1	0.00000000
You_Reference	Interactions	0.23868	1	0.00000000
Accept_Agree	Interpersonal relationships	−0.19135	1	0.00000064
Acknowledge	Interpersonal relationships	0.11188	1	0.00411453
Confront	Interpersonal relationships	0.00000	0	0.13340532
Inclusive	Interpersonal relationships	0.11965	1	0.00213317
Negative_Attribution	Interpersonal relationships	0.00000	0	0.28987217
Negative_Relation	Interpersonal relationships	−0.13780	1	0.00038839
Positive_Attribution	Interpersonal relationships	0.00000	0	0.28031950
Promise	Interpersonal relationships	−0.12624	1	0.00118143
Reassure	Interpersonal relationships	0.00000	0	0.13471862
Reinforce	Interpersonal relationships	0.00000	0	0.02847334

Table C.5—Continued

Language Characteristic	Language Category	Cohen's Distance	ANOVA Significant	P-Value
Self_Promise	Interpersonal relationships	0.00000	0	0.38050405
Aside	Narrative	0.00000	0	0.16578414
Biographical_Time	Narrative	0.00000	0	0.11376675
Narrative_Verbs	Narrative	−0.25810	1	0.00000000
Autobio	Personal perspective	0.00000	0	0.29225874
Confidence	Personal perspective	0.16487	1	0.00001970
Disclosure	Personal perspective	0.00000	0	0.02067596
FirstPer	Personal perspective	0.12770	1	0.00103264
Immediacy	Personal perspective	0.24204	1	0.00000000
Intensity	Personal perspective	0.12713	1	0.00108865
PrivateThinking	Personal perspective	0.12058	1	0.00196748
SelfDisclosure	Personal perspective	0.17430	1	0.00000616
SelfReluctance	Personal perspective	0.00000	0	0.17646008
SubjectivePercept	Personal perspective	0.17054	1	0.00000987
Uncertainty	Personal perspective	0.00000	0	0.06893928
CommonAuthorities	Public language	−0.15362	1	0.00007248
ConfirmedThght	Public language	0.00000	0	0.15791818
In_Media	Public language	−0.11286	1	0.00379643
ReceivedPOV	Public language	0.00000	0	0.12906423
Innovations	Public values	0.16221	1	0.00002701
Responsibility	Public values	−0.11486	1	0.00321579
StandardsNeg	Public values	−0.17875	1	0.00000348
StandardsPos	Public values	0.15692	1	0.00004992
Concessive	Reasoning	0.27597	1	0.00000000
Contingency	Reasoning	0.00000	0	0.01773065
DenyDisclaim	Reasoning	0.15109	1	0.00009595

Table C.5—Continued

Language Characteristic	Language Category	Cohen's Distance	ANOVA Significant	P-Value
DirectReasoning	Reasoning	0.00000	0	0.29053475
ReasonBackward	Reasoning	0.00000	0	0.02900260
ReasonForward	Reasoning	0.25960	1	0.00000000
Resistance	Reasoning	0.00000	0	0.34714170
Support	Reasoning	0.00000	0	0.07628866
Cause	Reporting	0.00000	0	0.34708277
Consequence	Reporting	0.12371	1	0.00148860
GenericEvents	Reporting	0.10800	1	0.00561769
MatureProcess	Reporting	0.00000	0	0.07106801
Precedent_Setting	Reporting	0.00000	0	0.38935504
RecurringEvents	Reporting	0.16362	1	0.00002287
ReportingEvents	Reporting	0.00000	0	0.39759639
ReportingStates	Reporting	0.47759	1	0.00000000
Sequence	Reporting	0.00000	0	0.35377882
Substitution	Reporting	0.00000	0	0.39704728
Transformation	Reporting	0.00000	0	0.03804867
Updates	Reporting	0.30442	1	0.00000000
Future_in_Past	Time	0.00000	0	0.21139571
PredictedFuture	Time	0.00000	0	0.27617919
ProjectAhead	Time	0.00000	0	0.19985822
ProjectBack	Time	−0.57472	1	0.00000000
SubjectiveTime	Time	0.00000	0	0.25849070
TimeDate	Time	0.32660	1	0.00000000
TimeDuration	Time	0.17108	1	0.00000923
TimeShift	Time	0.00000	0	0.10132469

Television Comparisons (Chapter Four)

Table C.6
Broadcast Television, Pre- and Post-2000

Language Characteristic	Language Category	Cohen's Distance	ANOVA Significant	P-Value
AbstractConcepts	Academic concepts	−0.42503	1	0.00000000
Attack_Citation	Academic concepts	0.00000	0	0.07389672
Authoritative_Citation	Academic concepts	−0.13631	1	0.00652666
Citations	Academic concepts	0.00000	0	0.25929373
CommunicatorRole	Academic concepts	0.00000	0	0.02558412
Contested_Citation	Academic concepts	−0.14319	1	0.00426833
LangRef	Academic concepts	0.00000	0	0.01926944
Metadiscourse	Academic concepts	0.00000	0	0.18449669
Neg_Citation	Academic concepts	0.00000	0	0.03183516
Precedent_Defending	Academic concepts	−0.13886	1	0.00558744
Quotation	Academic concepts	−2.93101	1	0.00000000
Repair_Citation	Academic concepts	−0.24230	1	0.00000096
Speculative_Citation	Academic concepts	0.00000	0	0.39888754
Neutral_Attribution	Characters	0.13383	1	0.00756589
PersonPronoun	Characters	0.25910	1	0.00000015
PersonProperty	Characters	0.00000	0	0.31053349
DialogCues	Descriptive language	−1.21925	1	0.00000000
Motions	Descriptive language	0.45117	1	0.00000000
OralCues	Descriptive language	0.42581	1	0.00000000
SceneShift	Descriptive language	0.14773	1	0.00318782
SenseObject	Descriptive language	0.00000	0	0.39780756
SenseProperty	Descriptive language	0.43343	1	0.00000000
SpaceRelation	Descriptive language	0.41076	1	0.00000000
ConfirmExperience	Directions	0.21340	1	0.00001726
ErrorRecovery	Directions	0.00000	0	0.39068506

Table C.6—Continued

Language Characteristic	Language Category	Cohen's Distance	ANOVA Significant	P-Value
Imperative	Directions	0.16056	1	0.00133237
Insist	Directions	0.00000	0	0.16311930
MoveBody	Directions	0.00000	0	0.26913973
Procedures	Directions	0.00000	0	0.28206251
Prohibitive	Directions	0.00000	0	0.22439511
Comparison	Elaboration	0.00000	0	0.38567919
Definition	Elaboration	0.00000	0	0.07604411
Example	Elaboration	−0.23363	1	0.00000238
Exceptions	Elaboration	−0.15496	1	0.00196685
Generalization	Elaboration	0.00000	0	0.12346006
Numbers	Elaboration	0.30324	1	0.00000000
Resemblances	Elaboration	0.00000	0	0.33458854
Specifiers	Elaboration	−0.22274	1	0.00000706
Anger	Emotion	0.00000	0	0.39887720
Apology	Emotion	0.14153	1	0.00473685
Fear	Emotion	0.00000	0	0.13927090
Negativity	Emotion	0.00000	0	0.02250175
Positivity	Emotion	0.27511	1	0.00000002
Reluctance	Emotion	0.00000	0	0.39888754
Sad	Emotion	0.16919	1	0.00071159
Attention_Grabber	Interactions	0.45428	1	0.00000000
Curiosity	Interactions	0.00000	0	0.02491696
Feedback	Interactions	0.00000	0	0.39265503
FollowUp	Interactions	0.00000	0	0.12213386
Future_Question	Interactions	0.00000	0	0.23741216
NegFeedback	Interactions	0.00000	0	0.39655924
OpenQuery	Interactions	0.16767	1	0.00079633
PosFeedback	Interactions	0.00000	0	0.02057768
PriorKnowledge	Interactions	0.00000	0	0.27821340
Question	Interactions	0.55248	1	0.00000000
Request	Interactions	0.00000	0	0.26117447

Table C.6—Continued

Language Characteristic	Language Category	Cohen's Distance	ANOVA Significant	P-Value
You_Attention	Interactions	0.62558	1	0.00000000
You_Reference	Interactions	0.50593	1	0.00000000
Accept_Agree	Interpersonal relationships	−0.16410	1	0.00103426
Acknowledge	Interpersonal relationships	0.93058	1	0.00000000
Confront	Interpersonal relationships	0.00000	0	0.39498564
Inclusive	Interpersonal relationships	0.56915	1	0.00000000
Negative_Attribution	Interpersonal relationships	0.00000	0	0.35258789
Negative_Relation	Interpersonal relationships	0.00000	0	0.03902520
Positive_Attribution	Interpersonal relationships	0.00000	0	0.35579904
Promise	Interpersonal relationships	0.00000	0	0.37781374
Reassure	Interpersonal relationships	0.00000	0	0.37492045
Reinforce	Interpersonal relationships	0.25990	1	0.00000014
Self_Promise	Interpersonal relationships	0.00000	0	0.31556710
Aside	Narrative	0.00000	0	0.38769176
Biographical_Time	Narrative	0.34255	1	0.00000000
Narrative_Verbs	Narrative	0.00000	0	0.35892327
Autobio	Personal perspective	0.27136	1	0.00000004
Confidence	Personal perspective	0.00000	0	0.17763739
Disclosure	Personal perspective	0.18202	1	0.00026373
FirstPer	Personal perspective	0.45267	1	0.00000000
Immediacy	Personal perspective	0.36304	1	0.00000000
Intensity	Personal perspective	0.34501	1	0.00000000
PrivateThinking	Personal perspective	−0.14161	1	0.00471382

Table C.6—Continued

Language Characteristic	Language Category	Cohen's Distance	ANOVA Significant	P-Value
SelfDisclosure	Personal perspective	0.00000	0	0.01246361
SelfReluctance	Personal perspective	0.00000	0	0.23546394
SubjectivePercept	Personal perspective	0.00000	0	0.36271951
Uncertainty	Personal perspective	0.00000	0	0.11258269
CommonAuthorities	Public language	−0.45764	1	0.00000000
ConfirmedThght	Public language	0.00000	0	0.33057384
In_Media	Public language	0.00000	0	0.39221195
ReceivedPOV	Public language	0.00000	0	0.24525207
Innovations	Public values	0.00000	0	0.13276823
Responsibility	Public values	0.00000	0	0.18474419
StandardsNeg	Public values	−0.36829	1	0.00000000
StandardsPos	Public values	0.00000	0	0.06273714
Concessive	Reasoning	−0.16809	1	0.00077234
Contingency	Reasoning	−0.38701	1	0.00000000
DenyDisclaim	Reasoning	−0.41475	1	0.00000000
DirectReasoning	Reasoning	0.00000	0	0.21982752
ReasonBackward	Reasoning	−0.28853	1	0.00000000
ReasonForward	Reasoning	0.67665	1	0.00000000
Resistance	Reasoning	−0.43350	1	0.00000000
Support	Reasoning	0.00000	0	0.01857514
Cause	Reporting	0.00000	0	0.39622310
Consequence	Reporting	0.00000	0	0.26277619
GenericEvents	Reporting	−0.14504	1	0.00379251
MatureProcess	Reporting	0.00000	0	0.19567819
Precedent_Setting	Reporting	0.00000	0	0.39873798
RecurringEvents	Reporting	0.00000	0	0.06603131
ReportingEvents	Reporting	0.00000	0	0.08365216
ReportingStates	Reporting	0.00000	0	0.28142576
Sequence	Reporting	0.25622	1	0.00000021

Table C.6—Continued

Language Characteristic	Language Category	Cohen's Distance	ANOVA Significant	P-Value
Substitution	Reporting	0.00000	0	0.10992622
Transformation	Reporting	0.00000	0	0.05530516
Updates	Reporting	0.19280	1	0.00010842
Future_in_Past	Time	0.00000	0	0.26698471
PredictedFuture	Time	−0.39521	1	0.00000000
ProjectAhead	Time	0.13913	1	0.00549469
ProjectBack	Time	−0.67354	1	0.00000000
SubjectiveTime	Time	0.00000	0	0.39888374
TimeDate	Time	−1.56661	1	0.00000000
TimeDuration	Time	0.00000	0	0.06961445
TimeShift	Time	0.00000	0	0.38375475

Table C.7
Broadcast Television Versus Cable Journalism, 2000–2017

Language Characteristic	Language Category	Cohen's Distance	ANOVA Significant	P-Value
AbstractConcepts	Academic concepts	−0.46404	1	0.00000000
Attack_Citation	Academic concepts	0.00000	0	0.02732527
Authoritative_Citation	Academic concepts	0.14921	1	0.00000858
Citations	Academic concepts	0.28938	1	0.00000000
CommunicatorRole	Academic concepts	0.11329	1	0.00080944
Contested_Citation	Academic concepts	−0.17767	1	0.00000010
LangRef	Academic concepts	0.00000	0	0.02235600
Metadiscourse	Academic concepts	0.54661	1	0.00000000
Neg_Citation	Academic concepts	0.00000	0	0.31419101
Precedent_Defending	Academic concepts	0.00000	0	0.16783734
Quotation	Academic concepts	0.00000	0	0.17306586
Repair_Citation	Academic concepts	0.00000	0	0.39889088
Speculative_Citation	Academic concepts	0.00000	0	0.33109279
Neutral_Attribution	Characters	0.34908	1	0.00000000

Table C.7—Continued

Language Characteristic	Language Category	Cohen's Distance	ANOVA Significant	P-Value
PersonPronoun	Characters	0.21950	1	0.00000000
PersonProperty	Characters	−0.38268	1	0.00000000
DialogCues	Descriptive language	−2.92338	1	0.00000000
Motions	Descriptive language	−0.66943	1	0.00000000
OralCues	Descriptive language	0.97718	1	0.00000000
SceneShift	Descriptive language	−0.21658	1	0.00000000
SenseObject	Descriptive language	−1.07030	1	0.00000000
SenseProperty	Descriptive language	−0.67913	1	0.00000000
SpaceRelation	Descriptive language	−0.77653	1	0.00000000
ConfirmExperience	Directions	0.00000	0	0.20640405
ErrorRecovery	Directions	0.00000	0	0.21160997
Imperative	Directions	0.23219	1	0.00000000
Insist	Directions	0.66786	1	0.00000000
MoveBody	Directions	0.00000	0	0.31284954
Procedures	Directions	0.13444	1	0.00006467
Prohibitive	Directions	0.00000	0	0.11993944
Comparison	Elaboration	−0.71572	1	0.00000000
Definition	Elaboration	0.00000	0	0.26020635
Example	Elaboration	0.25668	1	0.00000000
Exceptions	Elaboration	−0.08479	1	0.01236660
Generalization	Elaboration	0.23636	1	0.00000000
Numbers	Elaboration	−1.33541	1	0.00000000
Resemblances	Elaboration	0.19287	1	0.00000001
Specifiers	Elaboration	0.51812	1	0.00000000
Anger	Emotion	0.12309	1	0.00026471
Apology	Emotion	0.00000	0	0.32506898
Fear	Emotion	−0.30587	1	0.00000000
Negativity	Emotion	−0.69759	1	0.00000000
Positivity	Emotion	0.00000	0	0.23970845
Reluctance	Emotion	0.00000	0	0.39892862
Sad	Emotion	−0.18530	1	0.00000003

Table C.7—Continued

Language Characteristic	Language Category	Cohen's Distance	ANOVA Significant	P-Value
Attention_Grabber	Interactions	0.72938	1	0.00000000
Curiosity	Interactions	0.43843	1	0.00000000
Feedback	Interactions	0.00000	0	0.34343055
FollowUp	Interactions	0.14766	1	0.00001070
Future_Question	Interactions	0.23342	1	0.00000000
NegFeedback	Interactions	0.00000	0	0.39385551
OpenQuery	Interactions	0.38831	1	0.00000000
PosFeedback	Interactions	0.46672	1	0.00000000
PriorKnowledge	Interactions	0.38331	1	0.00000000
Question	Interactions	0.98315	1	0.00000000
Request	Interactions	0.33430	1	0.00000000
You_Attention	Interactions	1.24101	1	0.00000000
You_Reference	Interactions	0.86962	1	0.00000000
Accept_Agree	Interpersonal relationships	0.16919	1	0.00000040
Acknowledge	Interpersonal relationships	0.18714	1	0.00000002
Confront	Interpersonal relationships	0.00000	0	0.39538364
Inclusive	Interpersonal relationships	0.00000	0	0.35395318
Negative_Attribution	Interpersonal relationships	0.00000	0	0.26284278
Negative_Relation	Interpersonal relationships	−0.29718	1	0.00000000
Positive_Attribution	Interpersonal relationships	0.00000	0	0.19103637
Promise	Interpersonal relationships	−0.19940	1	0.00000000
Reassure	Interpersonal relationships	0.00000	0	0.04727412
Reinforce	Interpersonal relationships	0.24343	1	0.00000000
Self_Promise	Interpersonal relationships	0.12482	1	0.00021534
Aside	Narrative	0.37516	1	0.00000000
Biographical_Time	Narrative	−0.22739	1	0.00000000

Table C.7—Continued

Language Characteristic	Language Category	Cohen's Distance	ANOVA Significant	P-Value
Narrative_Verbs	Narrative	−0.38219	1	0.00000000
Autobio	Personal perspective	0.43974	1	0.00000000
Confidence	Personal perspective	0.86635	1	0.00000000
Disclosure	Personal perspective	0.00000	0	0.15343053
FirstPer	Personal perspective	0.85481	1	0.00000000
Immediacy	Personal perspective	−0.32877	1	0.00000000
Intensity	Personal perspective	0.46585	1	0.00000000
PrivateThinking	Personal perspective	0.59098	1	0.00000000
SelfDisclosure	Personal perspective	1.16026	1	0.00000000
SelfReluctance	Personal perspective	0.24748	1	0.00000000
SubjectivePercept	Personal perspective	0.33198	1	0.00000000
Uncertainty	Personal perspective	0.91948	1	0.00000000
CommonAuthorities	Public language	−0.19563	1	0.00000000
ConfirmedThght	Public language	0.48163	1	0.00000000
In_Media	Public language	0.00000	0	0.02393248
ReceivedPOV	Public language	−0.09116	1	0.00719821
Innovations	Public values	−0.41472	1	0.00000000
Responsibility	Public values	0.12555	1	0.00019712
StandardsNeg	Public values	0.00000	0	0.25240847
StandardsPos	Public values	−0.12458	1	0.00022158
Concessive	Reasoning	0.18274	1	0.00000004
Contingency	Reasoning	0.45662	1	0.00000000
DenyDisclaim	Reasoning	0.85025	1	0.00000000
DirectReasoning	Reasoning	0.17241	1	0.00000024
ReasonBackward	Reasoning	0.79027	1	0.00000000
ReasonForward	Reasoning	0.78000	1	0.00000000
Resistance	Reasoning	−0.08951	1	0.00830713
Support	Reasoning	0.10631	1	0.00169780
Cause	Reporting	−0.12653	1	0.00017487
Consequence	Reporting	0.00000	0	0.23537580
GenericEvents	Reporting	0.08731	1	0.01002686

Table C.7—Continued

Language Characteristic	Language Category	Cohen's Distance	ANOVA Significant	P-Value
MatureProcess	Reporting	−0.09230	1	0.00650383
Precedent_Setting	Reporting	−0.52156	1	0.00000000
RecurringEvents	Reporting	−0.28606	1	0.00000000
ReportingEvents	Reporting	0.21924	1	0.00000000
ReportingStates	Reporting	0.50560	1	0.00000000
Sequence	Reporting	−0.16792	1	0.00000049
Substitution	Reporting	−0.11795	1	0.00048137
Transformation	Reporting	−0.44747	1	0.00000000
Updates	Reporting	−0.38794	1	0.00000000
Future_in_Past	Time	0.00000	0	0.36174479
PredictedFuture	Time	−0.18469	1	0.00000003
ProjectAhead	Time	0.00000	0	0.09871549
ProjectBack	Time	0.00000	0	0.01841693
SubjectiveTime	Time	−0.32391	1	0.00000000
TimeDate	Time	0.00000	0	0.16814863
TimeDuration	Time	−0.95035	1	0.00000000
TimeShift	Time	0.11443	1	0.00071462

Online Versus Newspaper Comparisons (Chapter Five)

Table C.8
Online Versus Print Journalism, 2012–2017

Language Characteristic	Language Category	Cohen's Distance	ANOVA Significant	*P*-Value
AbstractConcepts	Academic concepts	−0.17120	1	0.00000000
Attack_Citation	Academic concepts	0.00000	0	0.22483783
Authoritative_Citation	Academic concepts	0.24275	1	0.00000000
Citations	Academic concepts	0.00000	0	0.16523736
CommunicatorRole	Academic concepts	0.27837	1	0.00000000
Contested_Citation	Academic concepts	0.33197	1	0.00000000
LangRef	Academic concepts	0.55695	1	0.00000000
Metadiscourse	Academic concepts	0.36217	1	0.00000000

Table C.8—Continued

Language Characteristic	Language Category	Cohen's Distance	ANOVA Significant	P-Value
Neg_Citation	Academic concepts	0.06368	1	0.00463075
Precedent_Defending	Academic concepts	−0.06910	1	0.00210030
Quotation	Academic concepts	0.44080	1	0.00000000
Repair_Citation	Academic concepts	0.15856	1	0.00000000
Speculative_Citation	Academic concepts	0.00000	0	0.30699094
Neutral_Attribution	Characters	−0.47554	1	0.00000000
PersonPronoun	Characters	−0.30316	1	0.00000000
PersonProperty	Characters	−0.90634	1	0.00000000
DialogCues	Descriptive language	0.47995	1	0.00000000
Motions	Descriptive language	−0.35958	1	0.00000000
OralCues	Descriptive language	0.43520	1	0.00000000
SceneShift	Descriptive language	−0.36905	1	0.00000000
SenseObject	Descriptive language	−0.70411	1	0.00000000
SenseProperty	Descriptive language	−0.36802	1	0.00000000
SpaceRelation	Descriptive language	−0.94006	1	0.00000000
ConfirmExperience	Directions	0.15120	1	0.00000000
ErrorRecovery	Directions	0.00000	0	0.12709121
Imperative	Directions	0.33746	1	0.00000000
Insist	Directions	0.53495	1	0.00000000
MoveBody	Directions	0.08268	1	0.00021847
Procedures	Directions	0.00000	0	0.39862666
Prohibitive	Directions	0.11001	1	0.00000068
Comparison	Elaboration	−0.20675	1	0.00000000
Definition	Elaboration	0.08438	1	0.00016017
Example	Elaboration	0.00000	0	0.20295074
Exceptions	Elaboration	0.00000	0	0.17065894
Generalization	Elaboration	0.32051	1	0.00000000
Numbers	Elaboration	−0.52691	1	0.00000000

Table C.8—Continued

Language Characteristic	Language Category	Cohen's Distance	ANOVA Significant	P-Value
Resemblances	Elaboration	0.00000	0	0.05777400
Specifiers	Elaboration	0.00000	0	0.01406398
Anger	Emotion	0.29429	1	0.00000000
Apology	Emotion	0.15317	1	0.00000000
Fear	Emotion	−0.05755	1	0.01047469
Negativity	Emotion	−0.16121	1	0.00000000
Positivity	Emotion	0.15448	1	0.00000000
Reluctance	Emotion	0.00000	0	0.39893482
Sad	Emotion	0.00000	0	0.31562451
Attention_Grabber	Interactions	0.35072	1	0.00000000
Curiosity	Interactions	0.16014	1	0.00000000
Feedback	Interactions	0.08012	1	0.00034561
FollowUp	Interactions	0.12869	1	0.00000001
Future_Question	Interactions	0.15194	1	0.00000000
NegFeedback	Interactions	0.08614	1	0.00011507
OpenQuery	Interactions	0.00000	0	0.39460133
PosFeedback	Interactions	0.14699	1	0.00000000
PriorKnowledge	Interactions	0.31496	1	0.00000000
Question	Interactions	0.50594	1	0.00000000
Request	Interactions	0.24498	1	0.00000000
You_Attention	Interactions	0.54715	1	0.00000000
You_Reference	Interactions	0.45783	1	0.00000000
Accept_Agree	Interpersonal relationships	0.00000	0	0.03825561
Acknowledge	Interpersonal relationships	0.22465	1	0.00000000
Confront	Interpersonal relationships	0.00000	0	0.11742596
Inclusive	Interpersonal relationships	0.78692	1	0.00000000
Negative_Attribution	Interpersonal relationships	0.10369	1	0.00000298
Negative_Relation	Interpersonal relationships	0.00000	0	0.01457067

Table C.8—Continued

Language Characteristic	Language Category	Cohen's Distance	ANOVA Significant	P-Value
Positive_Attribution	Interpersonal relationships	0.00000	0	0.25494116
Promise	Interpersonal relationships	0.00000	0	0.15502218
Reassure	Interpersonal relationships	0.00000	0	0.04148330
Reinforce	Interpersonal relationships	0.12101	1	0.00000004
Self_Promise	Interpersonal relationships	0.08254	1	0.00022410
Aside	Narrative	−0.09537	1	0.00001831
Biographical_Time	Narrative	−0.46495	1	0.00000000
Narrative_Verbs	Narrative	−0.23303	1	0.00000000
Autobio	Personal perspective	0.39466	1	0.00000000
Confidence	Personal perspective	0.63020	1	0.00000000
Disclosure	Personal perspective	0.17798	1	0.00000000
FirstPer	Personal perspective	0.68191	1	0.00000000
Immediacy	Personal perspective	0.62951	1	0.00000000
Intensity	Personal perspective	0.51380	1	0.00000000
PrivateThinking	Personal perspective	0.30891	1	0.00000000
SelfDisclosure	Personal perspective	0.72952	1	0.00000000
SelfReluctance	Personal perspective	0.09033	1	0.00005114
SubjectivePercept	Personal perspective	0.28894	1	0.00000000
Uncertainty	Personal perspective	0.00000	0	0.04189125
CommonAuthorities	Public language	0.08789	1	0.00008246
ConfirmedThght	Public language	0.26345	1	0.00000000
In_Media	Public language	0.22176	1	0.00000000
ReceivedPOV	Public language	0.00000	0	0.10564145
Innovations	Public values	0.00000	0	0.01658716

Table C.8—Continued

Language Characteristic	Language Category	Cohen's Distance	ANOVA Significant	P-Value
Responsibility	Public values	0.00000	0	0.01482011
StandardsNeg	Public values	0.18994	1	0.00000000
StandardsPos	Public values	0.27333	1	0.00000000
Concessive	Reasoning	−0.15131	1	0.00000000
Contingency	Reasoning	0.16071	1	0.00000000
DenyDisclaim	Reasoning	0.49659	1	0.00000000
DirectReasoning	Reasoning	0.19968	1	0.00000000
ReasonBackward	Reasoning	0.23423	1	0.00000000
ReasonForward	Reasoning	0.44401	1	0.00000000
Resistance	Reasoning	0.20952	1	0.00000000
Support	Reasoning	0.11568	1	0.00000017
Cause	Reporting	0.07689	1	0.00060332
Consequence	Reporting	0.00000	0	0.09918803
GenericEvents	Reporting	0.16442	1	0.00000000
MatureProcess	Reporting	0.00000	0	0.20106035
Precedent_Setting	Reporting	−0.13070	1	0.00000000
RecurringEvents	Reporting	−0.11610	1	0.00000015
ReportingEvents	Reporting	−0.14332	1	0.00000000
ReportingStates	Reporting	0.61782	1	0.00000000
Sequence	Reporting	0.00000	0	0.06445858
Substitution	Reporting	0.00000	0	0.01272121
Transformation	Reporting	−0.25903	1	0.00000000
Updates	Reporting	0.35322	1	0.00000000
Future_in_Past	Time	−0.07463	1	0.00087800
PredictedFuture	Time	0.32517	1	0.00000000
ProjectAhead	Time	0.17672	1	0.00000000
ProjectBack	Time	−0.65157	1	0.00000000
SubjectiveTime	Time	−0.15077	1	0.00000000
TimeDate	Time	0.00000	0	0.39560252
TimeDuration	Time	−0.59207	1	0.00000000
TimeShift	Time	−0.34262	1	0.00000000

Table C.9
Online Versus Print Journalism (reduced sample), 2012–2017

Language Characteristic	Language Category	Cohen's Distance	ANOVA Significant	P-Value
AbstractConcepts	Academic concepts	−0.25828	1	0.00000000
Attack_Citation	Academic concepts	0.00000	0	0.10671000
Authoritative_Citation	Academic concepts	−0.07467	1	0.00647815
Citations	Academic concepts	0.48378	1	0.00000000
CommunicatorRole	Academic concepts	−0.20696	1	0.00000000
Contested_Citation	Academic concepts	−0.19238	1	0.00000000
LangRef	Academic concepts	−0.43402	1	0.00000000
Metadiscourse	Academic concepts	−0.37300	1	0.00000000
Neg_Citation	Academic concepts	0.07830	1	0.00429675
Precedent_Defending	Academic concepts	0.15716	1	0.00000000
Quotation	Academic concepts	−0.27869	1	0.00000000
Repair_Citation	Academic concepts	0.00000	0	0.20955700
Speculative_Citation	Academic concepts	0.00000	0	0.31760899
Neutral_Attribution	Characters	0.57341	1	0.00000000
PersonPronoun	Characters	0.42283	1	0.00000000
PersonProperty	Characters	1.07519	1	0.00000000
DialogCues	Descriptive language	1.19834	1	0.00000000
Motions	Descriptive language	0.33296	1	0.00000000
OralCues	Descriptive language	−0.38925	1	0.00000000
SceneShift	Descriptive language	0.51401	1	0.00000000
SenseObject	Descriptive language	0.69046	1	0.00000000
SenseProperty	Descriptive language	0.45381	1	0.00000000
SpaceRelation	Descriptive language	0.85668	1	0.00000000
ConfirmExperience	Directions	−0.11068	1	0.00004700
ErrorRecovery	Directions	0.00000	0	0.10157599
Imperative	Directions	−0.34072	1	0.00000000
Insist	Directions	−0.61680	1	0.00000000

Table C.9—Continued

Language Characteristic	Language Category	Cohen's Distance	ANOVA Significant	P-Value
MoveBody	Directions	−0.12017	1	0.00000934
Procedures	Directions	0.00000	0	0.08795572
Prohibitive	Directions	−0.07772	1	0.00459355
Comparison	Elaboration	0.00000	0	0.15039537
Definition	Elaboration	−0.08629	1	0.00162779
Example	Elaboration	0.00000	0	0.12725034
Exceptions	Elaboration	0.00000	0	0.09810041
Generalization	Elaboration	−0.35835	1	0.00000000
Numbers	Elaboration	0.29214	1	0.00000000
Resemblances	Elaboration	0.00000	0	0.22889774
Specifiers	Elaboration	0.00000	0	0.36325444
Anger	Emotion	−0.21111	1	0.00000000
Apology	Emotion	−0.08737	1	0.00141685
Fear	Emotion	0.12059	1	0.00000868
Negativity	Emotion	0.19523	1	0.00000000
Positivity	Emotion	−0.27167	1	0.00000000
Reluctance	Emotion	0.00000	0	0.39892777
Sad	Emotion	0.00000	0	0.28070768
Attention_Grabber	Interactions	−0.39017	1	0.00000000
Curiosity	Interactions	−0.07846	1	0.00422168
Feedback	Interactions	−0.08487	1	0.00194874
FollowUp	Interactions	−0.08144	1	0.00296677
Future_Question	Interactions	−0.18633	1	0.00000000
NegFeedback	Interactions	−0.10434	1	0.00012850
OpenQuery	Interactions	0.00000	0	0.21725648
PosFeedback	Interactions	−0.11968	1	0.00001019
PriorKnowledge	Interactions	−0.34713	1	0.00000000
Question	Interactions	−0.49757	1	0.00000000
Request	Interactions	−0.11268	1	0.00003380
You_Attention	Interactions	−0.38937	1	0.00000000
You_Reference	Interactions	−0.33326	1	0.00000000

Table C.9—Continued

Language Characteristic	Language Category	Cohen's Distance	ANOVA Significant	P-Value
Accept_Agree	Interpersonal relationships	0.00000	0	0.15606162
Acknowledge	Interpersonal relationships	−0.24021	1	0.00000000
Confront	Interpersonal relationships	0.00000	0	0.17813430
Inclusive	Interpersonal relationships	−0.82534	1	0.00000000
Negative_Attribution	Interpersonal relationships	−0.11765	1	0.00001454
Negative_Relation	Interpersonal relationships	0.12180	1	0.00000698
Positive_Attribution	Interpersonal relationships	0.00000	0	0.06148336
Promise	Interpersonal relationships	−0.07185	1	0.00879319
Reassure	Interpersonal relationships	0.00000	0	0.08769689
Reinforce	Interpersonal relationships	−0.11985	1	0.00000990
Self_Promise	Interpersonal relationships	−0.07263	1	0.00809102
Aside	Narrative	0.07952	1	0.00372748
Biographical_Time	Narrative	0.54079	1	0.00000000
Narrative_Verbs	Narrative	0.53674	1	0.00000000
Autobio	Personal perspective	−0.33373	1	0.00000000
Confidence	Personal perspective	−0.62454	1	0.00000000
Disclosure	Personal perspective	0.00000	0	0.05694358
FirstPer	Personal perspective	−0.59563	1	0.00000000
Immediacy	Personal perspective	−0.57902	1	0.00000000
Intensity	Personal perspective	−0.57172	1	0.00000000
PrivateThinking	Personal perspective	−0.27275	1	0.00000000
SelfDisclosure	Personal perspective	−0.66018	1	0.00000000
SelfReluctance	Personal perspective	−0.07882	1	0.00404769

Table C.9—Continued

Language Characteristic	Language Category	Cohen's Distance	ANOVA Significant	P-Value
SubjectivePercept	Personal perspective	−0.30148	1	0.00000000
Uncertainty	Personal perspective	0.00000	0	0.07405878
CommonAuthorities	Public language	−0.18171	1	0.00000000
ConfirmedThght	Public language	−0.28224	1	0.00000000
In_Media	Public language	−0.12243	1	0.00000624
ReceivedPOV	Public language	0.00000	0	0.17963482
Innovations	Public values	0.00000	0	0.23988623
Responsibility	Public values	0.00000	0	0.39360987
StandardsNeg	Public values	−0.11902	1	0.00001145
StandardsPos	Public values	−0.45155	1	0.00000000
Concessive	Reasoning	0.00000	0	0.08388646
Contingency	Reasoning	−0.26966	1	0.00000000
DenyDisclaim	Reasoning	−0.41579	1	0.00000000
DirectReasoning	Reasoning	−0.25611	1	0.00000000
ReasonBackward	Reasoning	−0.14221	1	0.00000013
ReasonForward	Reasoning	−0.55779	1	0.00000000
Resistance	Reasoning	−0.15119	1	0.00000002
Support	Reasoning	−0.10057	1	0.00022720
Cause	Reporting	−0.09970	1	0.00025840
Consequence	Reporting	−0.09165	1	0.00080502
GenericEvents	Reporting	−0.31685	1	0.00000000
MatureProcess	Reporting	0.00000	0	0.31381187
Precedent_Setting	Reporting	0.08308	1	0.00243119
RecurringEvents	Reporting	0.07671	1	0.00515469
ReportingEvents	Reporting	0.19592	1	0.00000000
ReportingStates	Reporting	−0.46479	1	0.00000000
Sequence	Reporting	−0.08343	1	0.00233091
Substitution	Reporting	−0.08809	1	0.00129212
Transformation	Reporting	0.10389	1	0.00013773
Updates	Reporting	−0.22161	1	0.00000000

Table C.9—Continued

Language Characteristic	Language Category	Cohen's Distance	ANOVA Significant	P-Value
Future_in_Past	Time	0.09852	1	0.00030722
PredictedFuture	Time	−0.43620	1	0.00000000
ProjectAhead	Time	−0.33304	1	0.00000000
ProjectBack	Time	0.78299	1	0.00000000
SubjectiveTime	Time	0.09838	1	0.00031319
TimeDate	Time	−0.12134	1	0.00000759
TimeDuration	Time	0.32706	1	0.00000000
TimeShift	Time	0.28578	1	0.00000000

References

Aelieve, "List of the 20 Most Popular Liberal News Sites," webpage, 2018a. As of March 15, 2019:
https://aelieve.com/insights/website-rankings/category/news-media/most-popular-liberal-websites/

———, "List of the 20 Most Popular News Sites," webpage, 2018b. As of March 15, 2019:
https://aelieve.com/insights/website-rankings/category/news-media/most-popular-news-sites/

Airoldi, Edoardo M., Annelise G. Anderson, Stephen E. Fienberg, and Kiron K. Skinner, "Who Wrote Ronald Reagan's Radio Addresses?" *Bayesian Analysis*, Vol. 1, No. 2, 2006, pp. 289–320.

———, "Whose Ideas? Whose Words? Authorship of the Ronald Reagan Radio Addresses," *Political Science & Politics*, Vol. 40, No. 3, 2007, pp. 501–506.

Al-Malki, Amal, David Kaufer, Suguru Ishizaki, and Kira Dreher, *Arab Women in Arab News: Old Stereotypes and New Media*, New York: Bloomsbury Academic, 2012.

Bai, Xue, "Predicting Consumer Sentiments from Online Text," *Decision Support Systems*, Vol. 50, No. 4, 2011, pp. 732–742.

Battaglio, Stephen, "'ABC World News Tonight' Takes Ratings Crown but Broadcast News Audiences Continue to Shrink," *Los Angeles Times*, September 26, 2017.

Baum, Matthew A., and Yuri M. Zhukov, "Media Ownership and News Coverage of International Conflict," *Political Communication*, Vol. 36, No. 1, 2019, pp. 36–63.

Bialik, Kristen, and Katerina Eva Matsa, "Key Trends in Social and Digital News Media," Pew Research Center, October 4, 2017. As of March 15, 2019:
http://www.pewresearch.org/fact-tank/2017/10/04/key-trends-in-social-and-digital-news-media/

Bittermann, Jim, *World News Tonight with Peter Jennings*, ABC News, June 2, 1993.

Bock, Jessica, "The Grades Are In: New System Makes Finer Distinctions Among Districts; 'Perfect' Districts Lose Ranking with New Standards Education," *St. Louis Post-Dispatch*, August 23, 2013.

Bodine-Baron, Elizabeth, Todd C. Helmus, Madeline Magnuson, and Zev Winkelman, *Examining ISIS Support and Opposition Networks on Twitter*, Santa Monica, Calif.: RAND Corporation, RR-1328-OSD, 2016. As of March 15, 2019: https://www.rand.org/pubs/research_reports/RR1328.html

Borah, Porismita, "Conceptual Issues in Framing Theory: A Systematic Examination of a Decade's Literature," *Journal of Communication*, Vol. 61, No. 2, 2011, pp. 246–263.

Brittain, Amy, "The Crimes Against Them Were Terrifying, but the Judicial System Made It Worse," *Washington Post*, December 4, 2016.

Broomhall, Susan, ed., *Early Modern Emotions: An Introduction*, Abingdon, England: Routledge, 2016.

Carlson, Tucker, "Report: Trump Revealed Classified Info to Russians; Dems and Media Melt Down over Trump Presidency; Leftists Protest Gay Conservative Journalist; Cyberattack Impacted 200,000 Computers in 150 Countries," *Tucker Carlson Tonight*, Fox News Network, May 15, 2017

Carnegie Mellon University Department of English, "DocuScope: Computer-Aided Rhetorical Analysis," website, undated. As of March 15, 2019: https://www.cmu.edu/dietrich/english/research/docuscope.html

Carter, Richard F., and Bradley S. Greenberg, "Newspaper or Television: Which Do You Believe?" *Journalism Quarterly*, Vol. 42, Winter 1965, pp. 29–34.

Coe, Kevin, David Tewksbury, Bradley J. Bond, Kristin L. Drogos, Robert W. Porter, Ashley Yahn, and Yuanyuan Zhang, "Hostile News: Partisan Use and Perceptions of Cable News Programming," *Journal of Communication*, Vol. 58, No. 2, 2008, pp. 201–219.

Cohen, Jacob, *Statistical Power Analysis for the Behavioral Sciences*, Abingdon, England: Routledge Academic, 1988.

Cole, Jeffrey, Michael Suman, Phoebe Schramm, and Liuning Zhou, *Surveying the Digital Future 2017*, Los Angeles, Calif.: Center for the Digital Future at USC Annenberg, 2017. As of March 15, 2019: http://www.digitalcenter.org/wp-content/uploads/2013/10/2017-Digital-Future-Report.pdf

Collins, Jeffrey A., *Variations in Written English*, Washington, D.C.: U.S. Department of the Air Force, CI02-1189, 2003.

Cushman, John, Jr., "The Budget Struggle: Wealthy or Not, Taxpayers Will Find Plenty of Surprises," *New York Times*, August 8, 1993.

Darby, Brandon, "How I Spent My Time in Hugo Chávez's Venezuela," Breitbart News, March 6, 2013. As of March 15, 2019:
https://www.breitbart.com/national-security/2013/03/06/
my-experiences-in-hugo-chavez-venezuela-and-how-i-ended-up-there/

Degaetano, Stefania, and Elke Teich, "The Lexico-Grammar of Stance: An Exploratory Analysis of Scientific Texts," *Bochumer Linguistische Arbeitsberichte*, Vol. 3, 2011, pp. 57–66.

de Moraes, Lisa, "FNC Tops Cable in 2017, MSNBC Grows Most, CNN Bags Best Total Day on Record," *Deadline*, December 19, 2017. As of March 15, 2019:
https://deadline.com/2017/12/
fox-news-highest-ratings-cable-news-2017-1202230070/

Diehl, Trevor, Matthew Barnidge, and Homero Gil de Zúñiga, "Multi-Platform News Use and Political Participation Across Age Groups: Toward a Valid Metric of Platform Diversity and Its Effects," *Journalism & Mass Communication Quarterly*, September 20, 2018. As of March 18, 2019:
https://journals.sagepub.com/doi/pdf/10.1177/1077699018783960

Dixon, Travis L., and Charlotte L. Williams, "The Changing Misrepresentation of Race and Crime on Network and Cable News," *Journal of Communication*, Vol. 65, No. 1, 2014, pp. 24–39.

Dunaway, Johanna, and Regina G. Lawrence, "What Predicts the Game Frame? Media Ownership, Electoral Context, and Campaign News," *Political Communication*, Vol. 32, No. 1, 2015, pp. 43–60.

Dutta-Bergman, Mohan J., "Complementarity in Consumption of News Types Across Traditional and New Media," *Journal of Broadcasting & Electronic Media*, Vol. 48, No. 1, 2004, pp. 41–60.

Dutton, William H., "The Fifth Estate Emerging Through the Network of Networks," *Prometheus*, Vol. 27, No. 1, 2009, pp. 1–15.

Dvorkin, Lewis, "Inside Forbes: The State of the Digital News, or 25 Web Sites Captured in 3 Revealing Charts," *Forbes*, January 2016.

"Elizabeth's Story: Talks About Battle with Addiction and Anxiety," *World News Tonight with David Muir*, ABC, September 9, 2016.

Elliott, Andrea, "Amid Repressed Hopes, Reasons to Dream," *New York Times*, December 13, 2013.

Faraj, Samer, and Bijan Azad, "The Materiality of Technology: An Affordance Perspective," in Paul M. Leonardi, Bonnie A. Nardi, and Jannis Kallinikos, eds., *Materiality and Organizing*, Oxford, England: Oxford University Press, 2012, pp. 237–258.

Fedeli, Sophia, and Katerina Eva Matsa, "Use of Mobile Devices for News Continues to Grow, Outpacing Desktops and Laptops," Pew Research Center, July 17, 2018. As of March 15, 2019:
http://www.pewresearch.org/fact-tank/2018/07/17/use-of-mobile-devices-for-news-continues-to-grow-outpacing-desktops-and-laptops/

Finch, Maida A., Peter Goff, and Courtney Preston, "Language, Gender, and School-Leadership Labor Markets," *Leadership and Policy in Schools*, Vol. 17, 2018, pp. 1–20.

Fischer, Sara, "92% of Republicans Think Media Intentionally Reports Fake News," Axios, June 27, 2018.

Flaounas, Ilias, Omar Ali, Thomas Lansdall-Welfare, Tijl De Bie, Nick Mosdell, Justin Lewis, and Nello Cristianini, "Research Methods in the Age of Digital Journalism: Massive-Scale Automated Analysis of News-Content—Topics, Style and Gender," *Digital Journalism*, Vol. 1, No. 1, 2013, pp. 102–116.

"The Foxification of News," *The Economist*, July 7, 2011. As of March 15, 2019:
https://www.economist.com/special-report/2011/07/07/the-foxification-of-news

Gallup, "Confidence in Institutions," webpage, undated. As of March 18, 2019:
https://news.gallup.com/poll/1597/confidence-institutions.aspx

Gallup and Knight Foundation, *American Views: Trust, Media, and Democracy*, Washington, D.C.: Gallup, January 2018. As of March 15, 2019:
https://kf-site-production.s3.amazonaws.com/publications/pdfs/000/000/242/original/KnightFoundation_AmericansViews_Client_Report_010917_Final_Updated.pdf

Gaziano, Cecile, and Kristin McGrath, "Measuring the Concept of Credibility," *Journalism Quarterly*, Vol. 63, Autumn 1986, pp. 451–462.

Gibson, James J., *The Ecological Approach to Visual Perception*, London: Psychology Press and Routledge Classic Editions, reprint edition, 2014

Go, Eun, Kyung Han You, Eun Hwa Jung, and Hongjin Shim, "Why Do We Use Different Types of Websites and Assign Them Different Levels of Credibility? Structural Relations Among Users' Motives, Types of Websites, Information Credibility, and Trust in the Press," *Computers in Human Behavior*, Vol 54, January 2016, pp. 231–239.

Gottfried, Jeffrey, and Elisa Shearer, "Americans' Online News Use Is Closing In on TV News Use," Pew Research Center, September 7, 2017. As of March 15, 2019:
http://www.pewresearch.org/fact-tank/2017/09/07/americans-online-news-use-vs-tv-news-use/

Gunther, Albert C., "Biased Press or Biased Public?" *Public Opinion Quarterly*, Vol. 56, No. 2, 1992, pp. 147–167.

Hawkins, Robert P., Suzanne Pingree, Jacqueline Hitchon, Bradley W. Gorham, Prathana Kannaovakun, Eileen Gilligan, Barry Radler, Gudbjorg H. Kolbeins, and Toni Schmidt, "Predicting Selection and Activity in Television Genre Viewing," *Media Psychology*, Vol. 3, No. 3, 2001, pp. 237–264.

Helmus, Todd C., Elizabeth Bodine-Baron, Andrew Radin, Madeline Magnuson, Joshua Mendelsohn, William Marcellino, Andriy Bega, and Zev Winkelman, *Russian Social Media Influence: Understanding Russian Propaganda in Eastern Europe*, Santa Monica, Calif.: RAND Corporation, RR-237-OSD, 2018. As of March 15, 2019:
https://www.rand.org/pubs/research_reports/RR2237.html

Hitt, Matthew P., and Kathleen Searles, "Media Coverage and Public Approval of the US Supreme Court," *Political Communication*, Vol. 35, No. 4, 2018, pp. 1–21.

Ho, Daniel E., and Kevin M. Quinn, "Viewpoint Diversity and Media Consolidation: An Empirical Study," *Stanford Law Review*, Vol. 61, No. 4, 2009, pp. 781–868.

Hope, Jonathan, and Michael Witmore, "The Hundredth Psalm to the Tune of 'Green Sleeves': Digital Approaches to Shakespeare's Language of Genre," *Shakespeare Quarterly*, Vol. 61, No. 3, 2010, pp. 357–390.

Hu, Yongmei, David Kaufer, and Suguru Ishizaki, "Genre and Instinct," in Yang Cai, ed., *Computing with Instinct: Rediscovering Artificial Intelligence*, Berlin: Springer Science and Business Media, 2011, pp. 58–81.

Hunston, Susan, "Using a Corpus to Investigate Stance Quantitatively and Qualitatively," in Robert Englebretson, ed., *Stancetaking in Discourse*, Philadelphia, Pa.: John Benjamins Publishing, 2007, pp. 27–48.

Ishizaki, Suguru, and David Kaufer, "Computer-Aided Rhetorical Analysis," in Philip M. McCarthy and Chutima Boonthum-Denecke, eds., *Applied Natural Language Processing: Identification, Investigation and Resolution*, Hershey, Pa.: IGI Global, 2012, pp. 276–296.

Jakob, Nikolaus G. E., "No Alternatives? The Relationship Between Perceived Media Dependency, Use of Alternative Information Sources, and General Trust in Mass Media," *International Journal of Communication*, Vol. 4, 2010, pp. 589–606.

Johnson, Thomas J., and Barbara K. Kaye, "Cruising Is Believing? Comparing Internet and Traditional Sources on Media Credibility Measures," *Journalism & Mass Communication Quarterly*, Vol. 75, No. 2, 1998, pp. 325–340.

———, "Some Like It Lots: The Influence of Interactivity and Reliance on Credibility," *Computers in Human Behavior*, Vol. 61, August 1, 2016, pp. 136–145.

Jones, David A., "Why Americans Don't Trust the Media: A Preliminary Analysis," *Harvard International Journal of Press/Politics*, Vol. 9, No. 2, 2004, pp. 60–75.

Jones, Jeffrey, "U.S. Media Trust Continues to Recover From 2016 Low," Gallup, October 12, 2018.

Jurkowitz, Mark, Paul Hitlin, Amy Mitchell, Laura Houston Santhanam, Steve Adams, Monica Anderson, and Nancy Vogt, *The Changing TV News Landscape*, Washington, D.C.: Pew Research Center, March 17, 2013. As of March 15, 2019: http://www.journalism.org/2013/03/17/the-changing-tv-news-landscape/

Kahneman, Daniel, and Amos Tversky, "Choices, Values, and Frames," *American Psychologist*, Vol. 39, No. 4, 1984, pp. 341–350.

Karlsson, Michael, "Charting the Liquidity of Online News: Moving Towards a Method for Content Analysis of Online News," *International Communication Gazette*, Vol. 74, No. 4, 2012, pp. 385–402.

Kaufer, David, Suguru Ishizaki, Jeff Collins, and Pantelis Vlachos, "Teaching Language Awareness in Rhetorical Choice: Using IText and Visualization in Classroom Genre Assignments," *Journal of Business and Technical Communication*, Vol. 18, No. 3, 2004, pp. 361–402.

Kavanagh, Jennifer, and Michael D. Rich, *Truth Decay: An Initial Exploration of the Diminishing Role of Facts and Analysis in American Public Life*, Santa Monica, Calif.: RAND Corporation, RR-2314-RC, 2018. As of March 15, 2019: https://www.rand.org/pubs/research_reports/RR2314.html

Kayany, Joseph M., and Paul Yelsma, "Displacement Effects of Online Media in the Socio-Technical Contexts of Households," *Journal of Broadcasting & Electronic Media*, Vol. 44, No. 2, 2000, pp. 215–229.

Kennedy, Dan, "Print Is Dying, Digital Is No Savior: The Long, Ugly Decline of the Newspaper Business Continues Apace," commentary, WGBH News, January 26, 2016. As of March 15, 2019: https://www.wgbh.org/news/2016/01/26/local-news/print-dying-digital-no-savior-long-ugly-decline-newspaper-business-continues

Kian, Edward M., Michael Mondello, and John Vincent, "ESPN—The Women's Sports Network? A Content Analysis of Internet Coverage of March Madness," *Journal of Broadcasting & Electronic Media*, Vol. 53, No. 3, 2009, pp. 477–495.

Kiesling, Scott F., "Style as Stance," in Alexandra Jaffe, ed., *Stance: Sociolinguistic Perspectives*, New York: Oxford University Press, 2009, pp. 171–194.

Kiousis, Spiro, "Public Trust of Mistrust? Perceptions of Media Credibility in the Information Age," *Mass Communication and Society*, Vol. 4, No. 4, 2001, pp. 381–403.

Knight Foundation, "10 Reasons Why American Trust in the Media Is at an All-Time Low," Medium.com, January 15, 2018a. As of March 18, 2019: https://medium.com/trust-media-and-democracy/10-reasons-why-americans-dont-trust-the-media-d0630c125b9e

————, "An Online Experimental Platform to Assess Trust in the Media," webpage, July 18, 2018b. As of March 18, 2019:
https://knightfoundation.org/reports/
an-online-experimental-platform-to-assess-trust-in-the-media

Knight Foundation and Gallup Polling, *Indicators of News Media Trust*, Washington, D.C., September 11, 2018. As of February 6, 2019:
https://knightfoundation.org/reports/indicators-of-news-media-trust

Kohring, Matthias, and Jörg Matthes, "Trust in News Media: Development and Validation of a Multidimensional Scale," *Communication Research*, Vol. 34, No. 2, 2007, pp. 231–252.

Langin, Katie, "Fake News Spreads Faster Than True News on Twitter—Thanks to People, Not Bots," *Science Magazine*, March 8, 2018.

Langlois, Shawn, "How Biased Is Your News Source? You Probably Won't Agree with This Chart," *MarketWatch*, April 21, 2018. As of March 15, 2019:
https://www.marketwatch.com/story/how-biased-is-your-news-source-you-probably-wont-agree-with-this-chart-2018-02-28

Lee, Tien-Tsung, "Why They Don't Trust the Media: An Examination of Factors Predicting Trust," *American Behavioral Scientist*, Vol. 54, No. 1, 2010, pp. 8–21.

Leonardi, Paul M., "Theoretical Foundations for the Study of Sociomateriality," *Information and Organization*, Vol. 23, No. 2, 2013, pp. 59–76.

Lewis, Seth C., and Nikki Usher, "Open Source and Journalism: Toward New Frameworks for Imagining News Innovation," *Media, Culture & Society*, Vol. 35, No. 5, 2013, pp. 602–619.

Liebowitz, Stan J., and Alejandro Zentner, "Clash of the Titans: Does Internet Use Reduce Television Viewing?" *Review of Economics and Statistics*, Vol. 94, No. 1, 2012, pp. 234–245.

Lynch, Dianne, "The State of American Journalism," in *Looking at the Future of Journalism Education*, Miami, Fla.: Knight Foundation, 2015. As of March 15, 2019:
https://knightfoundation.org/features/je-the-state-of-american-journalism/

MacGregor, Phil, "Tracking the Online Audience," *Journalism Studies*, Vol. 8, No. 2, 2007, pp. 280–298.

Maier, Scott, "All the News Fit to Post? Comparing News Content on the Web to Newspapers, Television, and Radio," *Journalism & Mass Communication Quarterly*, Vol. 87, No. 3–4, 2010, pp. 548–562.

Marcellino, William M., "Talk Like a Marine: USMC Linguistic Acculturation and Civil–Military Argument," *Discourse Studies*, Vol. 16, No. 3, 2014, pp. 385–405.

————, "Revisioning Strategic Communication Through Rhetoric and Discourse Analysis," *Joint Forces Quarterly*, No. 76, 2015.

McChesney, Robert W., *Rich Media, Poor Democracy: Communication Politics in Dubious Times*, New York: New Press, 2015.

McGinty, Emma E., Hillary Samples, Sachini N. Bandara, Brendan Saloner, Marcus A. Bachhuber, and Colleen L. Barry, "The Emerging Public Discourse on State Legalization of Marijuana for Recreational Use in the US: Analysis of News Media Coverage, 2010–2014," *Preventive Medicine*, Vol. 90, 2016, pp. 114–120.

McIntyre, Douglas, "America's 100 Largest Newspapers," 24/7 Wall Street, January 24, 2017. As of March 15, 2019:
https://247wallst.com/media/2017/01/24/americas-100-largest-newspapers/

McKenzie, Carly T., Wilson Lowrey, Hal Hays, Jee Young Chung, and Chang Wan Woo, "Listening to News Audiences: The Impact of Community Structure and Economic Factors," *Mass Communication and Society*, Vol. 14, No. 3, 2011, pp. 375–395.

McLuhan, Marshall, *Understanding Media*, Cambridge, Mass.: MIT Press, reprint edition, 1994.

Media Bias/Fact Check, homepage, undated. As of March 15, 2019:
https://mediabiasfactcheck.com

Mierzejewska, Bozena I., Dobin Yim, Philip M. Napoli, Henry C. Lucas Jr., and Abrar Al-Hasan, "Evaluating Strategic Approaches to Competitive Displacement: The Case of the US Newspaper Industry," *Journal of Media Economics*, Vol. 30, No. 1, 2017, pp. 19–30.

Mitchell, Amy, ed., *State of the News Media, 2015*, Washington, D.C.: Pew Research Center, April 29, 2015.

Mitchell, Amy, Elisa Shearer, Jeffrey Gottfried, and Michael Barthel, "Pathways to News," Pew Research Center, July 2016. As of March 15, 2019:
http://www.journalism.org/2016/07/07/pathways-to-news/

Neuendorf, Kimberly A., *The Content Analysis Guidebook*, Thousand Oaks, Calif.: Sage, 2016.

Newhagen, John, and Clifford Nass, "Differential Criteria for Evaluating Credibility of Newspapers and TV News," *Journalism Quarterly*, Vol. 66, No. 2, 1989, pp. 277–284.

Newman, Nic, and David Levy, eds., *Digital News Report*, Oxford, England: Reuters Institute for the Study of Journalism, 2014. As of March 15, 2019:
http://www.digitalnewsreport.org/survey/2014/

Pantti, Mervi, "The Value of Emotion: An Examination of Television Journalists' Notions on Emotionality," *European Journal of Communication*, Vol. 25, No. 2, 2010, pp. 168–181.

Pearson, Catherine, "Proof Birth Control Access Is a Very, Very Big Deal to Women," Huffington Post, July 1, 2014. As of March 15, 2019: https://www.huffingtonpost.com/2014/07/01/birth-control-benefits-hobby-lobby_n_5545178.html

Pellechia, Marianne G., "Trends in Science Coverage: A Content Analysis of Three US Newspapers," *Public Understanding of Science*, Vol. 6, No. 1, 1997, pp. 49–68.

Peters, Chris, "Emotion Aside or Emotional Side? Crafting an 'Experience of Involvement' in the News," *Journalism*, Vol. 12, No. 3, 2011, pp. 297–316.

Pew Research Center, State of the News Media project, homepage, undated. As of March 15, 2019: http://www.pewresearch.org/topics/state-of-the-news-media/

———, *One-in-Ten Voters Online for Campaign '96*, 1996. As of March 18, 2019: http://assets.pewresearch.org/wp-content/uploads/sites/5/legacy-pdf/117.pdf

———, "Cable New Prime Time Viewership," webpage, March 13, 2006. As of March 15, 2019: http://www.journalism.org/numbers/cable-news-prime-time-viewership/.

———, "Internet/Broadband Fact Sheet," webpage, February 5, 2018a. As of March 15, 2019: http://www.pewinternet.org/fact-sheet/internet-broadband/

———, "Digital News Fact Sheet," State of the News Media project, webpage, June 6, 2018b. As of March 15, 2019: http://www.journalism.org/fact-sheet/digital-news/

———, "Newspapers Fact Sheet," State of the News Media project, webpage, June 13, 2018c. As of March 15, 2019: http://www.journalism.org/fact-sheet/newspapers/

———, "Network News Fact Sheet," State of the News Media project, webpage, July 25, 2018d. as of March 15, 2019: http://www.journalism.org/fact-sheet/network-news/

Pinsky, Drew, "Possible Reasons for Charlie Bothuell's 11 Day Disappearance; Story Behind the Woman Who Killed Her Own Son in the Midst of a Psychiatric Break; Oldest Daughter Held Little Patrick in Her Arms as He Died," *Dr. Drew*, CNN, July 2, 2014.

Polskin, Howard, "Who Gets the Most Traffic Among Conservative Websites," MediaShift, January 18, 2018. As of March 15, 2019: http://mediashift.org/2018/01/nine-insights-right-wing-website-traffic/

Prost, Charlene, "Bosley Gets Data on Park; Panel Drafted Report After Heavy Debate," *St. Louis Post-Dispatch*, November 7, 1994.

Rafail, Patrick, and John D. McCarthy, "Making the Tea Party Republican: Media Bias and Framing in Newspapers and Cable News," *Social Currents*, Vol. 5, No. 5, 2018.

Reinhardy, Scott, "Downsizing Effects on Personnel: The Case of Layoff Survivors in U.S. Newspapers," *Journal of Media Business Studies*, Vol. 7, No. 4, 2010, pp. 1–19.

Robles, Frances, "A Movie Date, a Text Message and a Fatal Shot," *New York Times*, January 22, 2014.

Schmidt, Christine, "Planted Stories? Fake News as Editorial Decisions? Trump or CNN? A Poll Examines the Public's Trust of Mainstream Media," Neiman Lab, April 3, 2018.

Shafer, Jack, "The Myth of the Terrorist Mastermind," Politico, November 16, 2015.

Shearer, Elisa, and Jeffrey Gottfried, *News Use Across Social Media Platforms 2017*, Washington, D.C.: Pew Research Center, September 7, 2017. As of March 15, 2019: http://www.journalism.org/2017/09/07/news-use-across-social-media-platforms-2017/

SimilarWeb, homepage, search thread for each outlet, conducted August-October 2018. As of October 2018: https://www.similarweb.com

Sobieraj, Sarah, and Jeffrey M. Berry, "From Incivility to Outrage: Political Discourse in Blogs, Talk Radio, and Cable News," *Political Communication*, Vol. 28, No. 1, 2011, pp. 19–41.

Stroud, Natalie Jomini, and Jae Kook Lee, "Perceptions of Cable News Credibility," *Mass Communication and Society*, Vol. 16, No. 1, 2013, pp. 67–88.

Stubbs, Michael, *Text and Corpus Analysis: Computer-Assisted Studies of Language and Culture*, Oxford, England: Blackwell, 1996.

Sunstein, Cass, *#Republic: Divided Democracy in the Age of Social Media*, Princeton, N.J.: Princeton University Press, 2018.

Szayna, Thomas S., Eric V. Larson, Angela O'Mahony, Sean Robson, Agnes Gereben Schaefer, Miriam Matthews, J. Michael Polich, Lynsay Ayer, Derek Eaton, William Marcellino, Lisa Miyashiro, Marek Posard, James Syme, Zev Winkelman, Cameron Wright, Megan Zander-Cotugno, and William Welser IV, *Considerations for Integrating Women into Closed Occupations in U.S. Special Operations Forces: Appendixes*, Santa Monica, Calif.: RAND Corporation, RR-1058/1-USSOCOM, 2015. As of March 18, 2019: https://www.rand.org/pubs/research_reports/RR1058.html

Tausczik, Yla R., and James W. Pennebaker, "The Psychological Meaning of Words: LIWC and Computerized Text Analysis Methods," *Journal of Language and Social Psychology*, Vol. 29, No. 1, 2010, pp. 24–54.

Tsfati, Yariv, and Jospeh N. Cappella, "Do People Watch What They Do Not Trust? Exploring the Association Between News Media Skepticism and Exposure," *Communication Research*, Vol. 30, No. 5, 2003, pp. 504–529.

Usher, Nikki, "Breaking News Production Processes in U.S. Metropolitan Newspapers: Immediacy and Journalistic Authority," *Journalism*, Vol. 19, No. 1, 2018, pp. 21–36.

Vaismoradi, Mojtaba, Hannele Turunen, and Terese Bondas, "Content Analysis and Thematic Analysis: Implications for Conducting a Qualitative Descriptive Study," *Nursing & Health Sciences*, Vol. 15, No. 3, 2013, pp. 398–405.

Valenzuela, Sebastián, Soledad Puente, and Pablo M. Flores, "Comparing Disaster News on Twitter and Television: An Intermedia Agenda Setting Perspective," *Journal of Broadcasting & Electronic Media*, Vol. 61, No. 4. 2017, pp. 615–637.

Vu, Hong Tien, "The Online Audience as Gatekeeper: The Influence of Reader Metrics on News Editorial Selection," *Journalism*, Vol. 15, No. 8, 2014, pp. 1094–1110.

Wagner, Kurt, and Rani Molla, "Facebook Is Not Getting Any Bigger in the United States," *Recode*, March 1, 2018. As of March 15, 2019: https://www.recode.net/2018/3/1/17063208/ facebook-us-growth-pew-research-users

Wanta, Wayne, and Yu-Wei Hu, "The Effects of Credibility, Reliance, and Exposure on Media Agenda-Setting: A Path Analysis Model," *Journalism Quarterly*, Vol. 71, No.1, 1994, pp. 90–98.

Westley, Bruce H., and Werner J. Severin, "Some Correlates of Media Credibility," *Journalism Quarterly*, Vol. 41, Summer 1964, pp. 325–335.

Westlund, Oscar, and Mathias A. Färdigh, "Accessing the News in an Age of Mobile Media: Tracing Displacing and Complementary Effects of Mobile News on Newspapers and Online News," *Mobile Media & Communication*, Vol. 3, No. 1, 2015, pp. 53–74.

Widholm, Andreas, "Tracing Online News in Motion: Time and Duration in the Study of Liquid Journalism," *Digital Journalism*, Vol. 4, No. 1, 2016, pp. 24–40.

Williams, Brian, "Environmental Group Concerned About Cell Phone Radiation," *NBC Nightly News*, NBC, September 10, 2009.

Winseck, Dwayne, "The State of Media Ownership and Media Markets: Competition or Concentration and Why Should We Care?" *Sociology Compass*, Vol. 2, No. 1, 2008, pp. 34–47.

Yu, Chong Ho, Angel Jannasch-Pennell, and Samuel DiGangi, "Compatibility Between Text Mining and Qualitative Research in the Perspectives of Grounded Theory, Content Analysis, and Reliability," *Qualitative Report*, Vol. 16, No. 3, 2011, pp. 730–744.

About the Authors

Jennifer Kavanagh is a senior political scientist at the RAND Corporation and associate director of the Strategy, Doctrine, and Resources Program in the RAND Arroyo Center. Her research focuses on U.S. political institutions and public opinion and their implications for U.S. foreign and domestic policy. Her work with RAND President and CEO Michael Rich defines Truth Decay as the diminishing reliance on facts, data, and analysis in U.S. political and civil discourse and describes its causes and consequences.

William Marcellino is a social and behavioral scientist at the RAND Corporation and a professor at the Pardee RAND Graduate School. He has a leading role at RAND in the development of analytic toolsets, including RAND-Lex, RAND's proprietary text analytics suite. Marcellino specializes in and teaches text analytics methods for big data sets (e.g., social media), as well as qualitative research methods.

Jonathan S. Blake is an associate political scientist at the RAND Corporation. His research interests include ethnicity, nationalism, and religion; conflict and post-conflict societies; social movements and collective political mobilization; and nontraditional security threats, such as the global refugee crisis and transnational criminal networks.

Shawn Smith is an assistant policy researcher at RAND and a Ph.D. student at the Pardee RAND Graduate School. Smith has worked in the private sector, using analytics and modeling to optimize business performance and customer acquisition. His transition to policy was largely motivated by RAND's ongoing work on Truth Decay, the examination of the diminishing role of facts, data, and analysis in American public life. Since joining RAND he has become a member of the Truth Decay project.

Steven Davenport is a doctoral candidate and assistant policy researcher at the Pardee RAND Graduate School. As a data scientist, he investigates questions in the public interest using quantitative and computational methods, including modeling, simulation, and data visualization.

Mahlet G. Tebeka is a doctoral candidate at the Pardee RAND Graduate School and an assistant policy researcher at the RAND Corporation. Her research interests include seeking innovative solutions to complex problems for health systems in low-resource settings. Tebeka has worked on several research areas at RAND, including health policy and Truth Decay.